hawkeye

MY LIFE AS A WEAPON

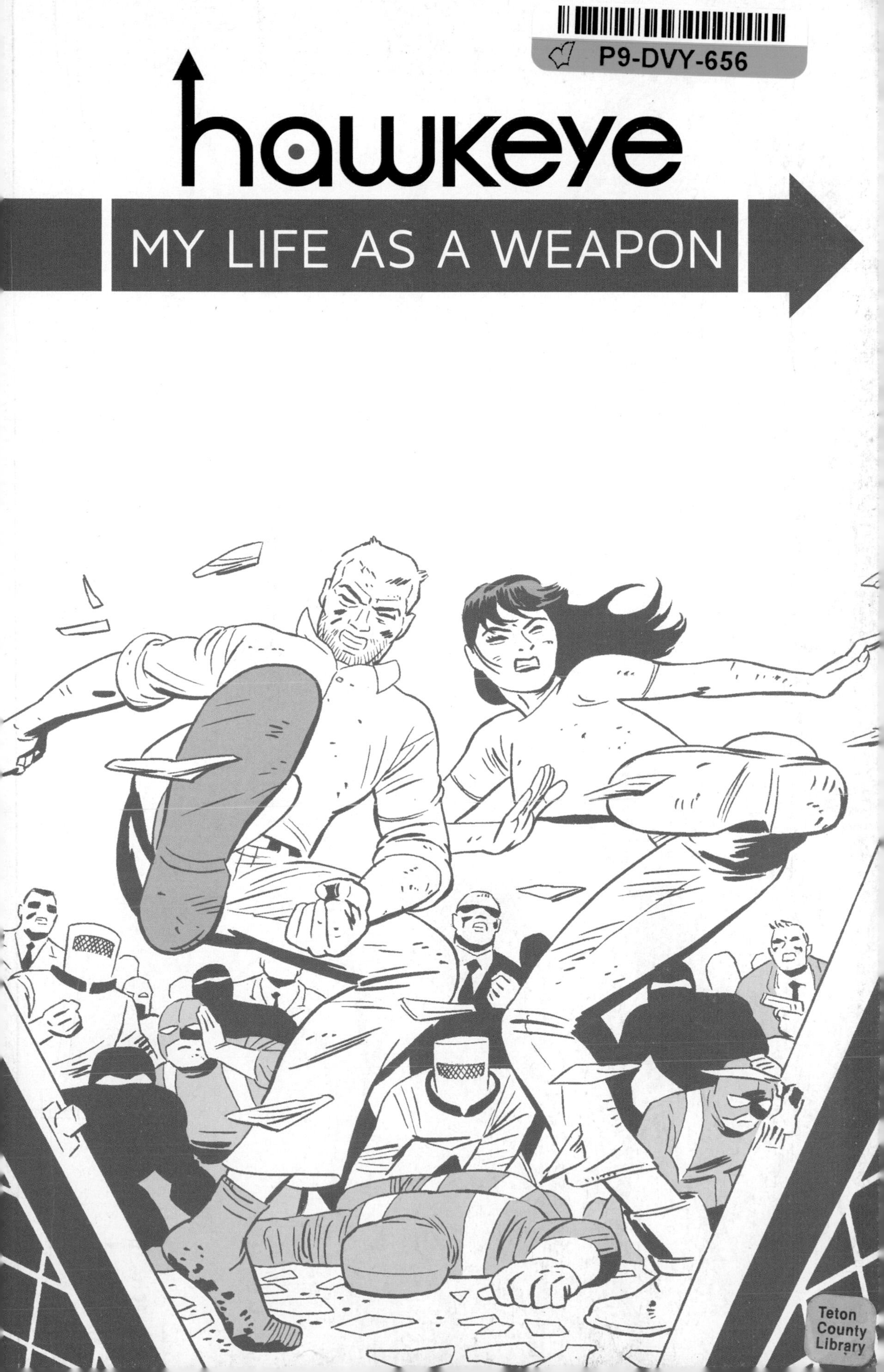

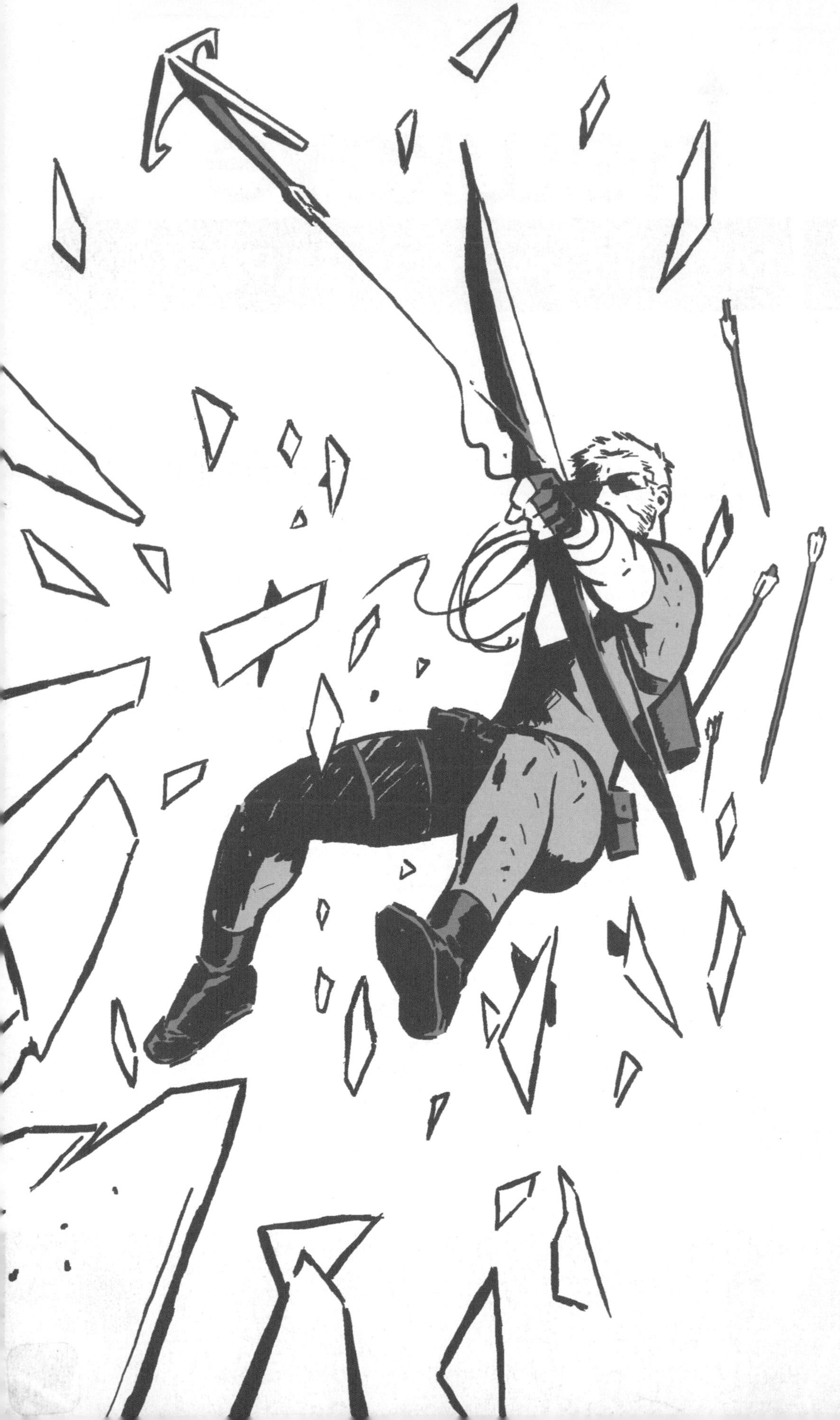

hawkeye

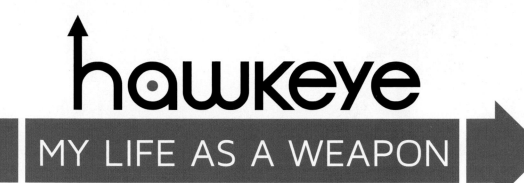

MY LIFE AS A WEAPON

MATT FRACTION
WRITER

DAVID AJA
ARTIST, #1-3

JAVIER PULIDO
ARTIST, #4-5

MATT HOLLINGSWORTH
COLOR ARTIST

CHRIS ELIOPOULOS
LETTERER

DAVID AJA
COVER ART

SANA AMANAT & TOM BRENNAN
ASSOCIATE EDITORS

STEPHEN WACKER
EDITOR

YOUNG AVENGERS PRESENTS #6

MATT FRACTION
WRITER

ALAN DAVIS
PENCILER

MARK FARMER
INKER

PAUL MOUNTS
COLORIST

VC'S CORY PETIT
LETTERER

JIM CHEUNG, JOHN DELL & JUSTIN PONSOR
COVER ART

MOLLY LAZER
ASSOCIATE EDITOR

TOM BREVOORT
EDITOR

COLLECTION EDITOR: **JENNIFER GRÜNWALD** • ASSISTANT EDITORS: **ALEX STARBUCK & NELSON RIBEIRO**
EDITOR, SPECIAL PROJECTS: **MARK D. BEAZLEY** • SENIOR EDITOR, SPECIAL PROJECTS: **JEFF YOUNGQUIST**
SVP OF PRINT & DIGITAL PUBLISHING SALES: **DAVID GABRIEL** • BOOK DESIGN: **JEFF POWELL**

EDITOR IN CHIEF: **AXEL ALONSO** • CHIEF CREATIVE OFFICER: **JOE QUESADA**
PUBLISHER: **DAN BUCKLEY** • EXECUTIVE PRODUCER: **ALAN FINE**

HAWKEYE VOL. 1: MY LIFE AS A WEAPON. Contains material originally published in magazine form as HAWKEYE #1-5 and YOUNG AVENGERS PRESENTS #6. Third printing 2013. ISBN# 978-0-7851-6562-0. Published by MARVEL WORLDWIDE, INC., a subsidiary of MARVEL ENTERTAINMENT, LLC. OFFICE OF PUBLICATION: 135 West 50th Street, New York, NY 10020. **Printed in the U.S.A.** ALAN FINE, EVP - Office of the President, Marvel Worldwide, Inc. and EVP & CMO Marvel Characters B.V.; DAN BUCKLEY, Publisher & President - Print, Animation & Digital Divisions; JOE QUESADA, Chief Creative Officer; TOM BREVOORT, SVP of Publishing; DAVID BOGART, SVP of Operations & Procurement, Publishing; C.B. CEBULSKI, SVP of Creator & Content Development; DAVID GABRIEL, SVP of Print & Digital Publishing Sales; JIM O'KEEFE, VP of Operations & Logistics; DAN CARR, Executive Director of Publishing Technology; SUSAN CRESPI, Editorial Operations Manager; ALEX MORALES, Publishing Operations Manager; STAN LEE, Chairman Emeritus. For information regarding advertising in Marvel Comics or on Marvel.com, please contact Niza Disla, Director of Marvel Partnerships, at ndisla@marvel.com. For Marvel subscription inquiries, please call 800-217-9158. **Manufactured between 4/24/2013 and 5/27/2013 by QUAD/GRAPHICS, VERSAILLES, KY, USA.**

09876543

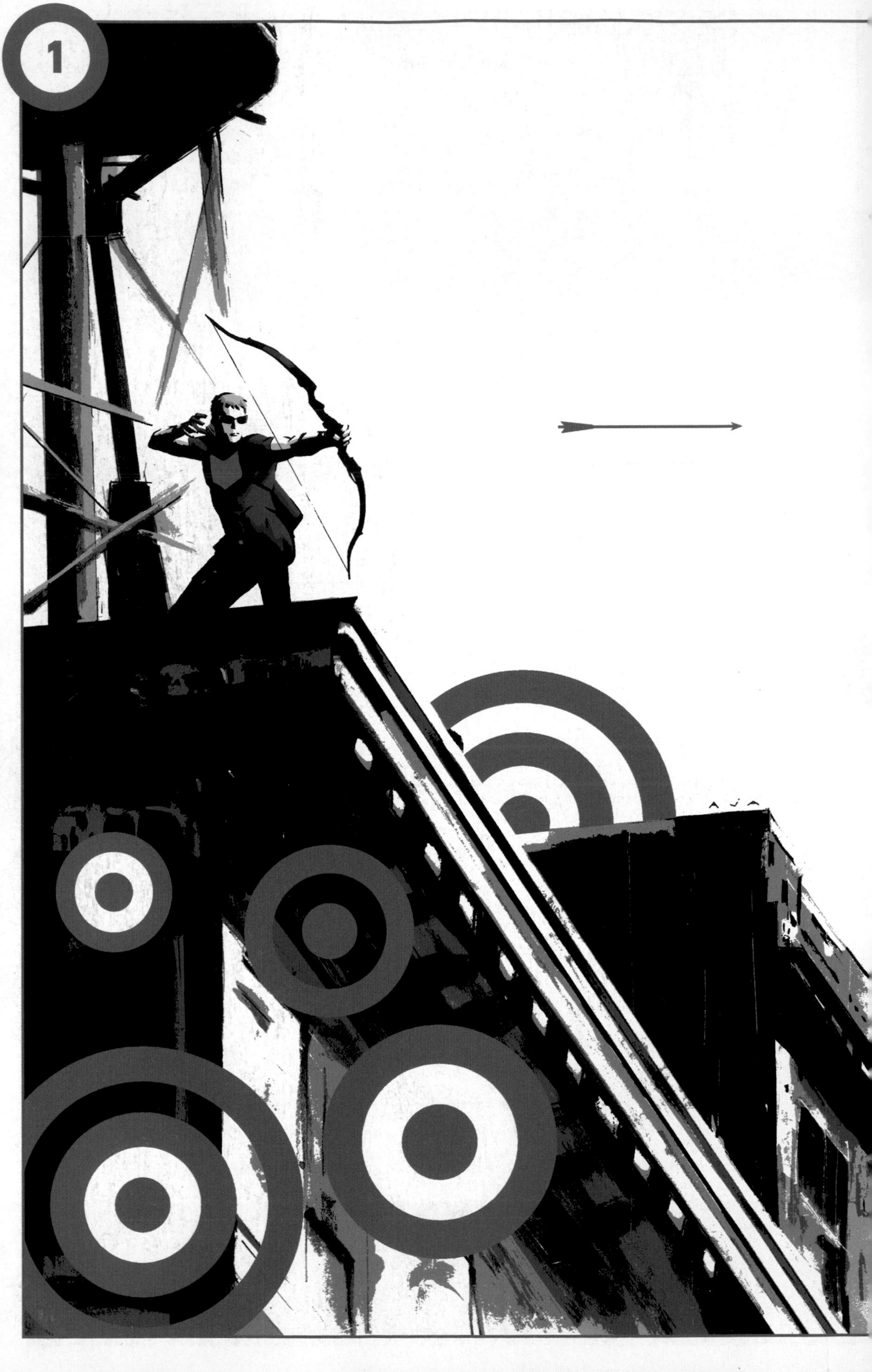
1

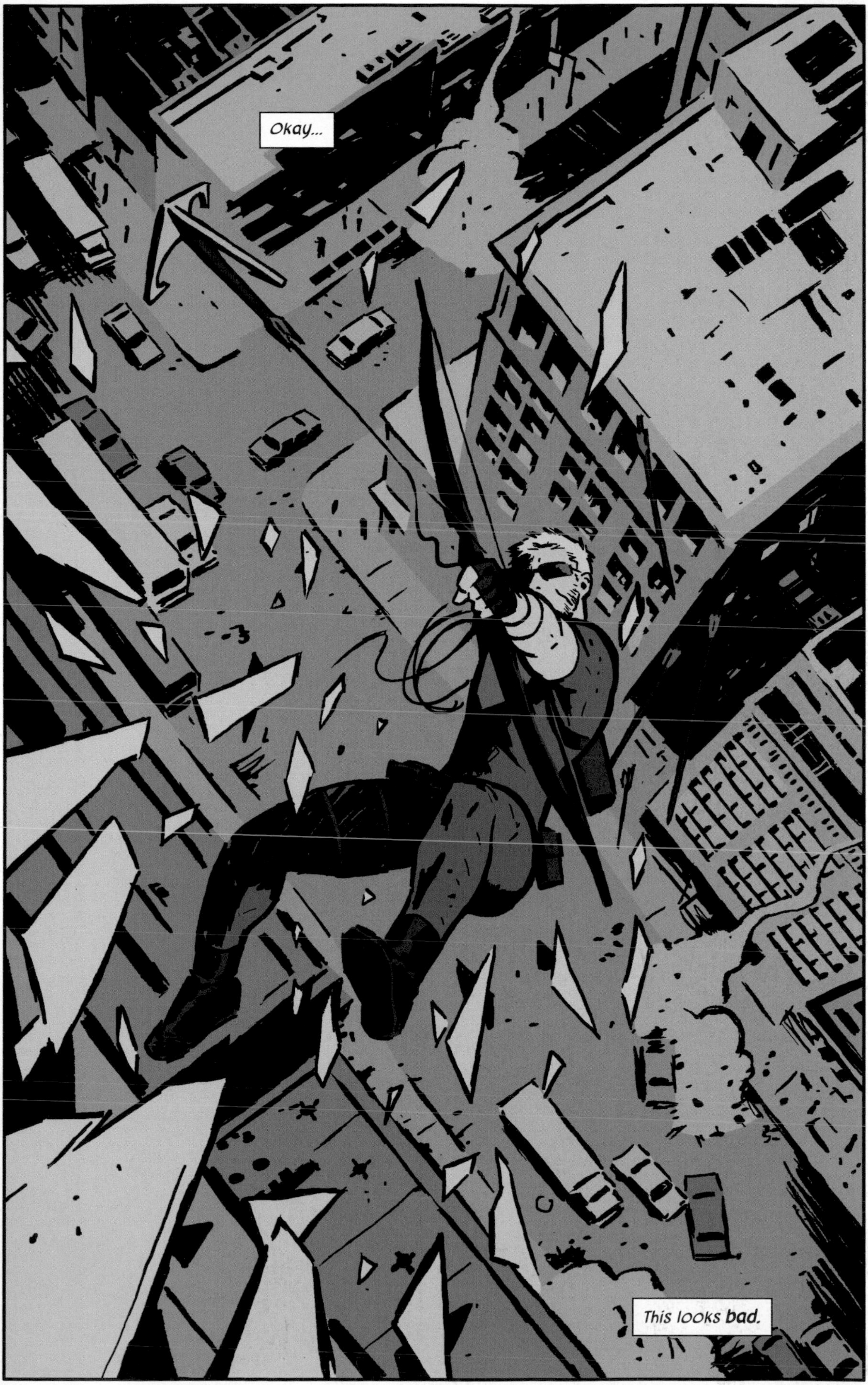
Okay...
This looks bad.

clint barton, a.k.a.

hawkeye,

became the greatest sharp-
shooter known to man.

he then joined the avengers.

this is what he does when
he's not being an avenger.

that's all you need to know.

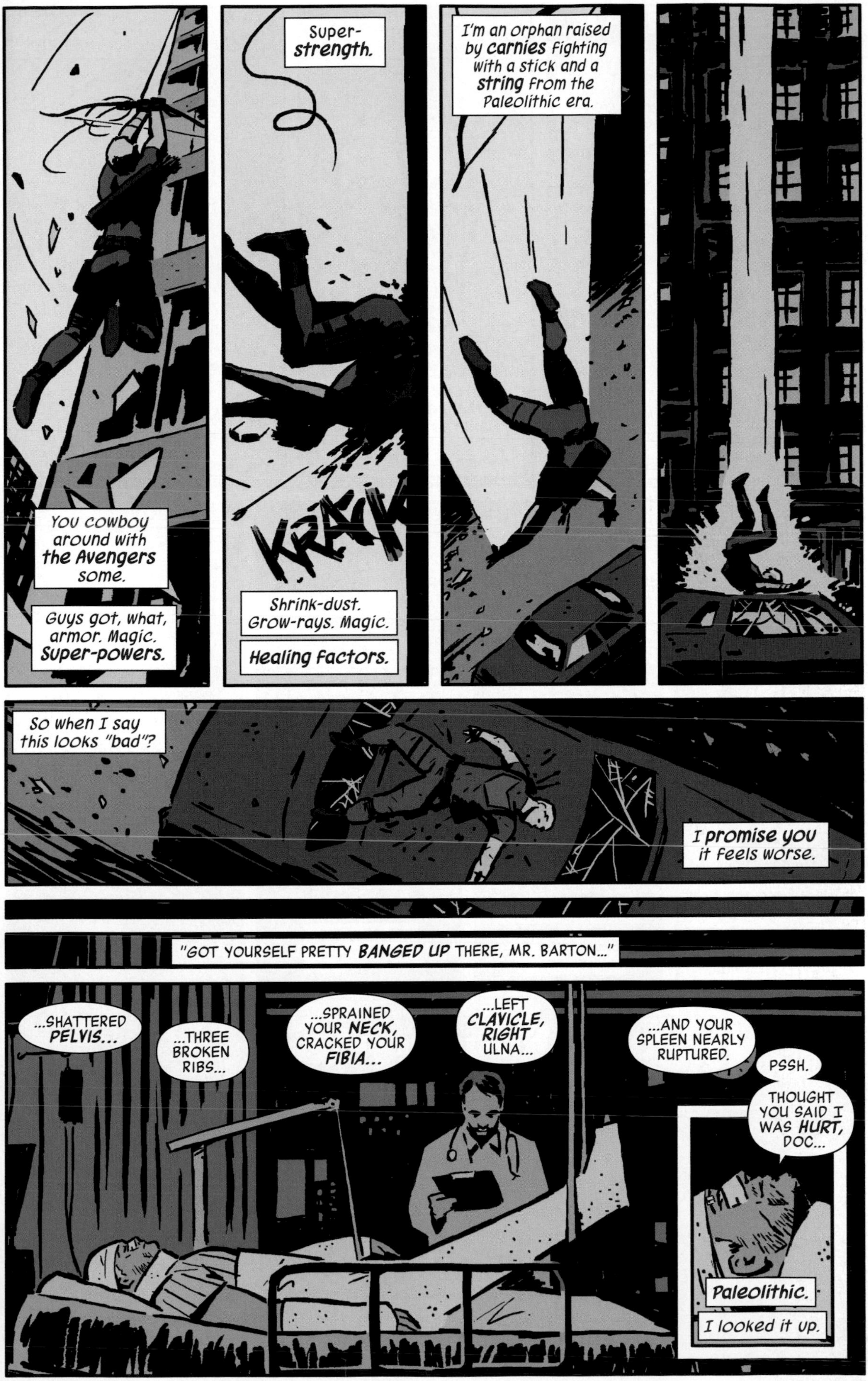

You cowboy around with the Avengers some.
Guys got, what, armor. Magic. Super-powers.
Super-strength.
KRACK
Shrink-dust. Grow-rays. Magic.
Healing factors.
I'm an orphan raised by carnies fighting with a stick and a string from the Paleolithic era.
So when I say this looks "bad"?
I promise you it feels worse.
"GOT YOURSELF PRETTY BANGED UP THERE, MR. BARTON..."
...SHATTERED PELVIS...
...THREE BROKEN RIBS...
...SPRAINED YOUR NECK, CRACKED YOUR FIBIA...
...LEFT CLAVICLE, RIGHT ULNA...
...AND YOUR SPLEEN NEARLY RUPTURED.
PSSH.
THOUGHT YOU SAID I WAS HURT, DOC...
Paleolithic.
I looked it up.

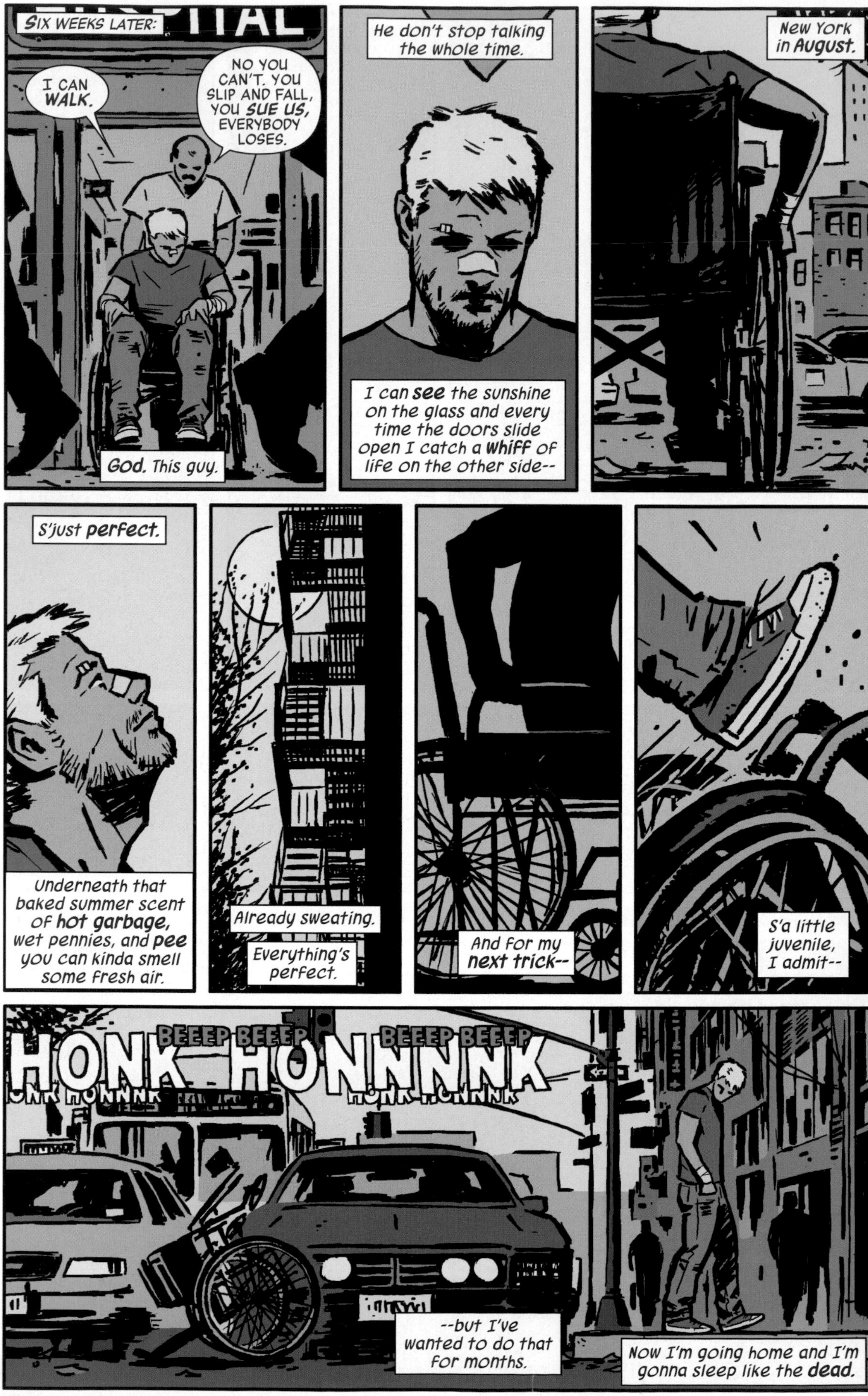

SIX WEEKS LATER:
I CAN WALK.
NO YOU CAN'T. YOU SLIP AND FALL, YOU SUE US, EVERYBODY LOSES.
God. This guy.
He don't stop talking the whole time.
I can see the sunshine on the glass and every time the doors slide open I catch a whiff of life on the other side--
New York in August.
S'just perfect.
Underneath that baked summer scent of hot garbage, wet pennies, and pee you can kinda smell some fresh air.
Already sweating.
Everything's perfect.
And for my next trick--
S'a little juvenile, I admit--
BEEEP BEEEP
HONK HONNNNK
BEEEP BEEEP
--but I've wanted to do that for months.
Now I'm going home and I'm gonna sleep like the dead.

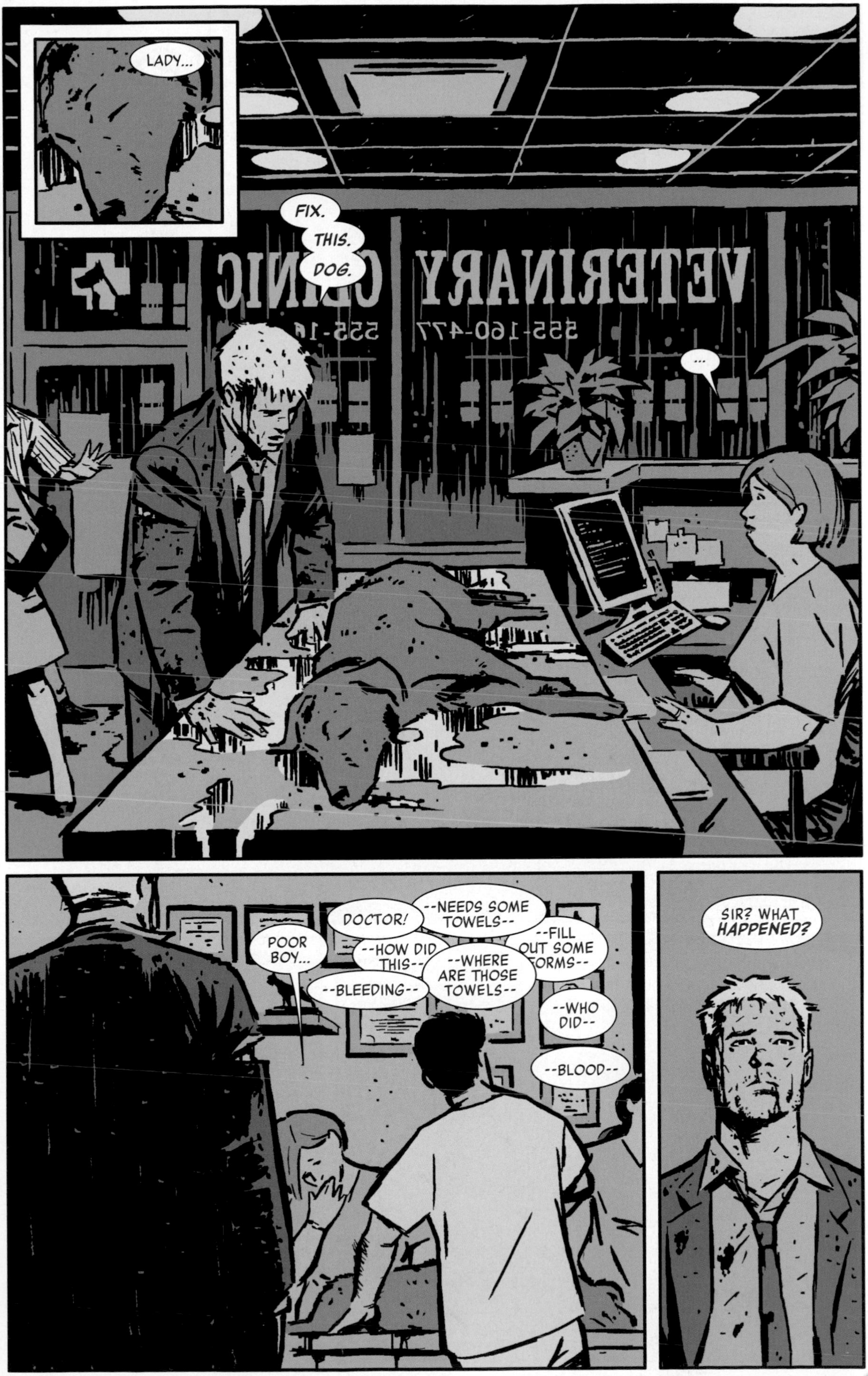
LADY...
FIX.
THIS.
DOG.
...
DOCTOR!
--NEEDS SOME TOWELS--
POOR BOY...
--HOW DID THIS--
--FILL OUT SOME FORMS--
--WHERE ARE THOSE TOWELS--
--BLEEDING--
--WHO DID--
--BLOOD--
SIR? WHAT *HAPPENED?*

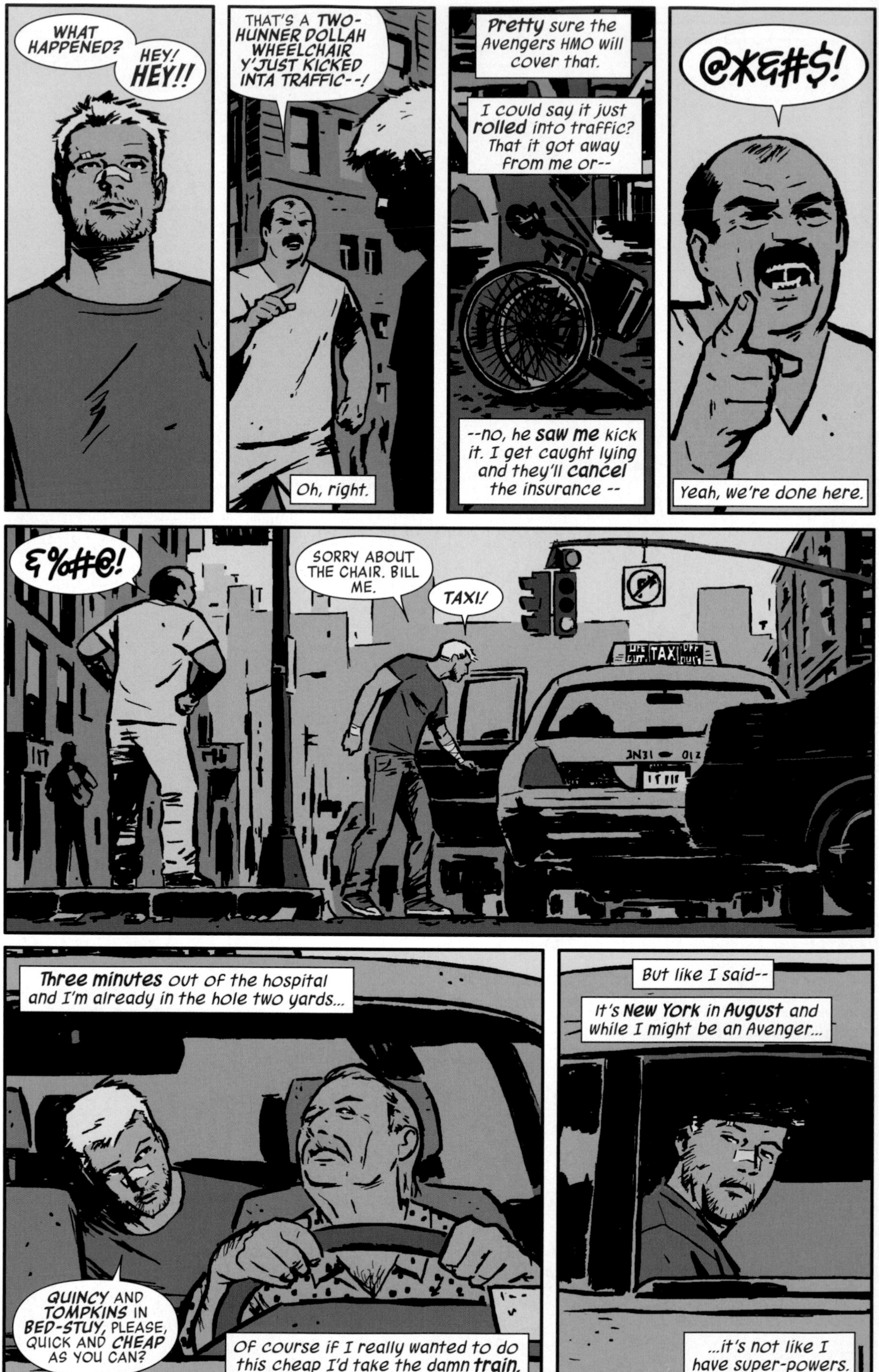
WHAT HAPPENED?
HEY! HEY!!
THAT'S A TWO-HUNNER DOLLAH WHEELCHAIR Y'JUST KICKED INTA TRAFFIC--!
Oh, right.
Pretty sure the Avengers HMO will cover that.
I could say it just rolled into traffic? That it got away from me or--
--no, he saw me kick it. I get caught lying and they'll cancel the insurance --
@✻&#$!
Yeah, we're done here.
&%#@!
SORRY ABOUT THE CHAIR. BILL ME.
TAXI!
TAXI
Three minutes out of the hospital and I'm already in the hole two yards...
QUINCY AND TOMPKINS IN BED-STUY, PLEASE, QUICK AND CHEAP AS YOU CAN?
Of course if I really wanted to do this cheap I'd take the damn train.
But like I said--
It's New York in August and while I might be an Avenger...
...it's not like I have super-powers.

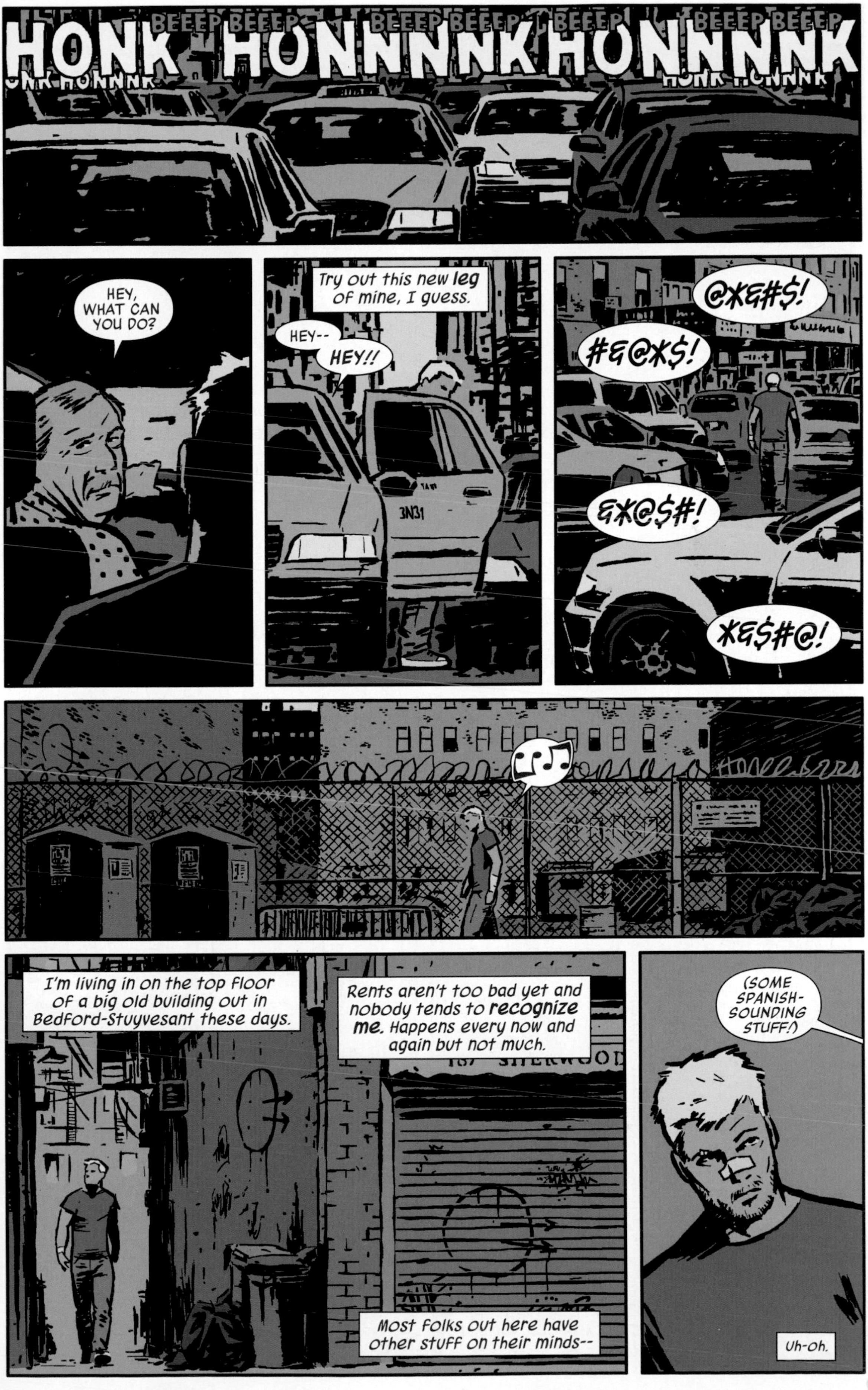
BEEEP BEEEP
HONK HONNNNK HONNNNK
BEEEP BEEEP BEEEP BEEEP BEEEP
HONK HONNNNK
HEY, WHAT CAN YOU DO?
Try out this new leg of mine, I guess.
HEY--
HEY!!
@*&#$!
#&@*$!
&*@$#!
*&$#@!
I'm living in on the top floor of a big old building out in Bedford-Stuyvesant these days.
Rents aren't too bad yet and nobody tends to recognize me. Happens every now and again but not much.
Most folks out here have other stuff on their minds--
(SOME SPANISH-SOUNDING STUFF.)
Uh-oh.

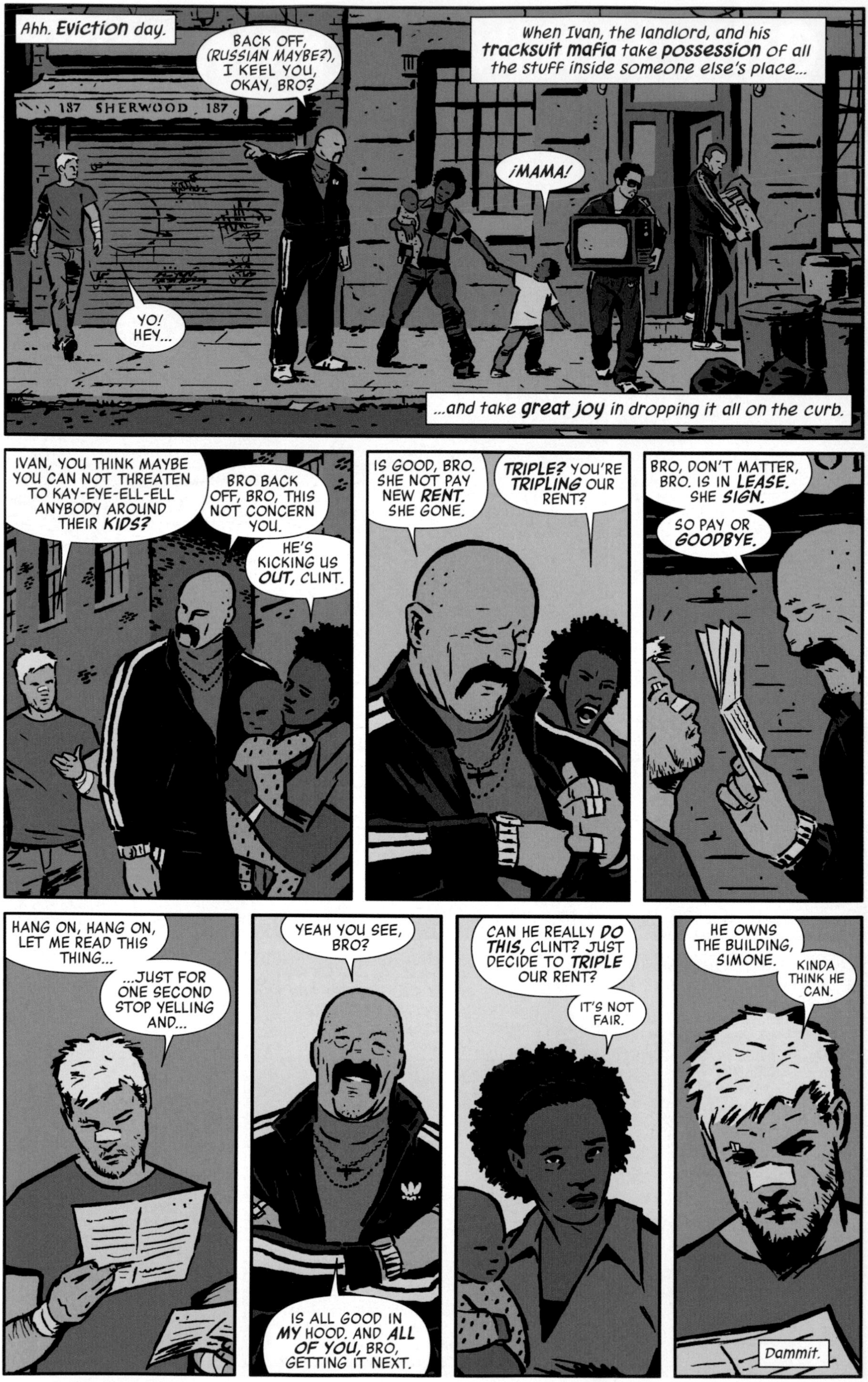

Ahh. Eviction day.
BACK OFF, (RUSSIAN MAYBE?), I KEEL YOU, OKAY, BRO?
When Ivan, the landlord, and his tracksuit mafia take possession of all the stuff inside someone else's place...
187 SHERWOOD 187
¡MAMA!
YO! HEY...
...and take great joy in dropping it all on the curb.
IVAN, YOU THINK MAYBE YOU CAN NOT THREATEN TO KAY-EYE-ELL-ELL ANYBODY AROUND THEIR KIDS?
BRO BACK OFF, BRO, THIS NOT CONCERN YOU.
HE'S KICKING US OUT, CLINT.
IS GOOD, BRO. SHE NOT PAY NEW RENT. SHE GONE.
TRIPLE? YOU'RE TRIPLING OUR RENT?
BRO, DON'T MATTER, BRO. IS IN LEASE. SHE SIGN.
SO PAY OR GOODBYE.
HANG ON, HANG ON, LET ME READ THIS THING...
...JUST FOR ONE SECOND STOP YELLING AND...
YEAH YOU SEE, BRO?
IS ALL GOOD IN MY HOOD. AND ALL OF YOU, BRO, GETTING IT NEXT.
CAN HE REALLY DO THIS, CLINT? JUST DECIDE TO TRIPLE OUR RENT?
IT'S NOT FAIR.
HE OWNS THE BUILDING, SIMONE.
KINDA THINK HE CAN.
Dammit.

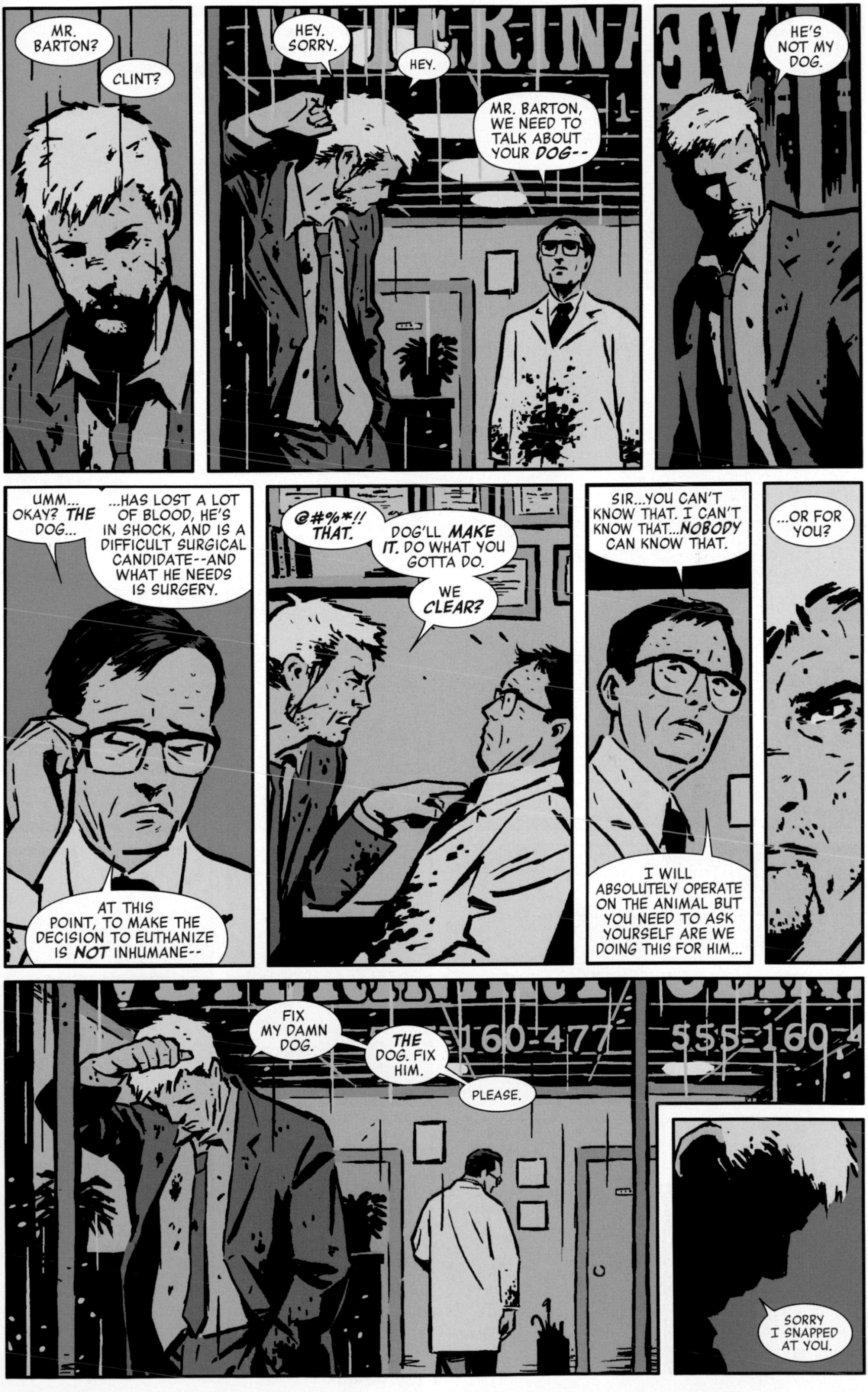
MR. BARTON?
CLINT?
HEY. SORRY.
HEY.
MR. BARTON, WE NEED TO TALK ABOUT YOUR DOG--
HE'S NOT MY DOG.
UMM... OKAY? THE DOG...
...HAS LOST A LOT OF BLOOD, HE'S IN SHOCK, AND IS A DIFFICULT SURGICAL CANDIDATE--AND WHAT HE NEEDS IS SURGERY.
AT THIS POINT, TO MAKE THE DECISION TO EUTHANIZE IS NOT INHUMANE--
@#%*!! THAT.
DOG'LL MAKE IT. DO WHAT YOU GOTTA DO.
WE CLEAR?
SIR...YOU CAN'T KNOW THAT. I CAN'T KNOW THAT...NOBODY CAN KNOW THAT.
I WILL ABSOLUTELY OPERATE ON THE ANIMAL BUT YOU NEED TO ASK YOURSELF ARE WE DOING THIS FOR HIM...
...OR FOR YOU?
FIX MY DAMN DOG.
THE DOG. FIX HIM.
PLEASE.
SORRY I SNAPPED AT YOU.

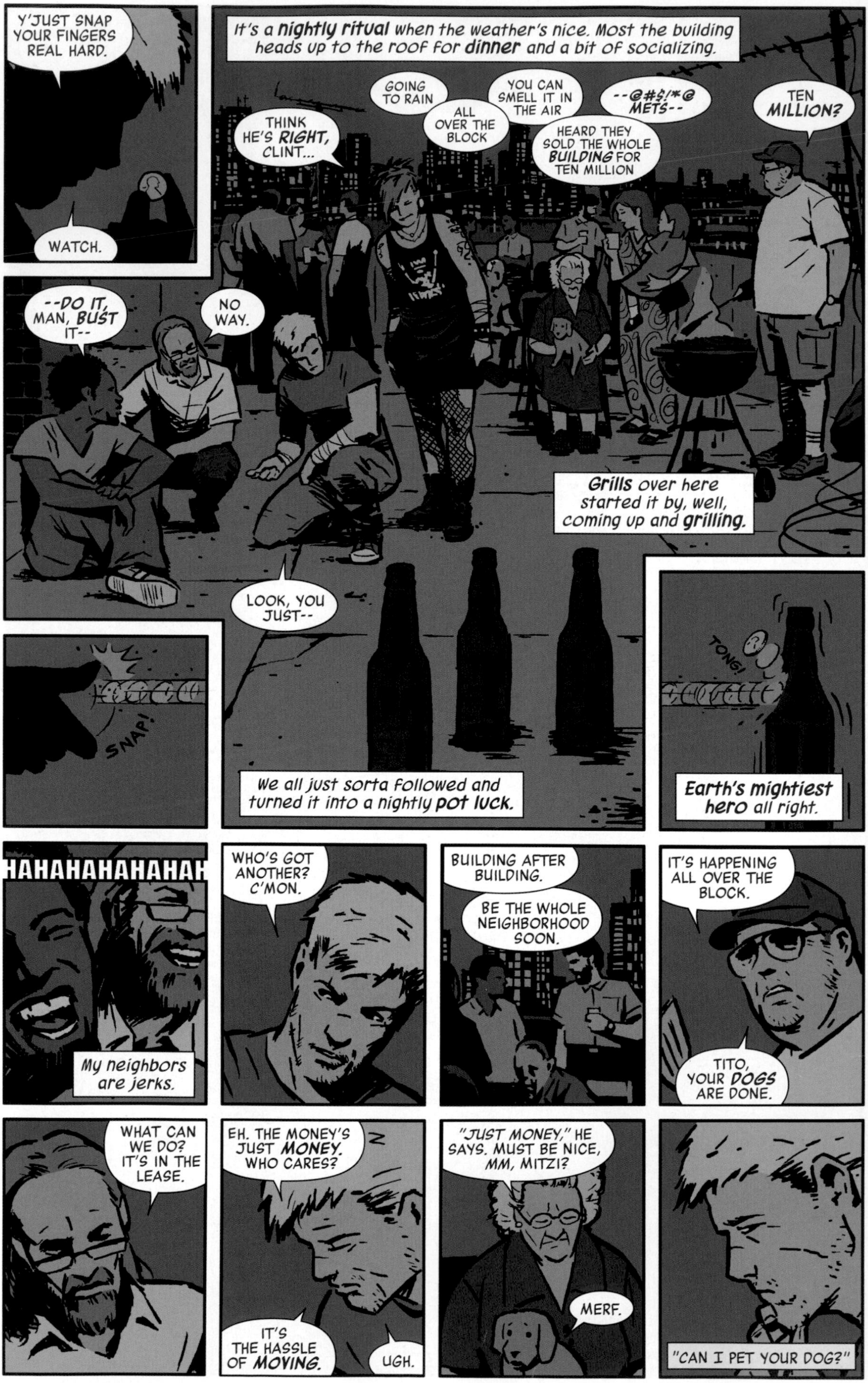
Y'JUST SNAP YOUR FINGERS REAL HARD.
WATCH.
It's a nightly ritual when the weather's nice. Most the building heads up to the roof for dinner and a bit of socializing.
THINK HE'S RIGHT, CLINT...
GOING TO RAIN
ALL OVER THE BLOCK
YOU CAN SMELL IT IN THE AIR
--@#$!*@ METS--
HEARD THEY SOLD THE WHOLE BUILDING FOR TEN MILLION
TEN MILLION?
--DO IT, MAN, BUST IT--
NO WAY.
Grills over here started it by, well, coming up and grilling.
LOOK, YOU JUST--
SNAP!
We all just sorta followed and turned it into a nightly pot luck.
TONG!
Earth's mightiest hero all right.
HAHAHAHAHAHAH
My neighbors are jerks.
WHO'S GOT ANOTHER? C'MON.
BUILDING AFTER BUILDING.
BE THE WHOLE NEIGHBORHOOD SOON.
IT'S HAPPENING ALL OVER THE BLOCK.
TITO, YOUR DOGS ARE DONE.
WHAT CAN WE DO? IT'S IN THE LEASE.
EH. THE MONEY'S JUST MONEY. WHO CARES?
IT'S THE HASSLE OF MOVING.
UGH.
"JUST MONEY," HE SAYS. MUST BE NICE, MM, MITZI?
MERF.
"CAN I PET YOUR DOG?"

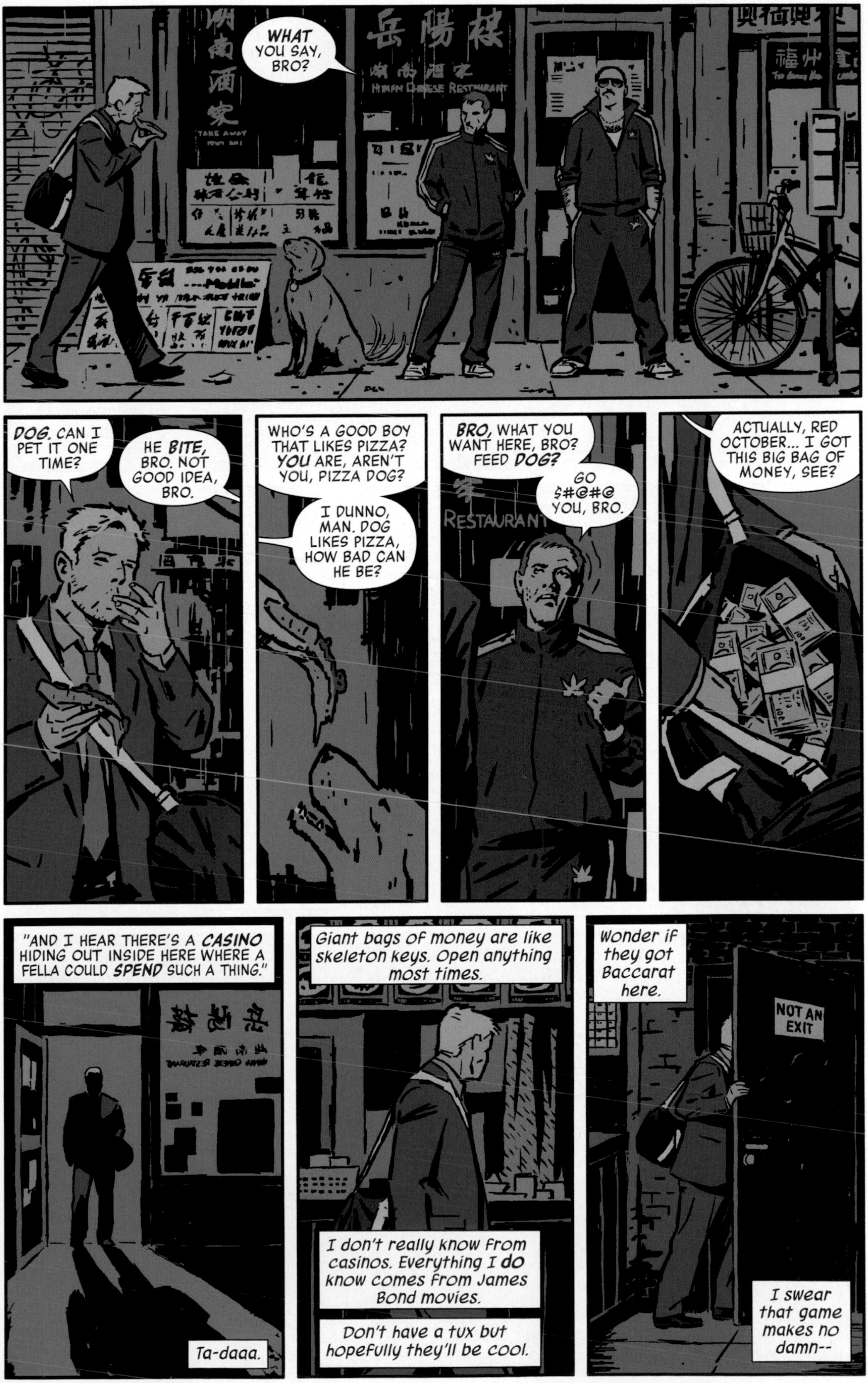
WHAT YOU SAY, BRO?
DOG. CAN I PET IT ONE TIME?
HE BITE, BRO. NOT GOOD IDEA, BRO.
WHO'S A GOOD BOY THAT LIKES PIZZA? YOU ARE, AREN'T YOU, PIZZA DOG?
I DUNNO, MAN. DOG LIKES PIZZA, HOW BAD CAN HE BE?
BRO, WHAT YOU WANT HERE, BRO? FEED DOG?
GO $#@#@ YOU, BRO.
ACTUALLY, RED OCTOBER... I GOT THIS BIG BAG OF MONEY, SEE?
"AND I HEAR THERE'S A CASINO HIDING OUT INSIDE HERE WHERE A FELLA COULD SPEND SUCH A THING."
Ta-daaa.
Giant bags of money are like skeleton keys. Open anything most times.
I don't really know from casinos. Everything I do know comes from James Bond movies.
Don't have a tux but hopefully they'll be cool.
Wonder if they got Baccarat here.
NOT AN EXIT
I swear that game makes no damn--

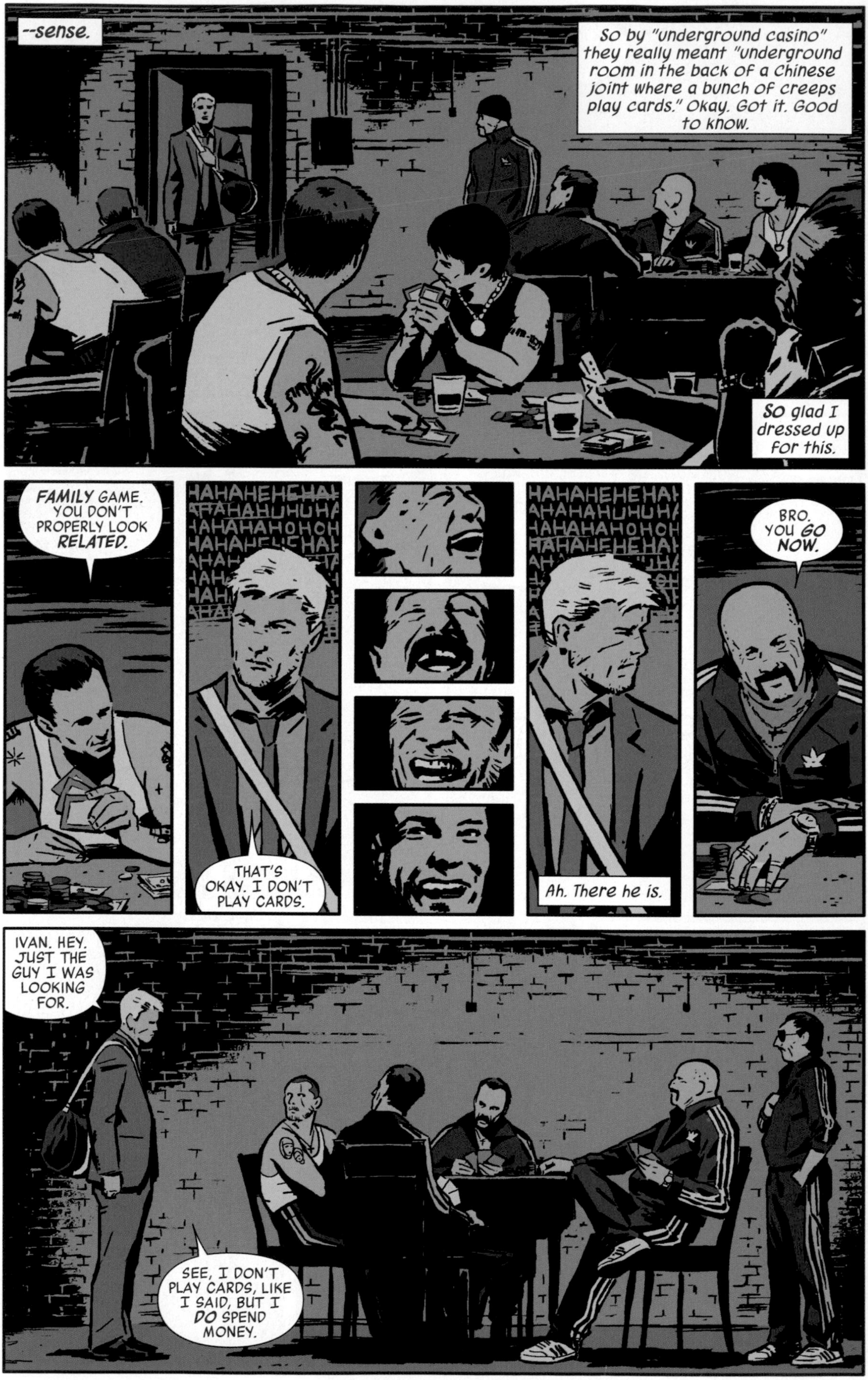
--sense.
So by "underground casino" they really meant "underground room in the back of a Chinese joint where a bunch of creeps play cards." Okay. Got it. Good to know.
So glad I dressed up for this.
FAMILY GAME. YOU DON'T PROPERLY LOOK RELATED.
HAHAHEHEHAH AHAHAHUHUHA HAHAHAHOHOH HAHAHEHEHAH
THAT'S OKAY. I DON'T PLAY CARDS.
HAHAHEHEHAH AHAHAHUHUHA HAHAHAHOHOH HAHAHEHEHAH
Ah. There he is.
BRO. YOU GO NOW.
IVAN. HEY. JUST THE GUY I WAS LOOKING FOR.
SEE, I DON'T PLAY CARDS, LIKE I SAID, BUT I DO SPEND MONEY.

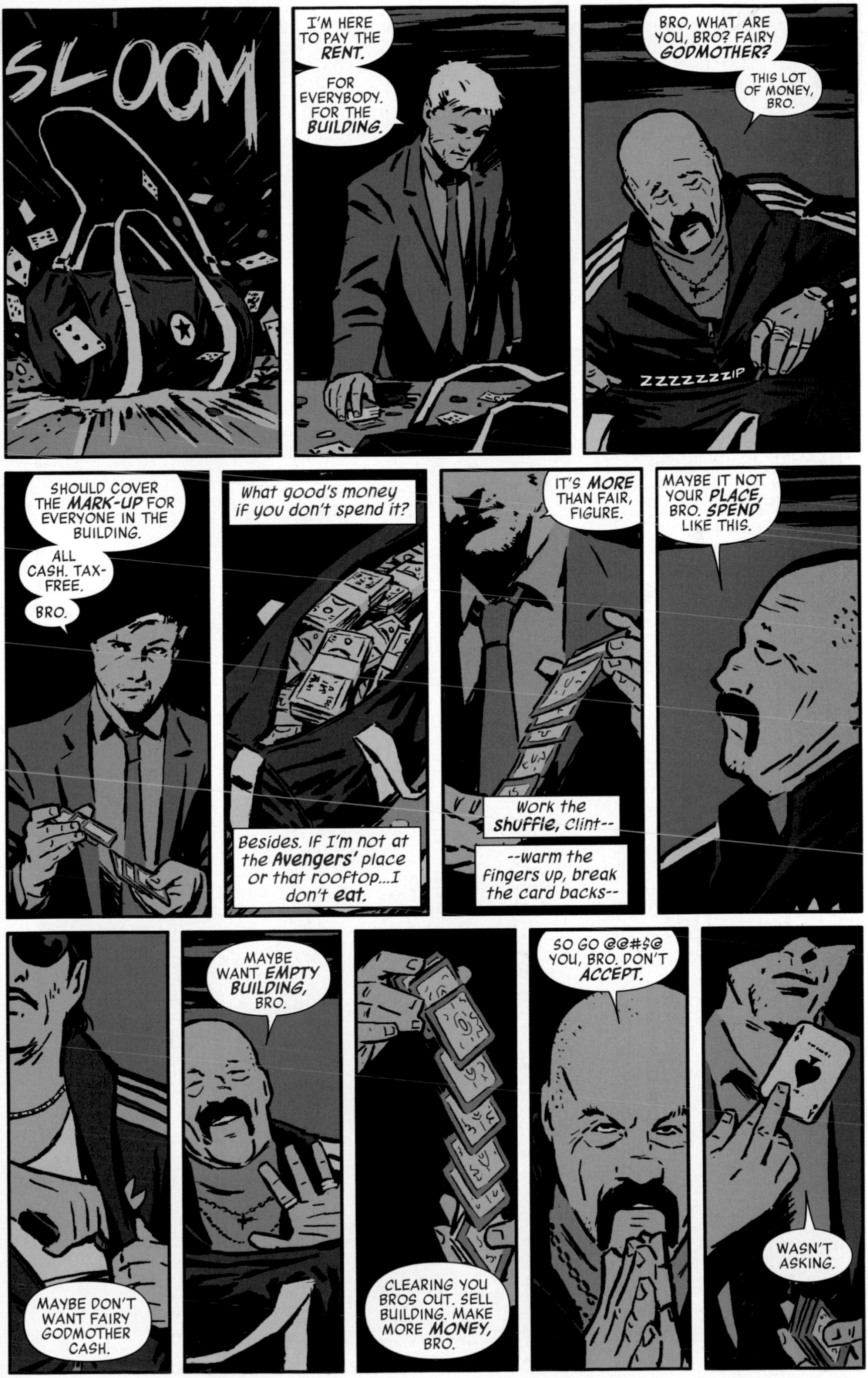
SLOOM
I'M HERE TO PAY THE RENT.
FOR EVERYBODY. FOR THE BUILDING.
BRO, WHAT ARE YOU, BRO? FAIRY GODMOTHER?
THIS LOT OF MONEY, BRO.
ZZZZZZZIP
SHOULD COVER THE MARK-UP FOR EVERYONE IN THE BUILDING.
ALL CASH. TAX-FREE.
BRO.
What good's money if you don't spend it?
Besides. If I'm not at the Avengers' place or that rooftop...I don't eat.
IT'S MORE THAN FAIR, FIGURE.
Work the shuffle, Clint--
--warm the fingers up, break the card backs--
MAYBE IT NOT YOUR PLACE, BRO. SPEND LIKE THIS.
MAYBE DON'T WANT FAIRY GODMOTHER CASH.
MAYBE WANT EMPTY BUILDING, BRO.
CLEARING YOU BROS OUT. SELL BUILDING. MAKE MORE MONEY, BRO.
SO GO @@#$@ YOU, BRO. DON'T ACCEPT.
WASN'T ASKING.

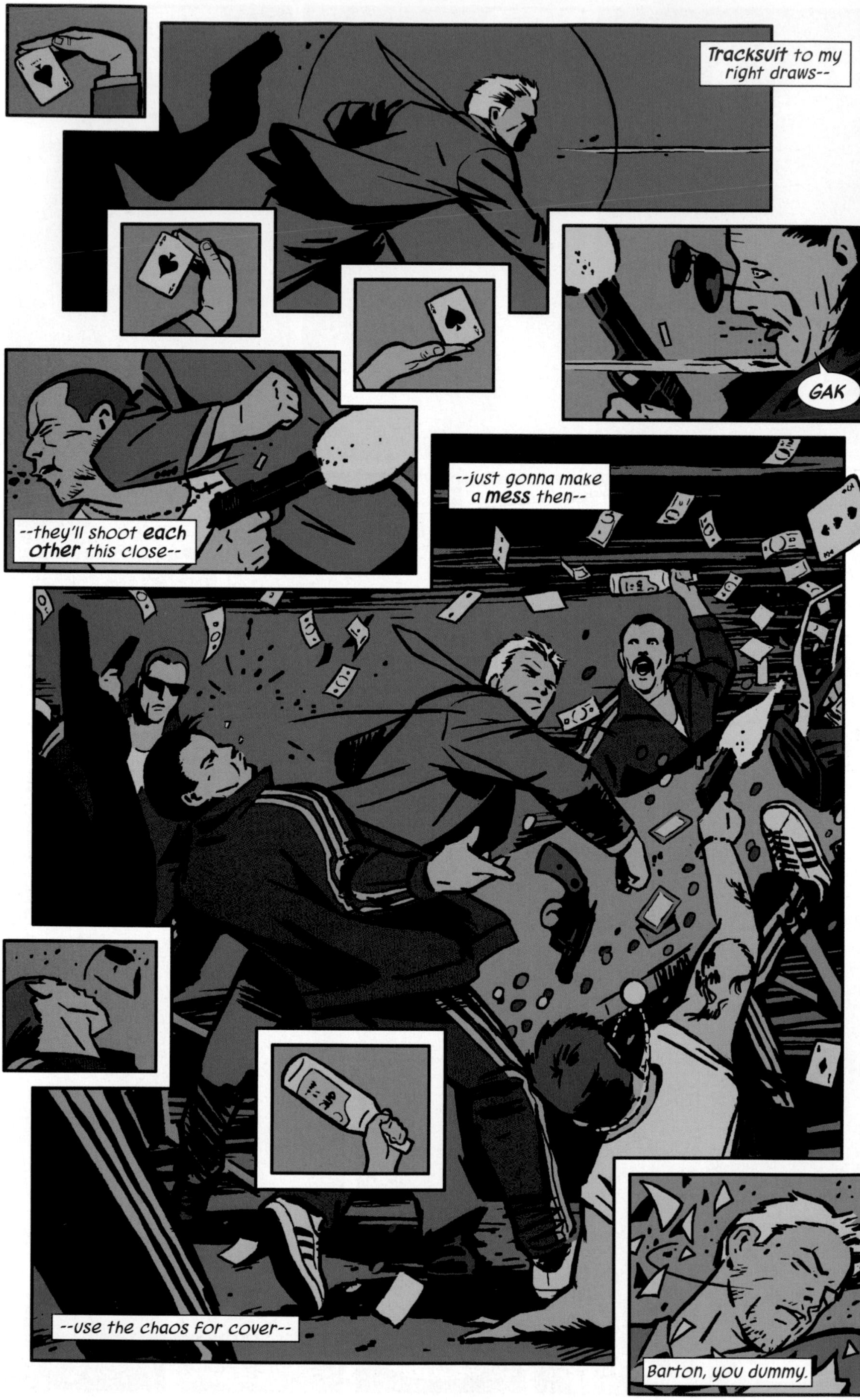
Tracksuit to my right draws--
GAK
--they'll shoot each other this close--
--just gonna make a mess then--
--use the chaos for cover--
Barton, you dummy.

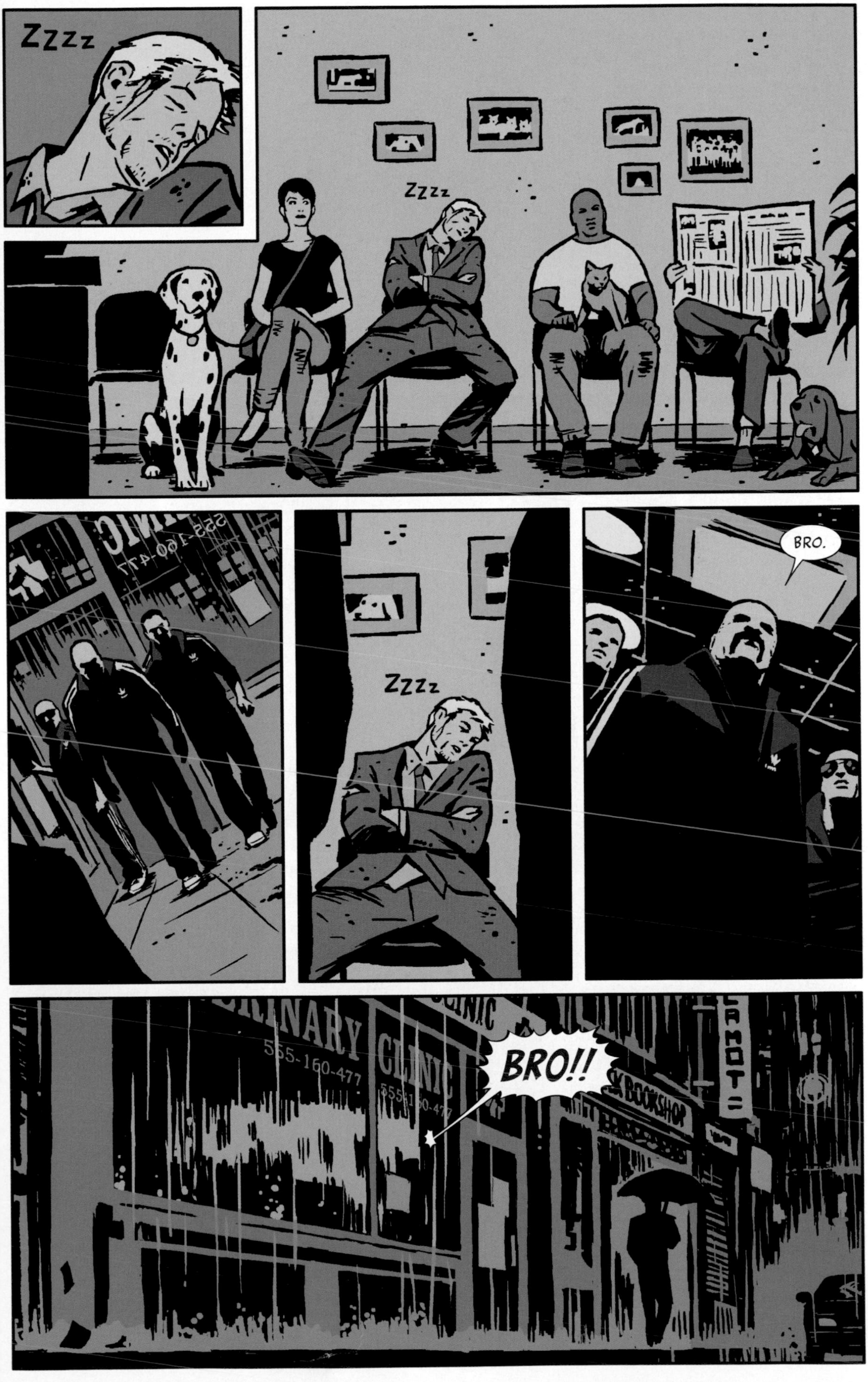
Zzzz
Zzzz
Zzzz
BRO.
RINARY
CLINIC
555-160-477
BRO!!
BOOKSHOP

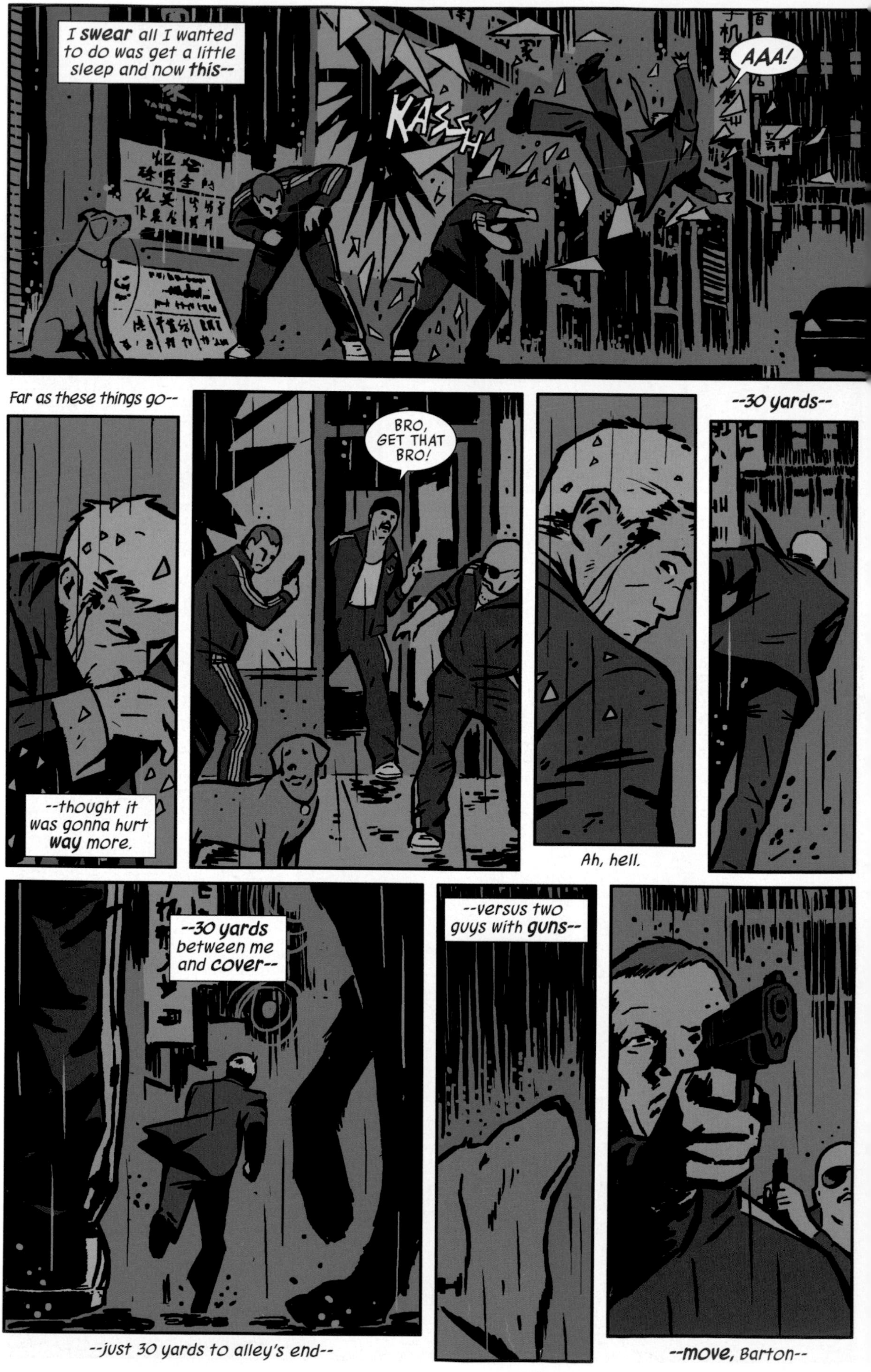
I swear all I wanted to do was get a little sleep and now this--
KASSH
AAA!
Far as these things go--
--thought it was gonna hurt way more.
BRO, GET THAT BRO!
Ah, hell.
--30 yards--
--30 yards between me and cover--
--just 30 yards to alley's end--
--versus two guys with guns--
--move, Barton--

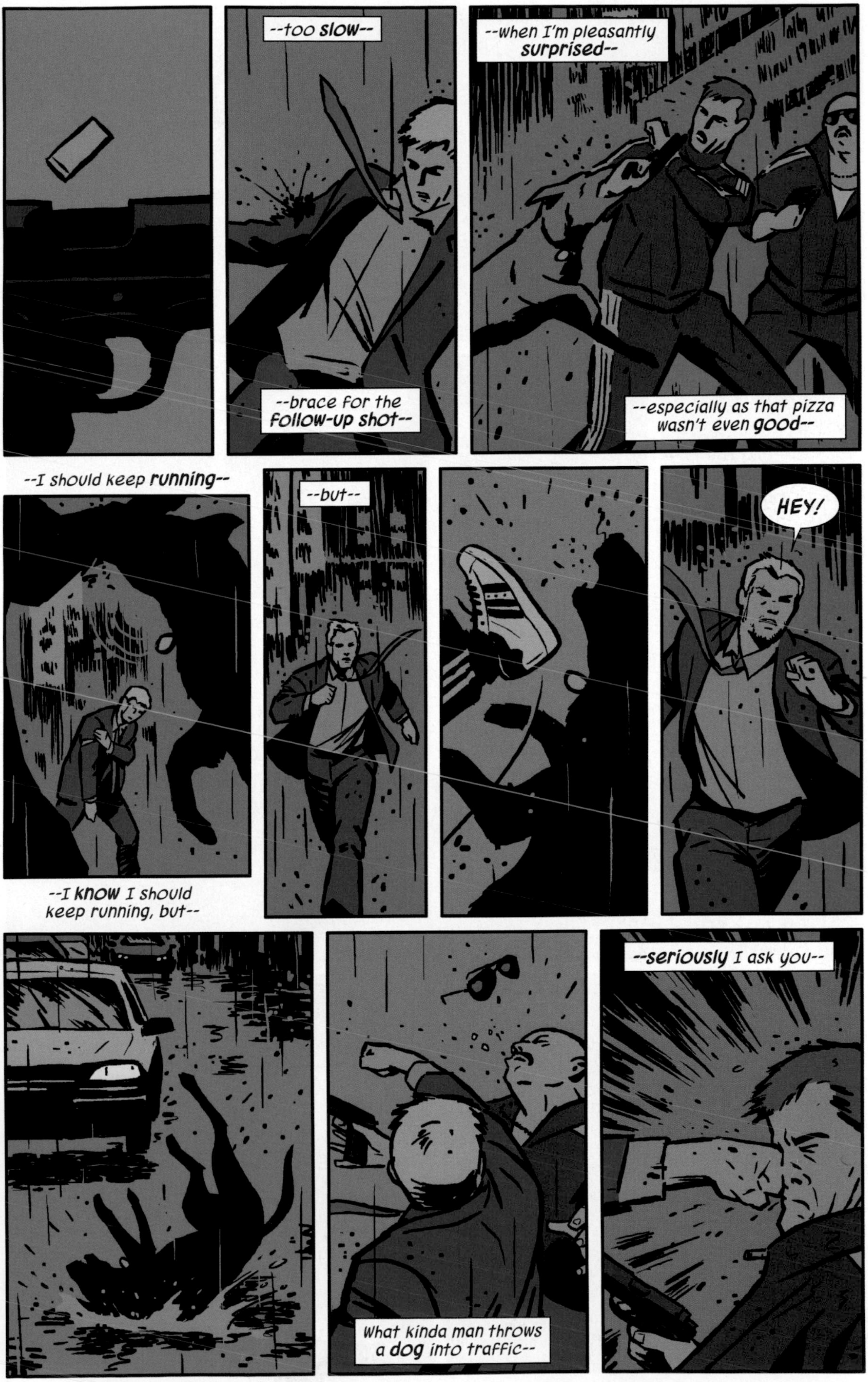
--too slow--
--brace for the follow-up shot--
--when I'm pleasantly surprised--
--especially as that pizza wasn't even good--
--I should keep running--
--I know I should keep running, but--
--but--
HEY!
What kinda man throws a dog into traffic--
--seriously I ask you--

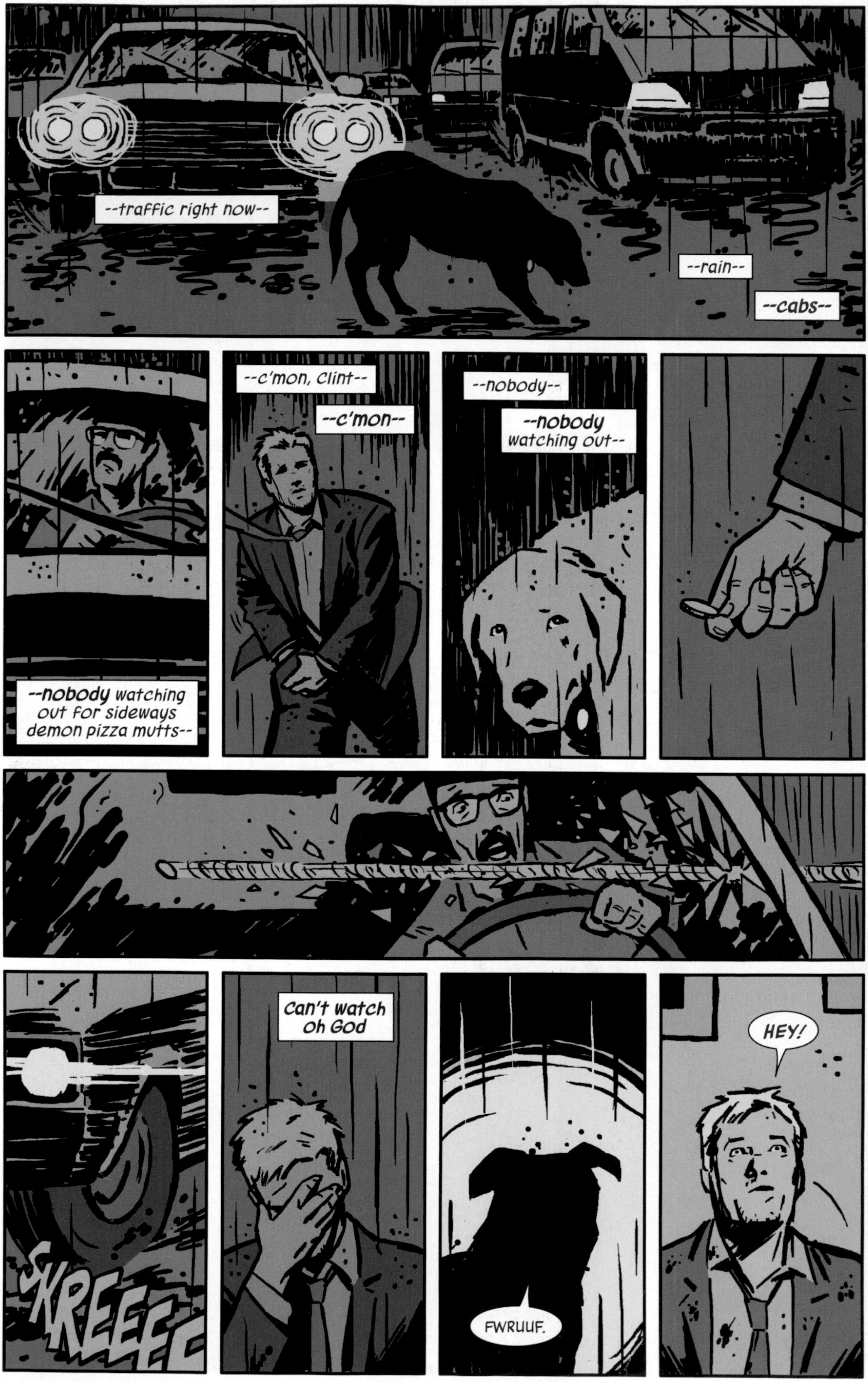
--traffic right now--
--rain--
--cabs--
--nobody watching out for sideways demon pizza mutts--
--c'mon, Clint--
--c'mon--
--nobody--
--nobody watching out--
SKREEEE
Can't watch oh God
FWRUUF.
HEY!

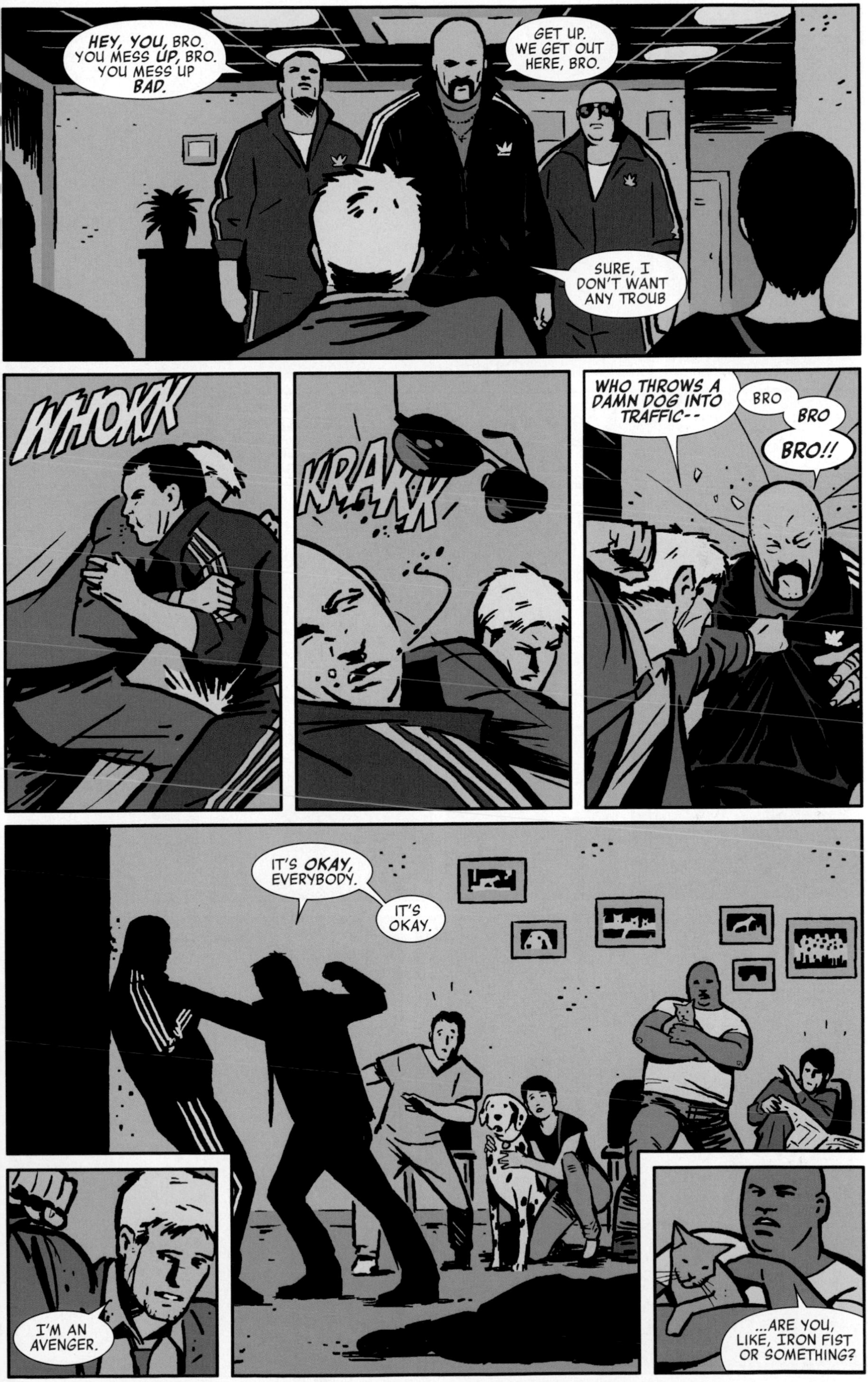
HEY, YOU, BRO. YOU MESS UP, BRO. YOU MESS UP BAD.
GET UP. WE GET OUT HERE, BRO.
SURE, I DON'T WANT ANY TROUB
WHOKK
KRAKK
WHO THROWS A DAMN DOG INTO TRAFFIC--
BRO
BRO
BRO!!
IT'S OKAY, EVERYBODY.
IT'S OKAY.
I'M AN AVENGER.
...ARE YOU, LIKE, IRON FIST OR SOMETHING?

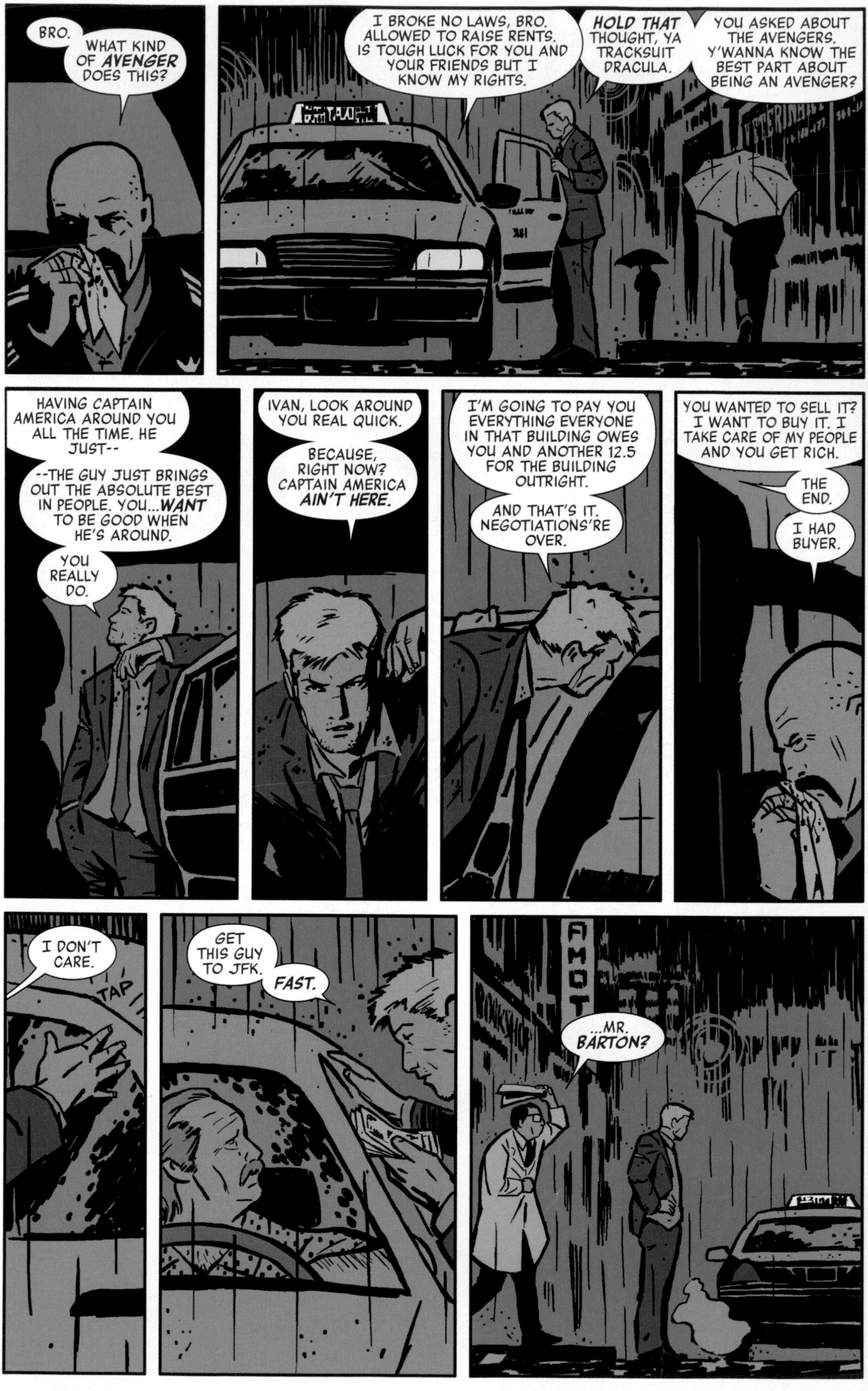
BRO.
WHAT KIND OF AVENGER DOES THIS?
I BROKE NO LAWS, BRO. ALLOWED TO RAISE RENTS. IS TOUGH LUCK FOR YOU AND YOUR FRIENDS BUT I KNOW MY RIGHTS.
HOLD THAT THOUGHT, YA TRACKSUIT DRACULA.
YOU ASKED ABOUT THE AVENGERS. Y'WANNA KNOW THE BEST PART ABOUT BEING AN AVENGER?
HAVING CAPTAIN AMERICA AROUND YOU ALL THE TIME. HE JUST--
--THE GUY JUST BRINGS OUT THE ABSOLUTE BEST IN PEOPLE. YOU...WANT TO BE GOOD WHEN HE'S AROUND.
YOU REALLY DO.
IVAN, LOOK AROUND YOU REAL QUICK.
BECAUSE, RIGHT NOW? CAPTAIN AMERICA AIN'T HERE.
I'M GOING TO PAY YOU EVERYTHING EVERYONE IN THAT BUILDING OWES YOU AND ANOTHER 12.5 FOR THE BUILDING OUTRIGHT.
AND THAT'S IT. NEGOTIATIONS'RE OVER.
YOU WANTED TO SELL IT? I WANT TO BUY IT. I TAKE CARE OF MY PEOPLE AND YOU GET RICH.
THE END.
I HAD BUYER.
I DON'T CARE.
TAP
GET THIS GUY TO JFK.
FAST.
...MR. BARTON?

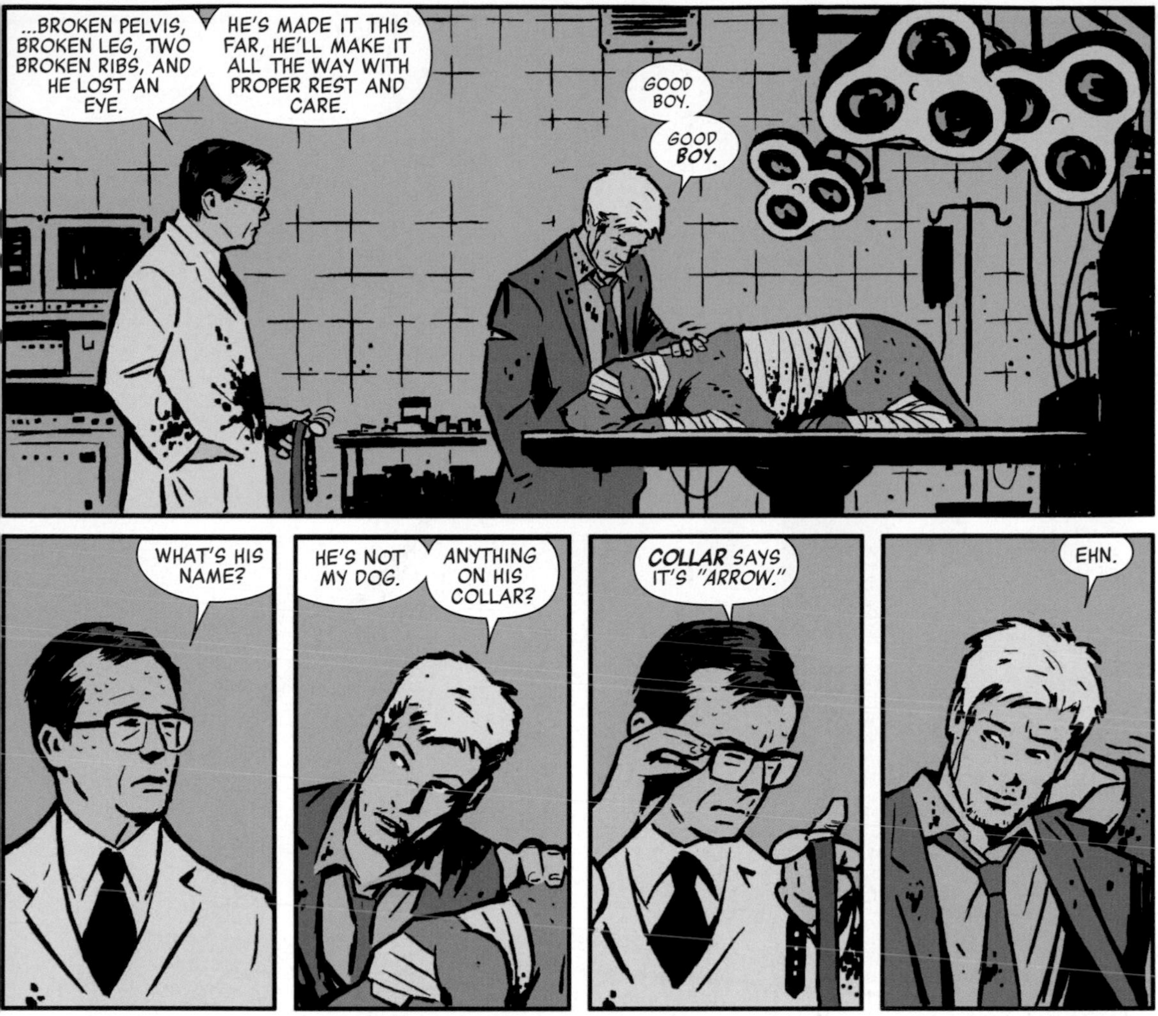
...BROKEN PELVIS, BROKEN LEG, TWO BROKEN RIBS, AND HE LOST AN EYE.
HE'S MADE IT THIS FAR, HE'LL MAKE IT ALL THE WAY WITH PROPER REST AND CARE.
GOOD BOY.
GOOD BOY.
WHAT'S HIS NAME?
HE'S NOT MY DOG.
ANYTHING ON HIS COLLAR?
COLLAR SAYS IT'S "ARROW."
EHN.

lucky hawkeye
a clint barton adventure

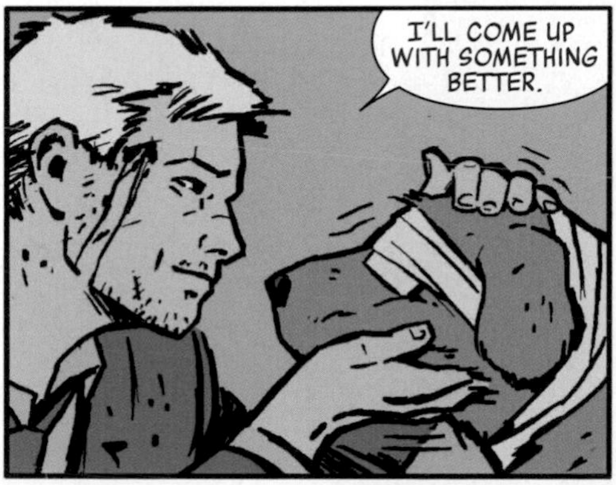
I'LL COME UP WITH SOMETHING BETTER.

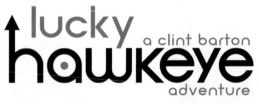

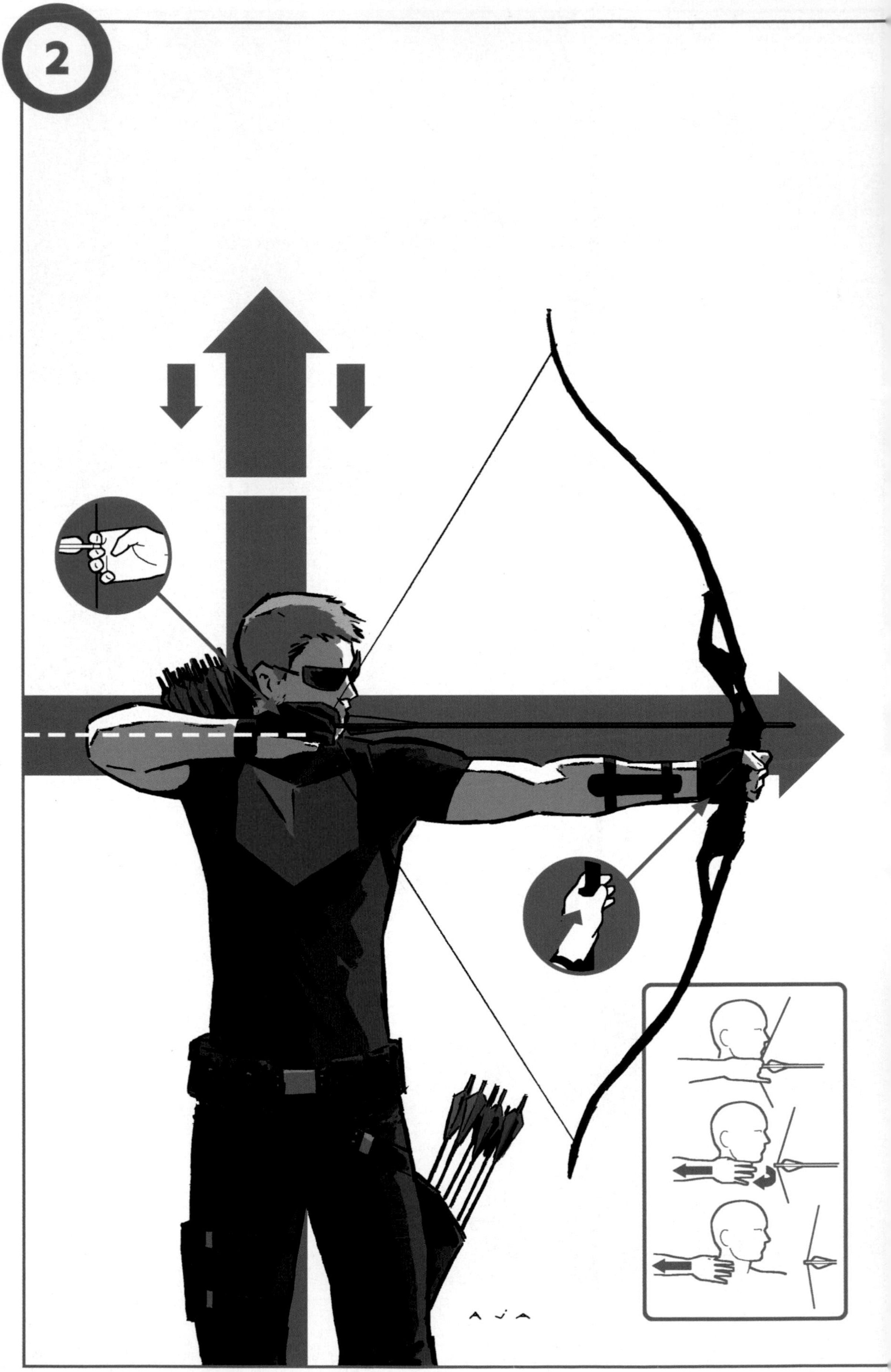
2

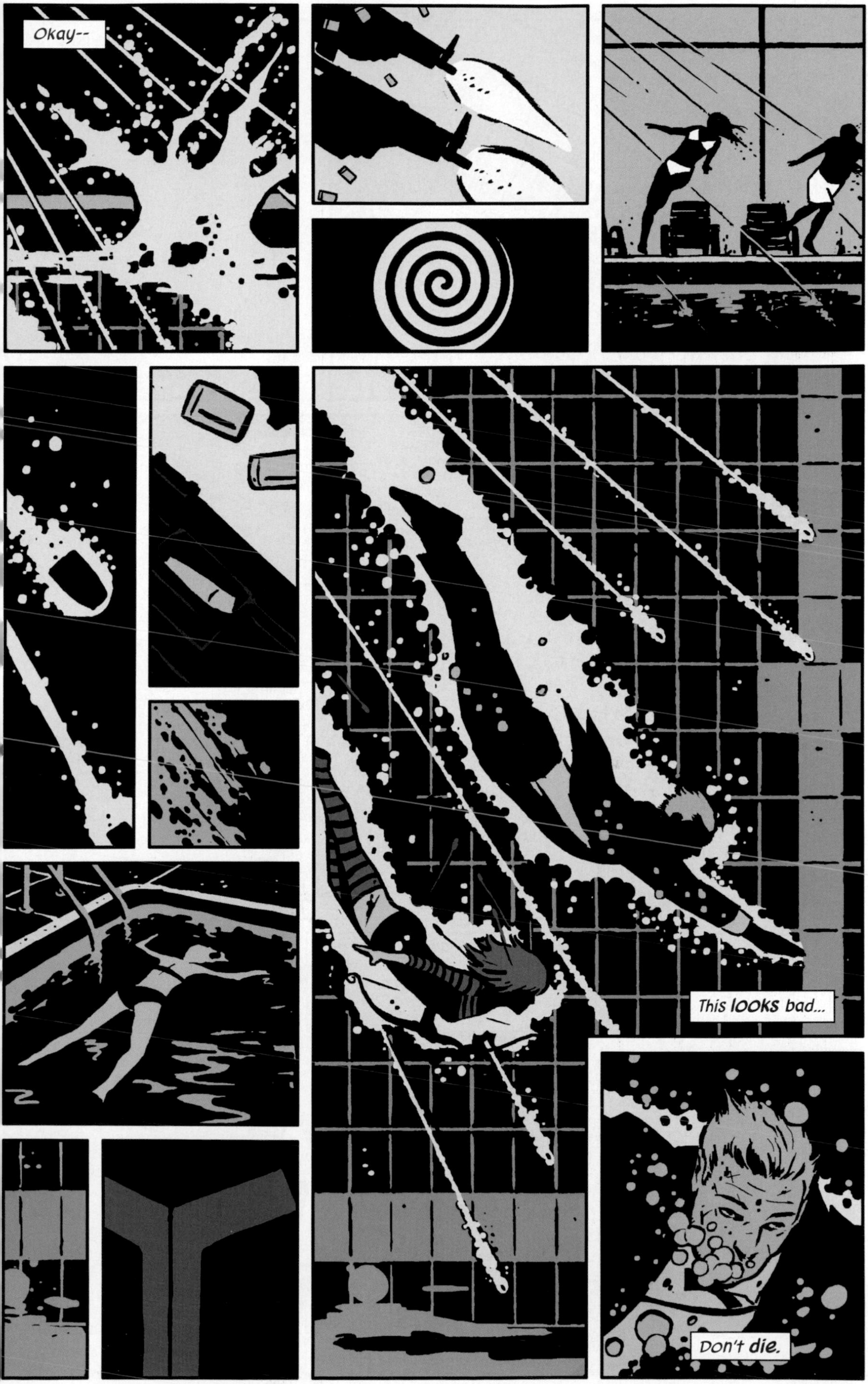
Okay--
This looks bad...
Don't die.

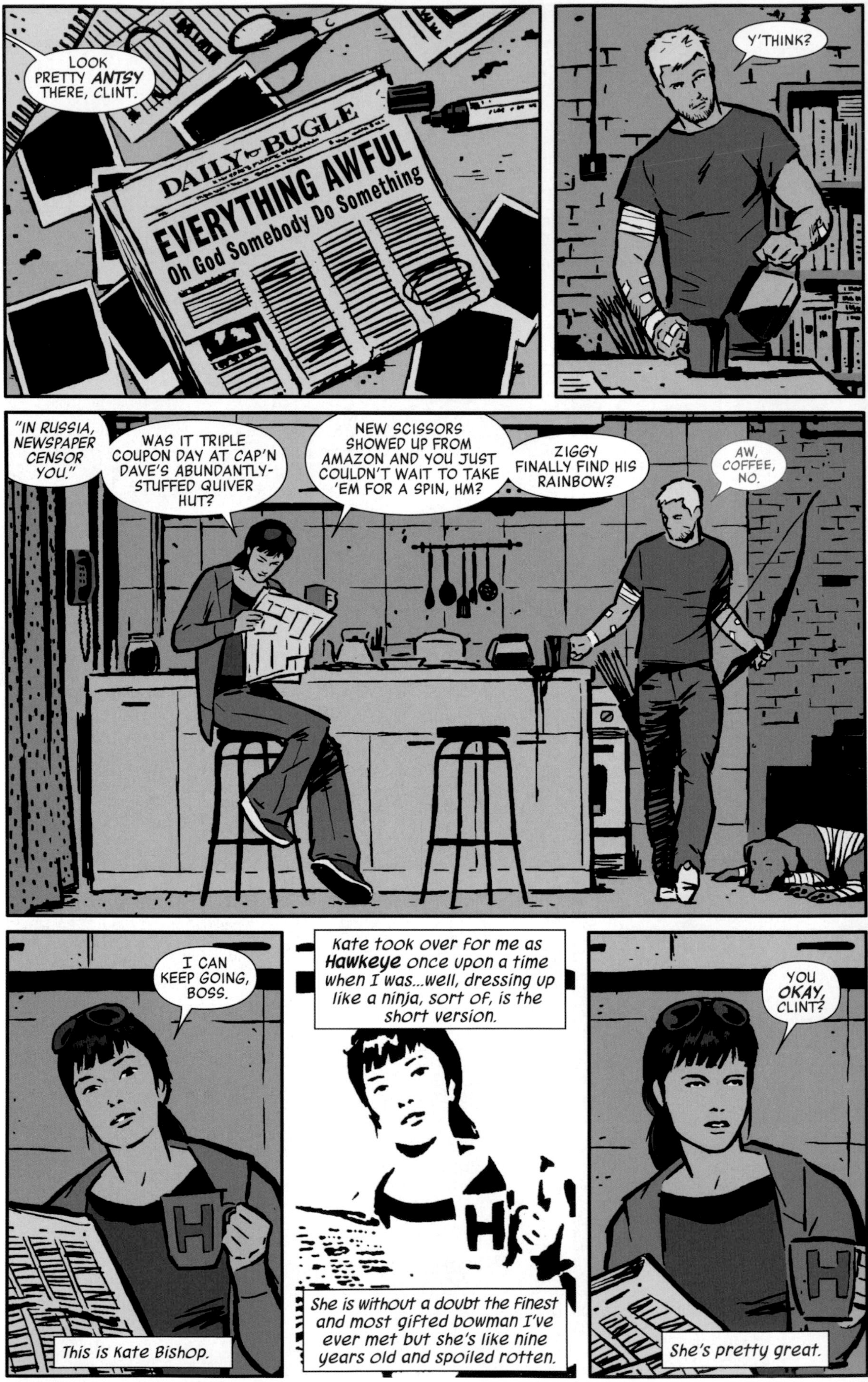

LOOK PRETTY ANTSY THERE, CLINT.
DAILY BUGLE
EVERYTHING AWFUL
Oh God Somebody Do Something
Y'THINK?
"IN RUSSIA, NEWSPAPER CENSOR YOU."
WAS IT TRIPLE COUPON DAY AT CAP'N DAVE'S ABUNDANTLY-STUFFED QUIVER HUT?
NEW SCISSORS SHOWED UP FROM AMAZON AND YOU JUST COULDN'T WAIT TO TAKE 'EM FOR A SPIN, HM?
ZIGGY FINALLY FIND HIS RAINBOW?
AW, COFFEE, NO.
I CAN KEEP GOING, BOSS.
This is Kate Bishop.
Kate took over for me as Hawkeye once upon a time when I was...well, dressing up like a ninja, sort of, is the short version.
She is without a doubt the finest and most gifted bowman I've ever met but she's like nine years old and spoiled rotten.
YOU OKAY, CLINT?
She's pretty great.

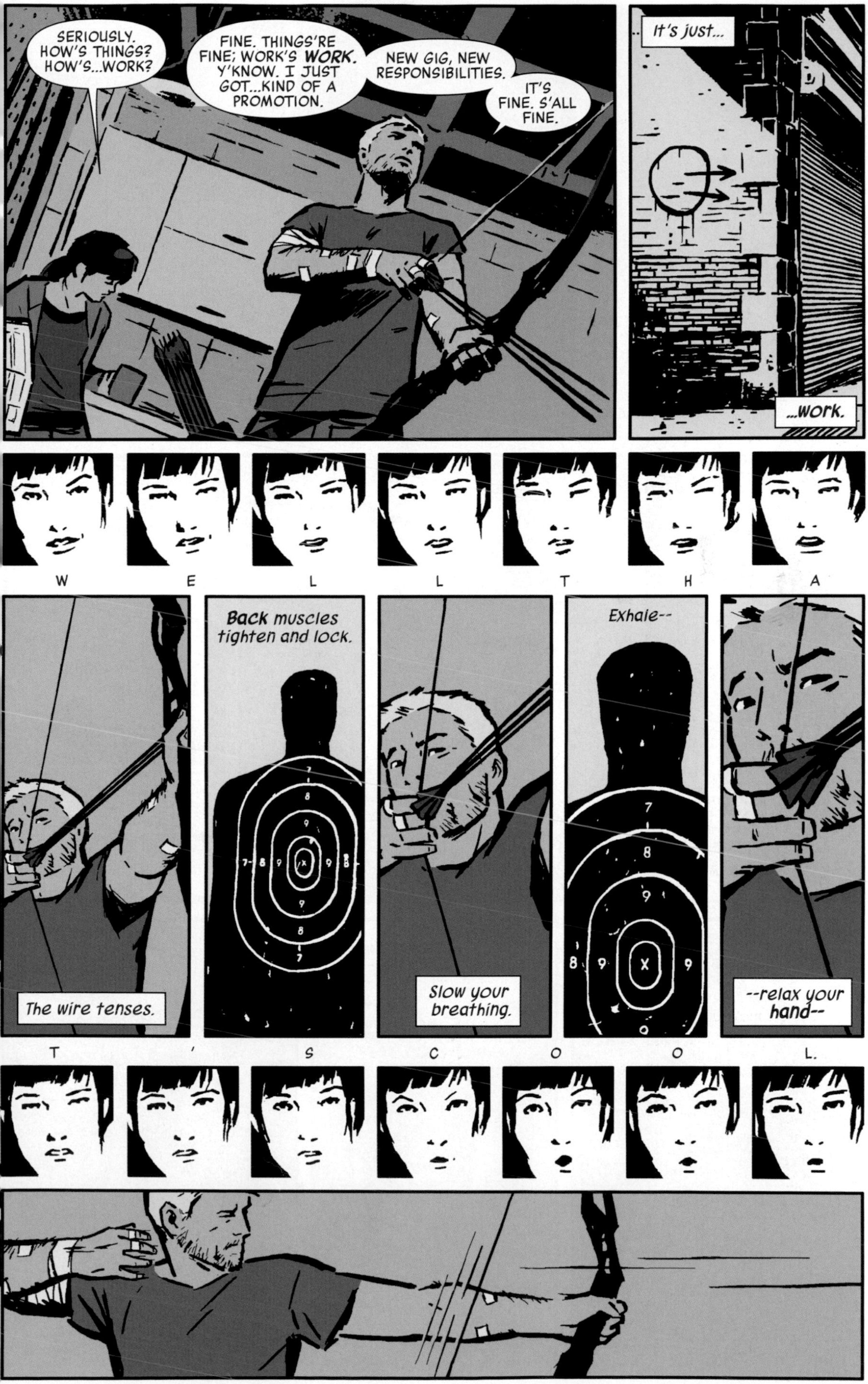
SERIOUSLY. HOW'S THINGS? HOW'S...WORK?
FINE. THINGS'RE FINE; WORK'S WORK. Y'KNOW. I JUST GOT...KIND OF A PROMOTION.
NEW GIG, NEW RESPONSIBILITIES.
IT'S FINE. S'ALL FINE.
It's just...
...work.
W E L L T H A
The wire tenses.
Back muscles tighten and lock.
Slow your breathing.
Exhale--
--relax your hand--
T ' S C O O L.

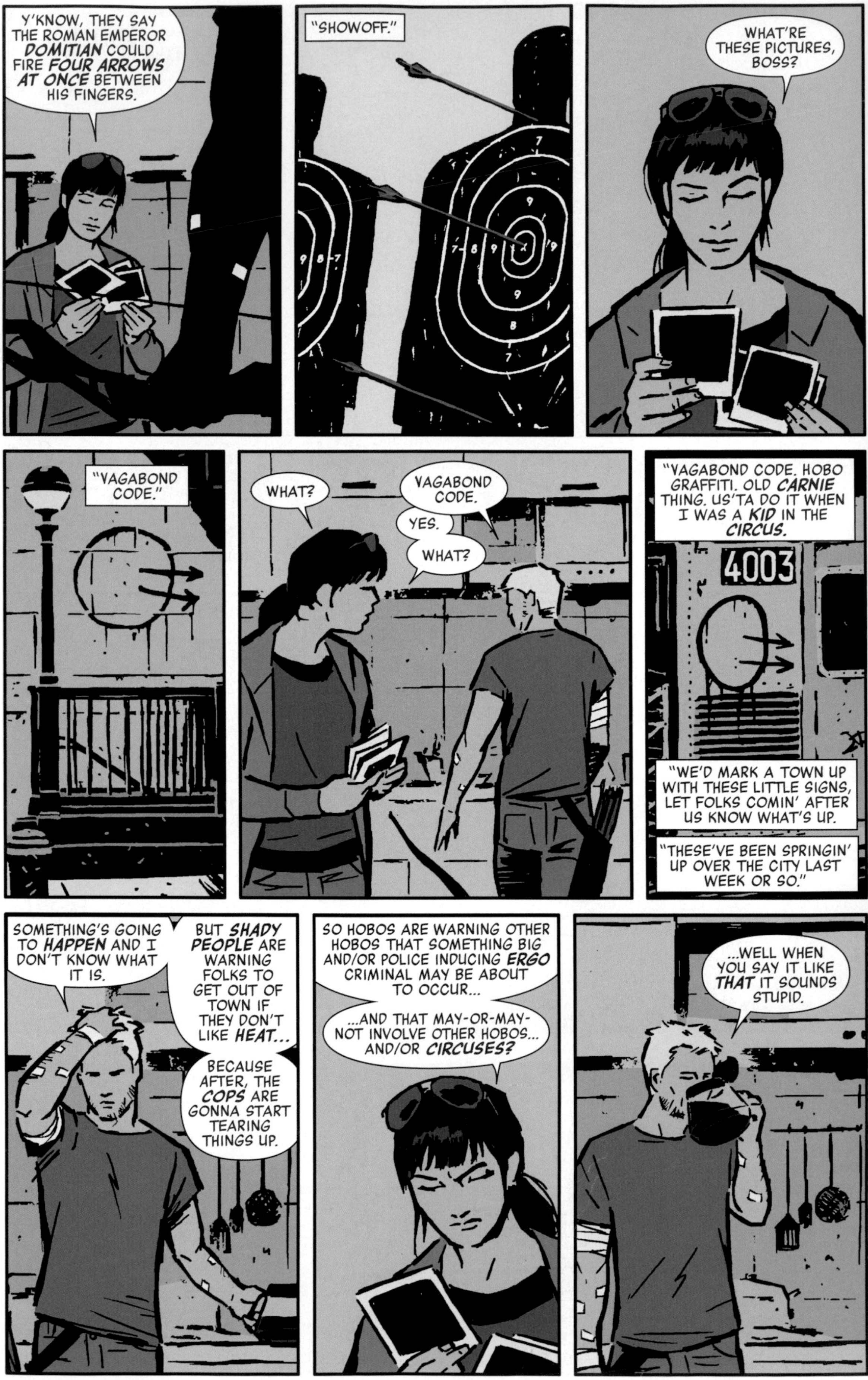
Y'KNOW, THEY SAY THE ROMAN EMPEROR DOMITIAN COULD FIRE FOUR ARROWS AT ONCE BETWEEN HIS FINGERS.
"SHOWOFF."
WHAT'RE THESE PICTURES, BOSS?
"VAGABOND CODE."
WHAT?
VAGABOND CODE.
YES.
WHAT?
"VAGABOND CODE. HOBO GRAFFITI. OLD CARNIE THING. US'TA DO IT WHEN I WAS A KID IN THE CIRCUS.
4003
"WE'D MARK A TOWN UP WITH THESE LITTLE SIGNS, LET FOLKS COMIN' AFTER US KNOW WHAT'S UP.
"THESE'VE BEEN SPRINGIN' UP OVER THE CITY LAST WEEK OR SO."
SOMETHING'S GOING TO HAPPEN AND I DON'T KNOW WHAT IT IS.
BUT SHADY PEOPLE ARE WARNING FOLKS TO GET OUT OF TOWN IF THEY DON'T LIKE HEAT...
BECAUSE AFTER, THE COPS ARE GONNA START TEARING THINGS UP.
SO HOBOS ARE WARNING OTHER HOBOS THAT SOMETHING BIG AND/OR POLICE INDUCING ERGO CRIMINAL MAY BE ABOUT TO OCCUR...
...AND THAT MAY-OR-MAY-NOT INVOLVE OTHER HOBOS... AND/OR CIRCUSES?
...WELL WHEN YOU SAY IT LIKE THAT IT SOUNDS STUPID.

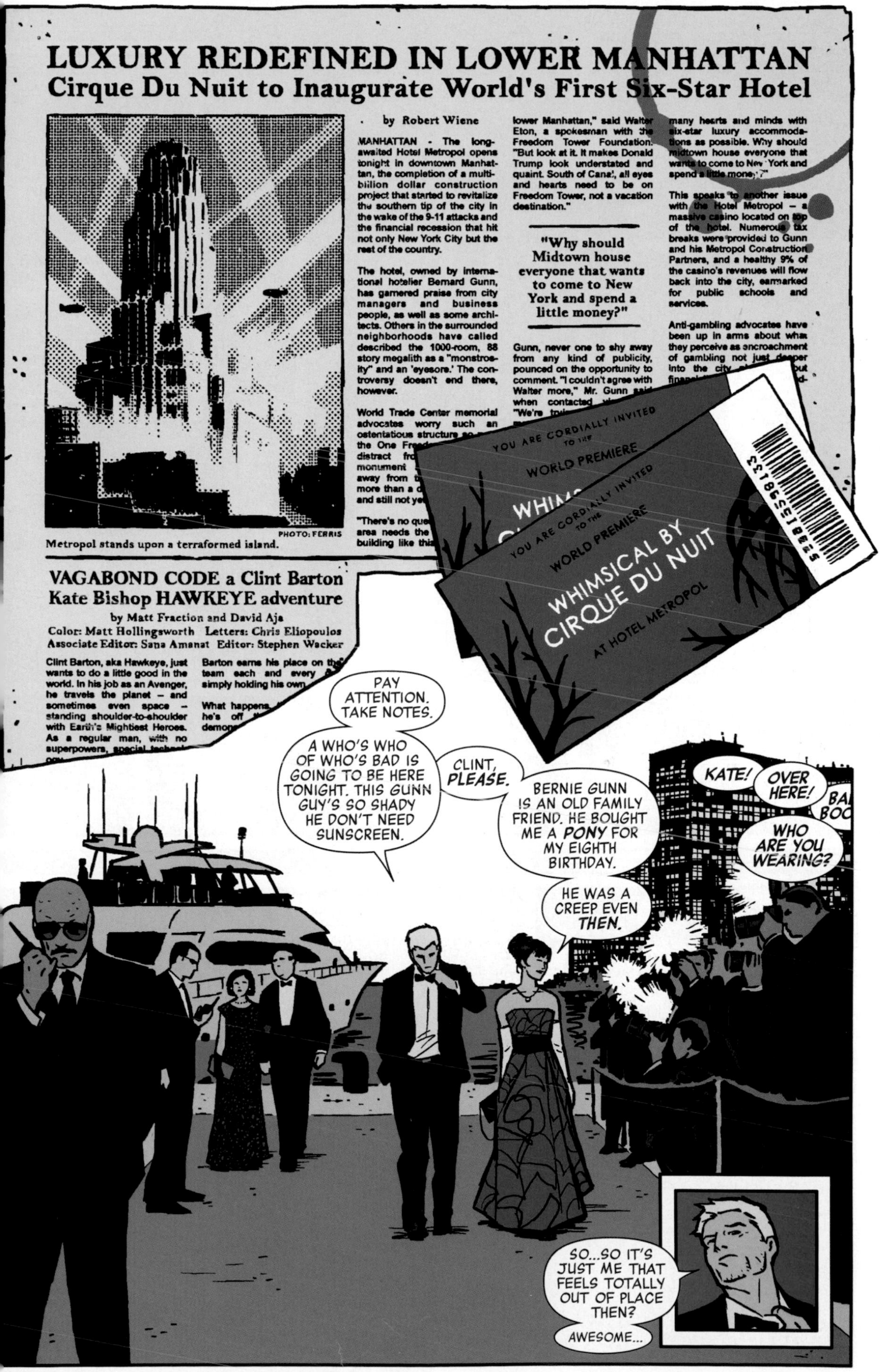

LUXURY REDEFINED IN LOWER MANHATTAN
Cirque Du Nuit to Inaugurate World's First Six-Star Hotel
by Robert Wiene
MANHATTAN - The long-awaited Hotel Metropol opens tonight in downtown Manhattan, the completion of a multi-billion dollar construction project that started to revitalize the southern tip of the city in the wake of the 9-11 attacks and the financial recession that hit not only New York City but the rest of the country.
The hotel, owned by international hotelier Bernard Gunn, has garnered praise from city managers and business people, as well as some architects. Others in the surrounded neighborhoods have called described the 1000-room, 88 story megalith as a "monstrosity" and an 'eyesore.' The controversy doesn't end there, however.
World Trade Center memorial advocates worry such an ostentatious structure
the One
distract
monument
away from
more than a
and still not
"There's no
area needs the
building like
lower Manhattan," said Walter Eton, a spokesman with the Freedom Tower Foundation. "But look at it. It makes Donald Trump look understated and quaint. South of Canal, all eyes and hearts need to be on Freedom Tower, not a vacation destination."
"Why should Midtown house everyone that wants to come to New York and spend a little money?"
Gunn, never one to shy away from any kind of publicity, pounced on the opportunity to comment. "I couldn't agree with Walter more," Mr. Gunn
when contacted
"We're
many hearts and minds with six-star luxury accommodations as possible. Why should midtown house everyone that wants to come to New York and spend a little money?"
This speaks to another issue with the Hotel Metropol – a massive casino located on top of the hotel. Numerous tax breaks were provided to Gunn and his Metropol Construction Partners, and a healthy 9% of the casino's revenues will flow back into the city, earmarked for public schools and services.
Anti-gambling advocates have been up in arms about what they perceive as encroachment of gambling not just deeper into the city
PHOTO: FERRIS
Metropol stands upon a terraformed island.
VAGABOND CODE a Clint Barton Kate Bishop HAWKEYE adventure
by Matt Fraction and David Aja
Color: Matt Hollingsworth Letters: Chris Eliopoulos
Associate Editor: Sana Amanat Editor: Stephen Wacker
Clint Barton, aka Hawkeye, just wants to do a little good in the world. In his job as an Avenger, he travels the planet – and sometimes even space – standing shoulder-to-shoulder with Earth's Mightiest Heroes. As a regular man, with no superpowers,
Barton earns his place on the team each and every
simply holding his own
What happens
he's off
YOU ARE CORDIALLY INVITED TO THE
WORLD PREMIERE
YOU ARE CORDIALLY INVITED TO THE
WORLD PREMIERE
WHIMSICAL BY CIRQUE DU NUIT
AT HOTEL METROPOL
PAY ATTENTION. TAKE NOTES.
A WHO'S WHO OF WHO'S BAD IS GOING TO BE HERE TONIGHT. THIS GUNN GUY'S SO SHADY HE DON'T NEED SUNSCREEN.
CLINT, PLEASE.
BERNIE GUNN IS AN OLD FAMILY FRIEND. HE BOUGHT ME A PONY FOR MY EIGHTH BIRTHDAY.
HE WAS A CREEP EVEN THEN.
KATE!
OVER HERE!
WHO ARE YOU WEARING?
SO...SO IT'S JUST ME THAT FEELS TOTALLY OUT OF PLACE THEN?
AWESOME...

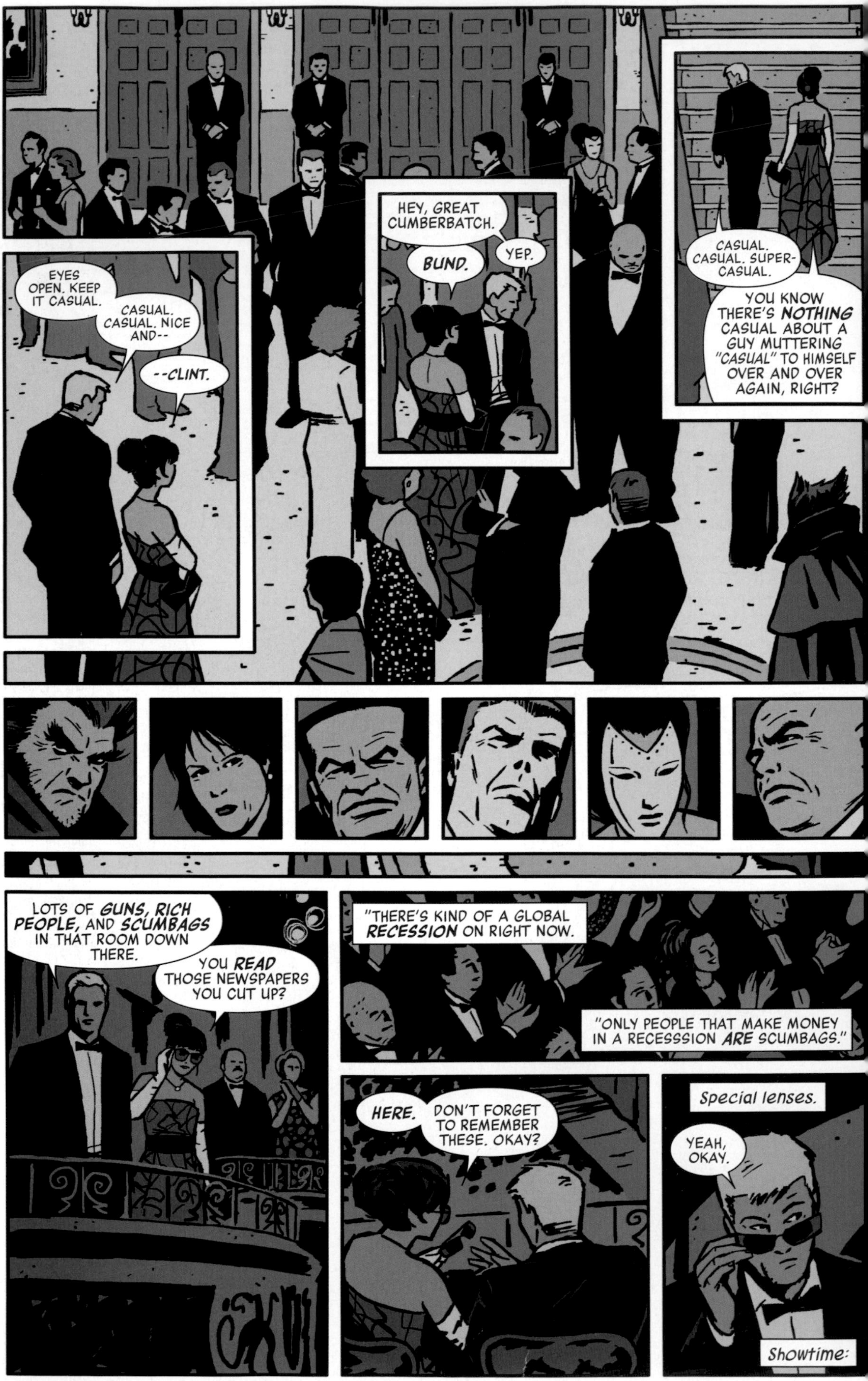
EYES OPEN. KEEP IT CASUAL.
CASUAL. CASUAL. NICE AND--
--CLINT.
HEY, GREAT CUMBERBATCH.
BUND.
YEP.
CASUAL. CASUAL. SUPER-CASUAL.
YOU KNOW THERE'S NOTHING CASUAL ABOUT A GUY MUTTERING "CASUAL" TO HIMSELF OVER AND OVER AGAIN, RIGHT?
LOTS OF GUNS, RICH PEOPLE, AND SCUMBAGS IN THAT ROOM DOWN THERE.
YOU READ THOSE NEWSPAPERS YOU CUT UP?
"THERE'S KIND OF A GLOBAL RECESSION ON RIGHT NOW.
"ONLY PEOPLE THAT MAKE MONEY IN A RECESSSION ARE SCUMBAGS."
HERE.
DON'T FORGET TO REMEMBER THESE. OKAY?
Special lenses.
YEAH, OKAY.
Showtime:

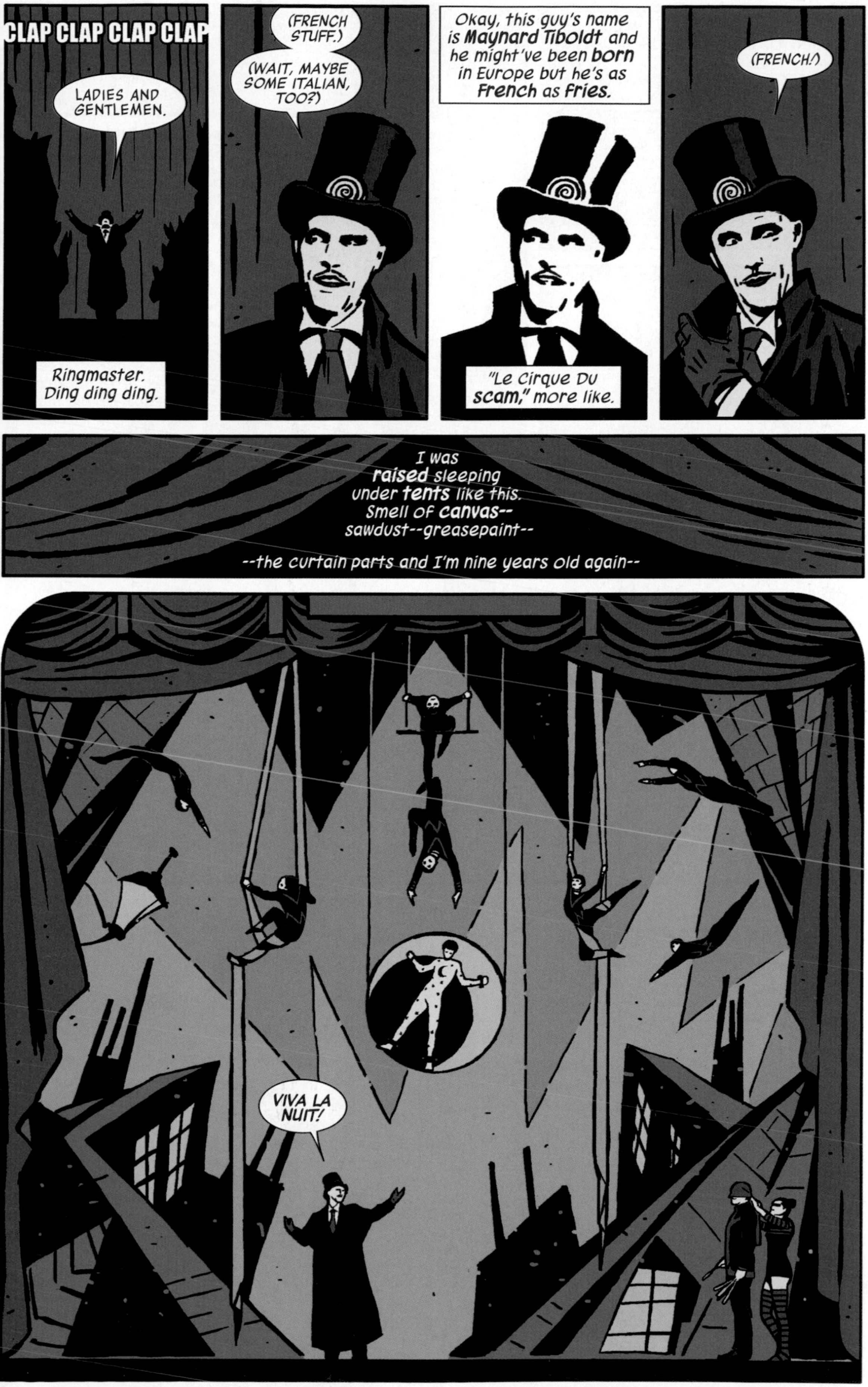
CLAP CLAP CLAP CLAP
LADIES AND GENTLEMEN.
Ringmaster. Ding ding ding.
(FRENCH STUFF.)
(WAIT, MAYBE SOME ITALIAN, TOO?)
Okay, this guy's name is Maynard Tiboldt and he might've been born in Europe but he's as French as fries.
"Le Cirque Du scam," more like.
(FRENCH!)
I was raised sleeping under tents like this. Smell of canvas-- sawdust--greasepaint--
--the curtain parts and I'm nine years old again--
VIVA LA NUIT!

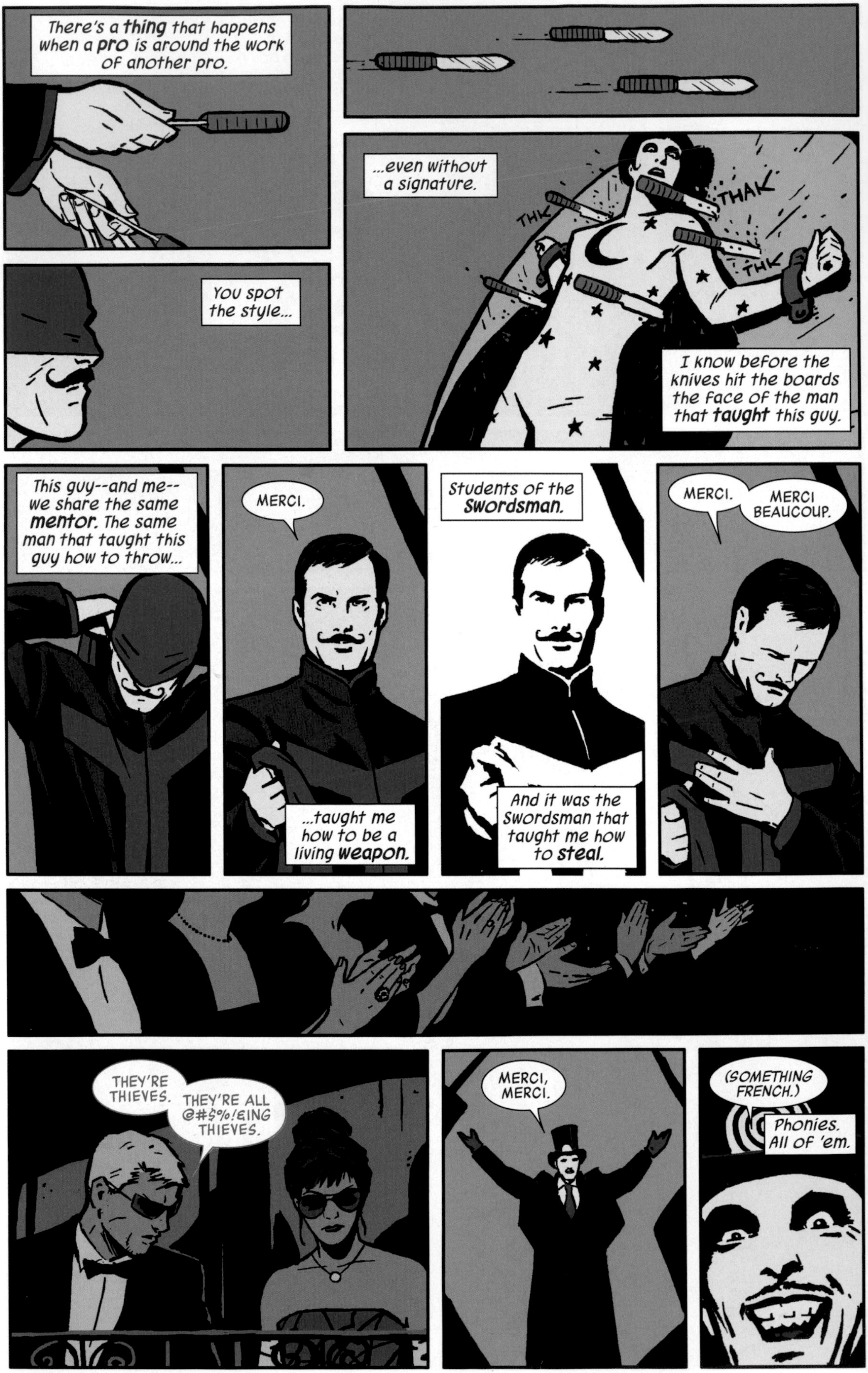
There's a thing that happens when a pro is around the work of another pro.
You spot the style...
...even without a signature.
THK
THAK
THK
I know before the knives hit the boards the face of the man that taught this guy.
This guy--and me--we share the same mentor. The same man that taught this guy how to throw...
MERCI.
...taught me how to be a living weapon.
Students of the Swordsman.
And it was the Swordsman that taught me how to steal.
MERCI.
MERCI BEAUCOUP.
THEY'RE THIEVES.
THEY'RE ALL @#$%!€ING THIEVES.
MERCI, MERCI.
(SOMETHING FRENCH.)
Phonies. All of 'em.

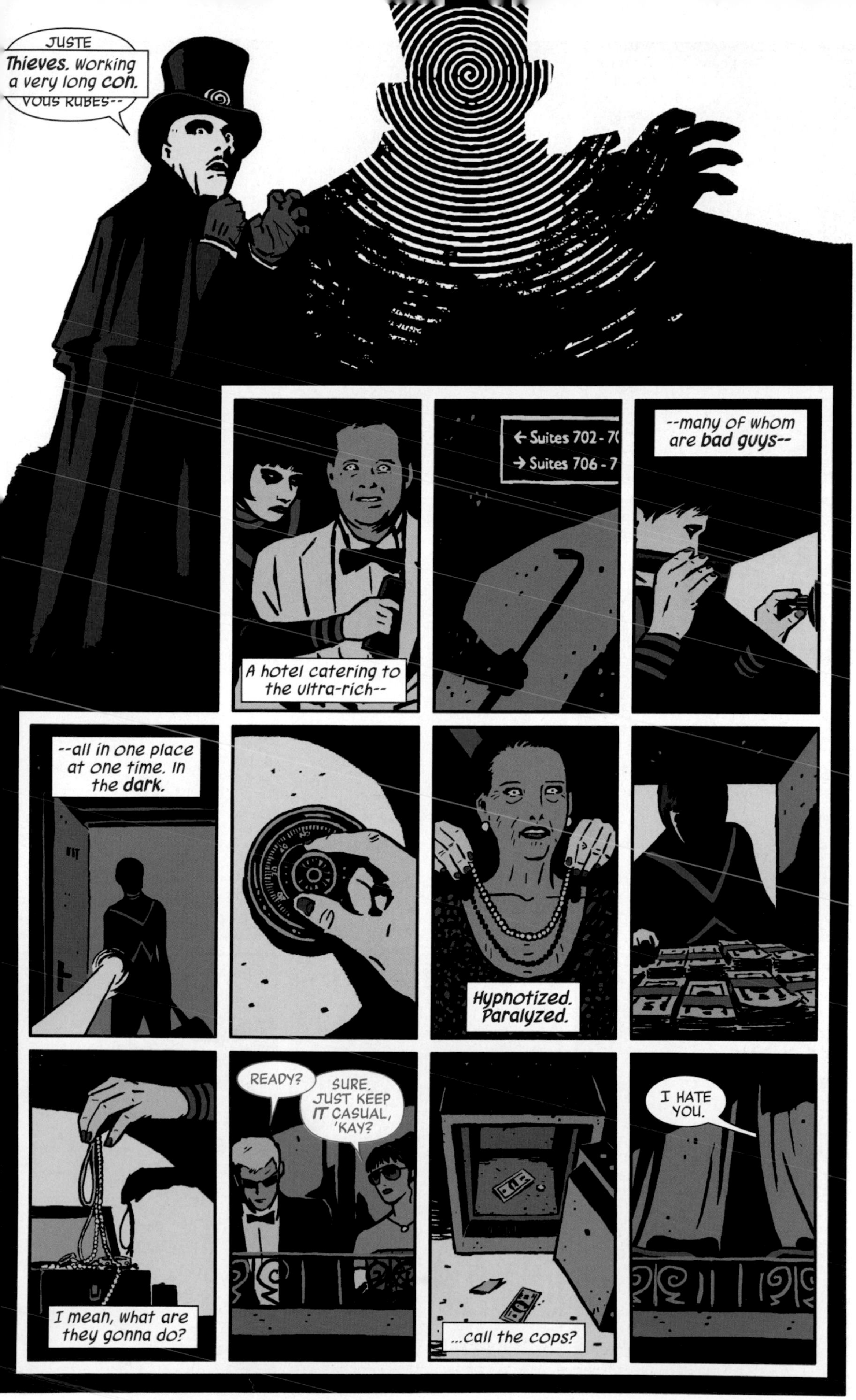
JUSTE
Thieves. Working a very long con.
VOUS RUBES--
A hotel catering to the ultra-rich--
← Suites 702 - 70
→ Suites 706 - 7
--many of whom are bad guys--
--all in one place at one time. In the dark.
Hypnotized. Paralyzed.
I mean, what are they gonna do?
READY?
SURE. JUST KEEP IT CASUAL, 'KAY?
...call the cops?
I HATE YOU.

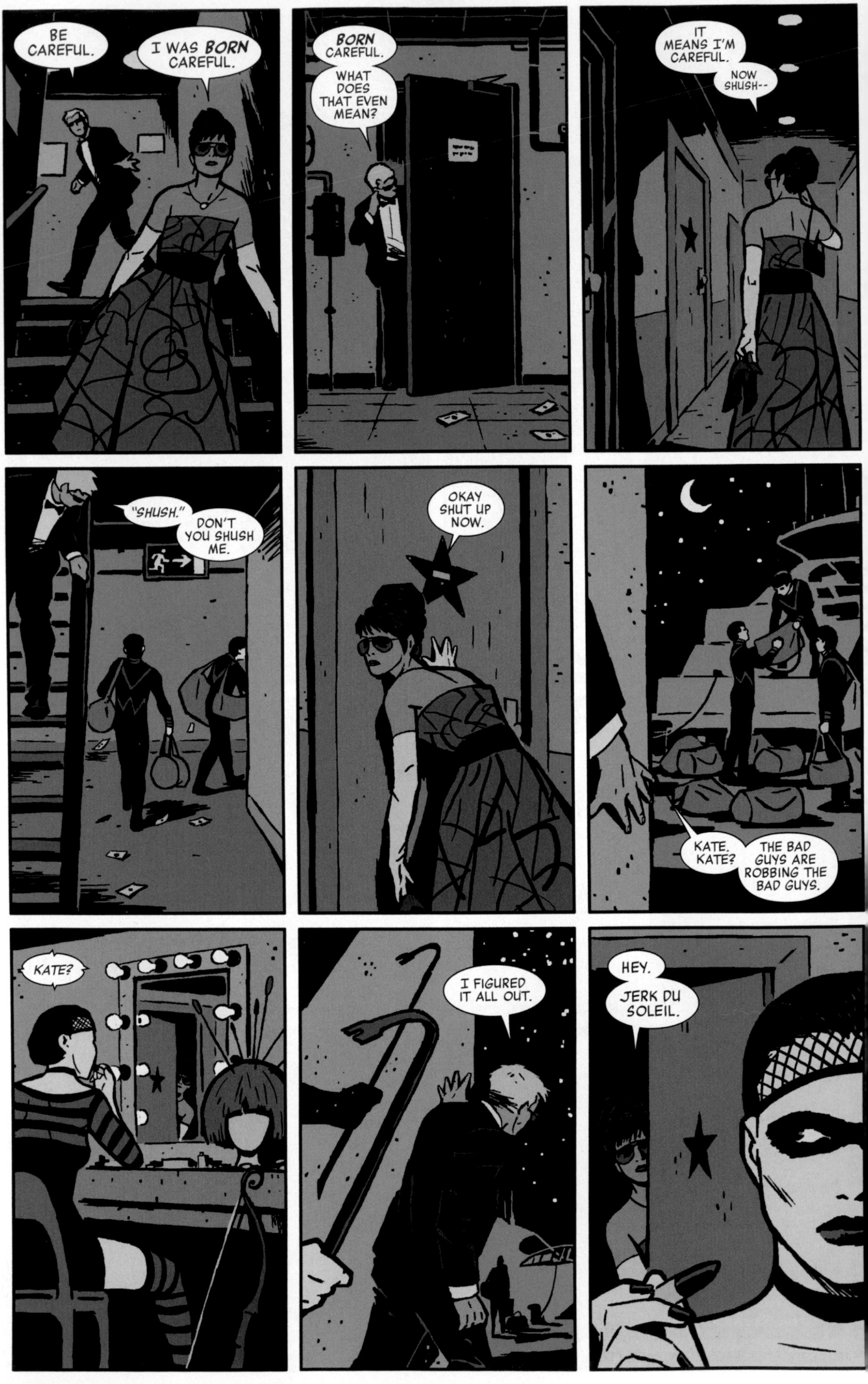
BE CAREFUL.
I WAS BORN CAREFUL.
BORN CAREFUL.
WHAT DOES THAT EVEN MEAN?
IT MEANS I'M CAREFUL.
NOW SHUSH--
"SHUSH."
DON'T YOU SHUSH ME.
OKAY SHUT UP NOW.
KATE. KATE?
THE BAD GUYS ARE ROBBING THE BAD GUYS.
KATE?
I FIGURED IT ALL OUT.
HEY.
JERK DU SOLEIL.

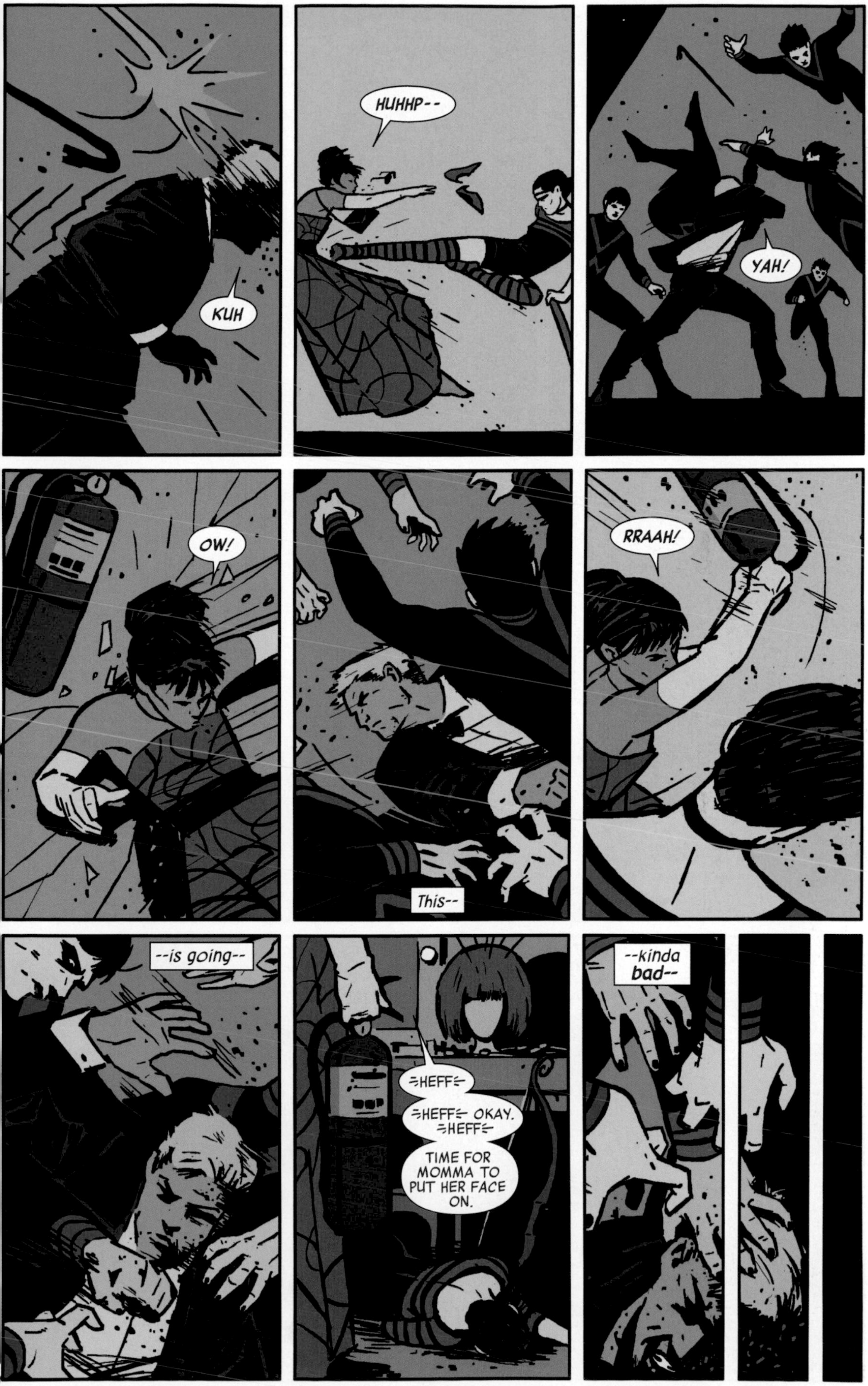
KUH
HUHHP--
YAH!
OW!
This--
RRAAH!
--is going--
=HEFF=
=HEFF= OKAY. =HEFF=
TIME FOR MOMMA TO PUT HER FACE ON.
--kinda bad--

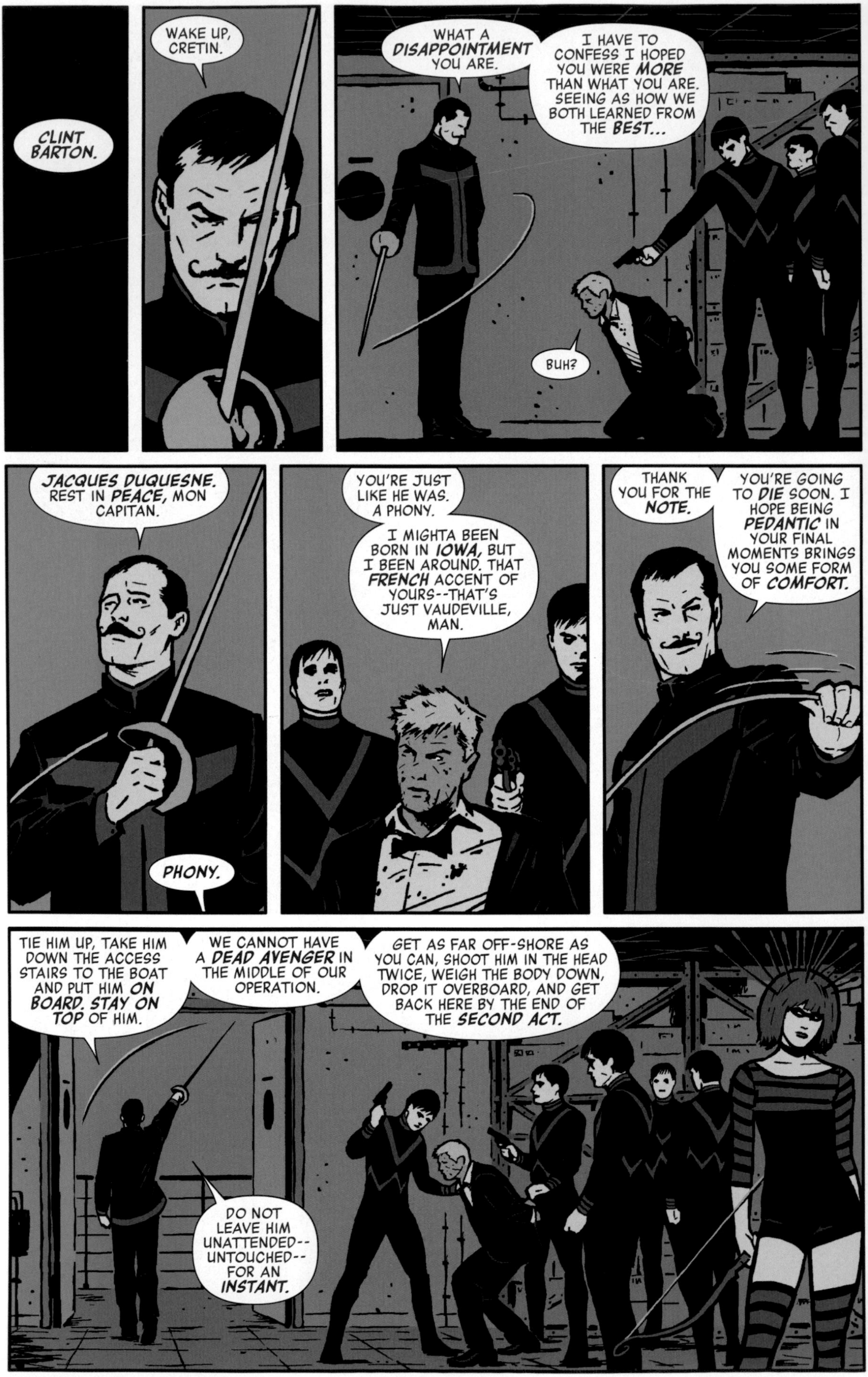
CLINT BARTON.
WAKE UP, CRETIN.
WHAT A DISAPPOINTMENT YOU ARE.
I HAVE TO CONFESS I HOPED YOU WERE MORE THAN WHAT YOU ARE. SEEING AS HOW WE BOTH LEARNED FROM THE BEST...
BUH?
JACQUES DUQUESNE. REST IN PEACE, MON CAPITAN.
PHONY.
YOU'RE JUST LIKE HE WAS. A PHONY.
I MIGHTA BEEN BORN IN IOWA, BUT I BEEN AROUND. THAT FRENCH ACCENT OF YOURS--THAT'S JUST VAUDEVILLE, MAN.
THANK YOU FOR THE NOTE.
YOU'RE GOING TO DIE SOON. I HOPE BEING PEDANTIC IN YOUR FINAL MOMENTS BRINGS YOU SOME FORM OF COMFORT.
TIE HIM UP, TAKE HIM DOWN THE ACCESS STAIRS TO THE BOAT AND PUT HIM ON BOARD. STAY ON TOP OF HIM.
WE CANNOT HAVE A DEAD AVENGER IN THE MIDDLE OF OUR OPERATION.
GET AS FAR OFF-SHORE AS YOU CAN, SHOOT HIM IN THE HEAD TWICE, WEIGH THE BODY DOWN, DROP IT OVERBOARD, AND GET BACK HERE BY THE END OF THE SECOND ACT.
DO NOT LEAVE HIM UNATTENDED-- UNTOUCHED-- FOR AN INSTANT.

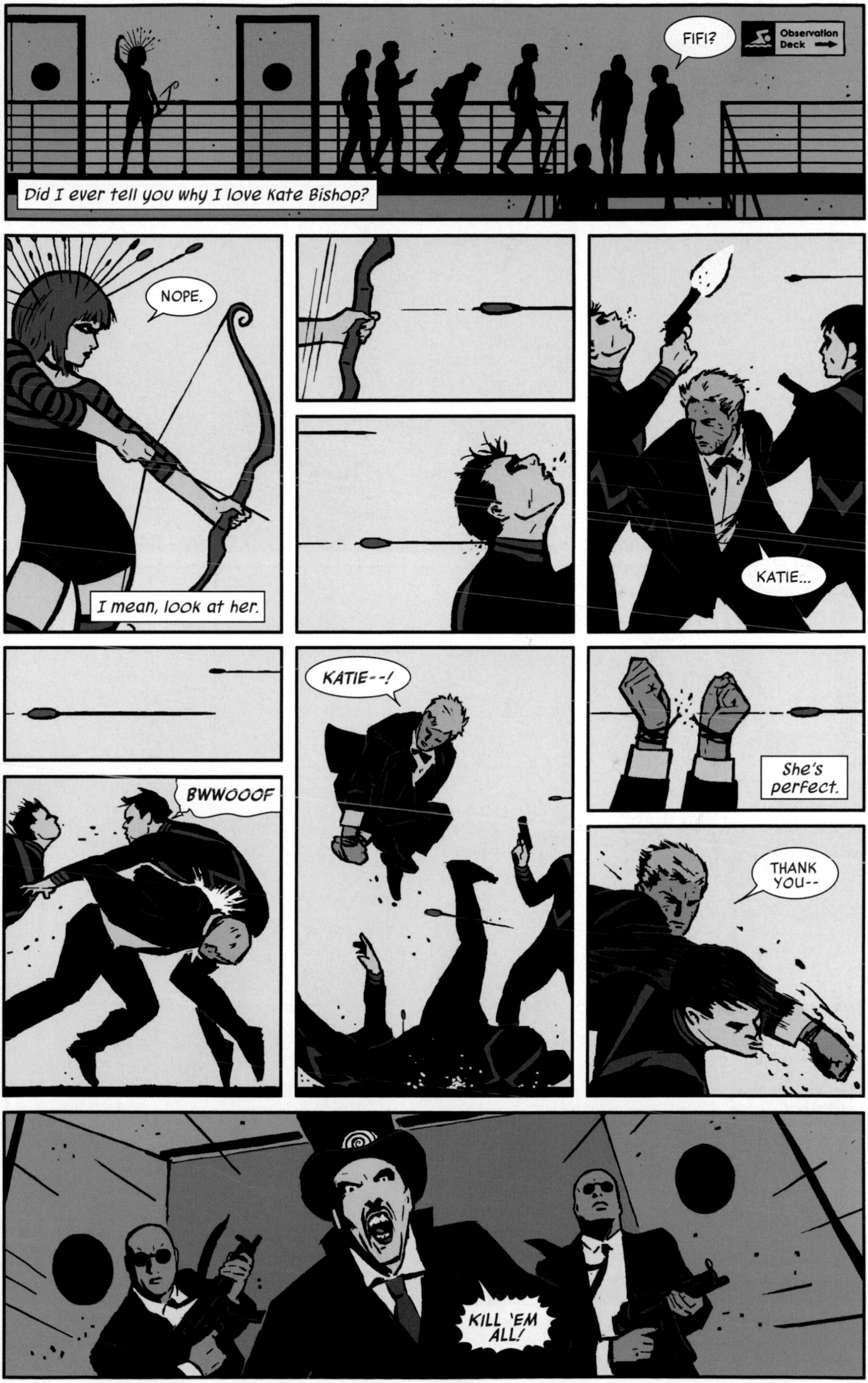
Observation Deck
FIFI?
Did I ever tell you why I love Kate Bishop?
NOPE.
I mean, look at her.
KATIE...
KATIE--!
She's perfect.
BWWOOOF
THANK YOU--
KILL 'EM ALL!

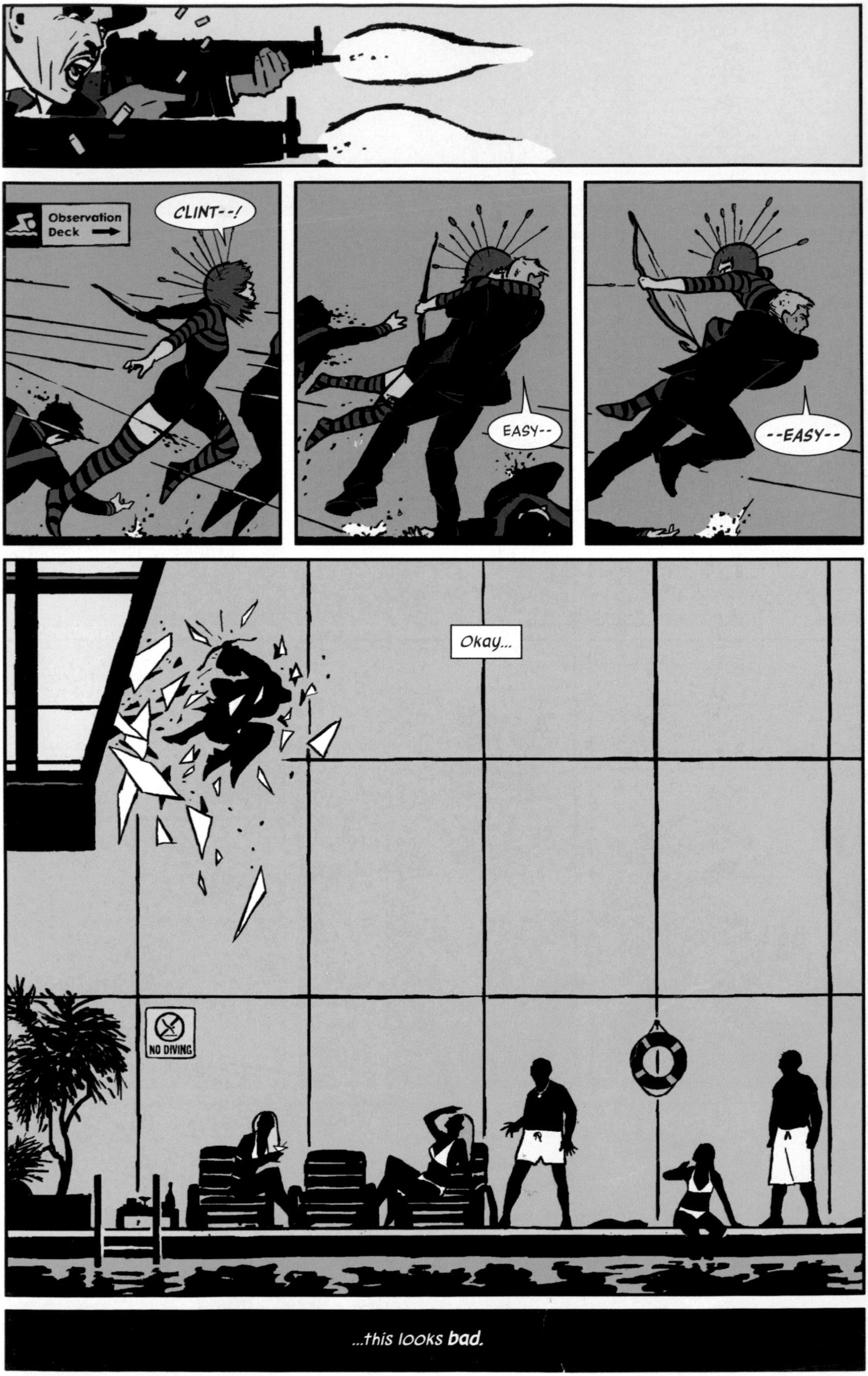
Observation Deck
CLINT--!
EASY--
--EASY--
Okay...
NO DIVING
...this looks bad.

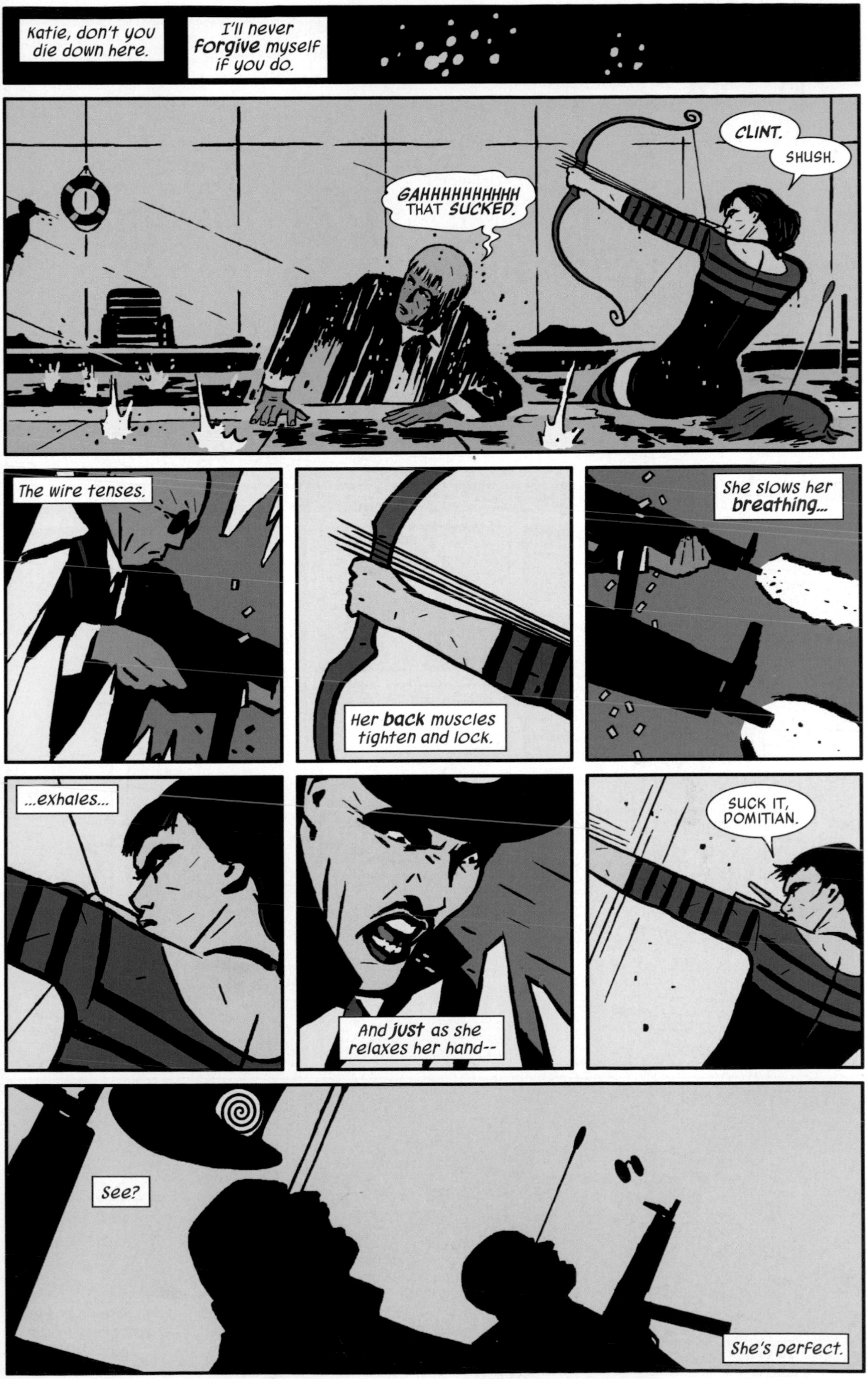
Katie, don't you die down here.
I'll never forgive myself if you do.
GAHHHHHHHHHH THAT SUCKED.
CLINT.
SHUSH.
The wire tenses.
Her back muscles tighten and lock.
She slows her breathing...
...exhales...
And just as she relaxes her hand--
SUCK IT, DOMITIAN.
See?
She's perfect.

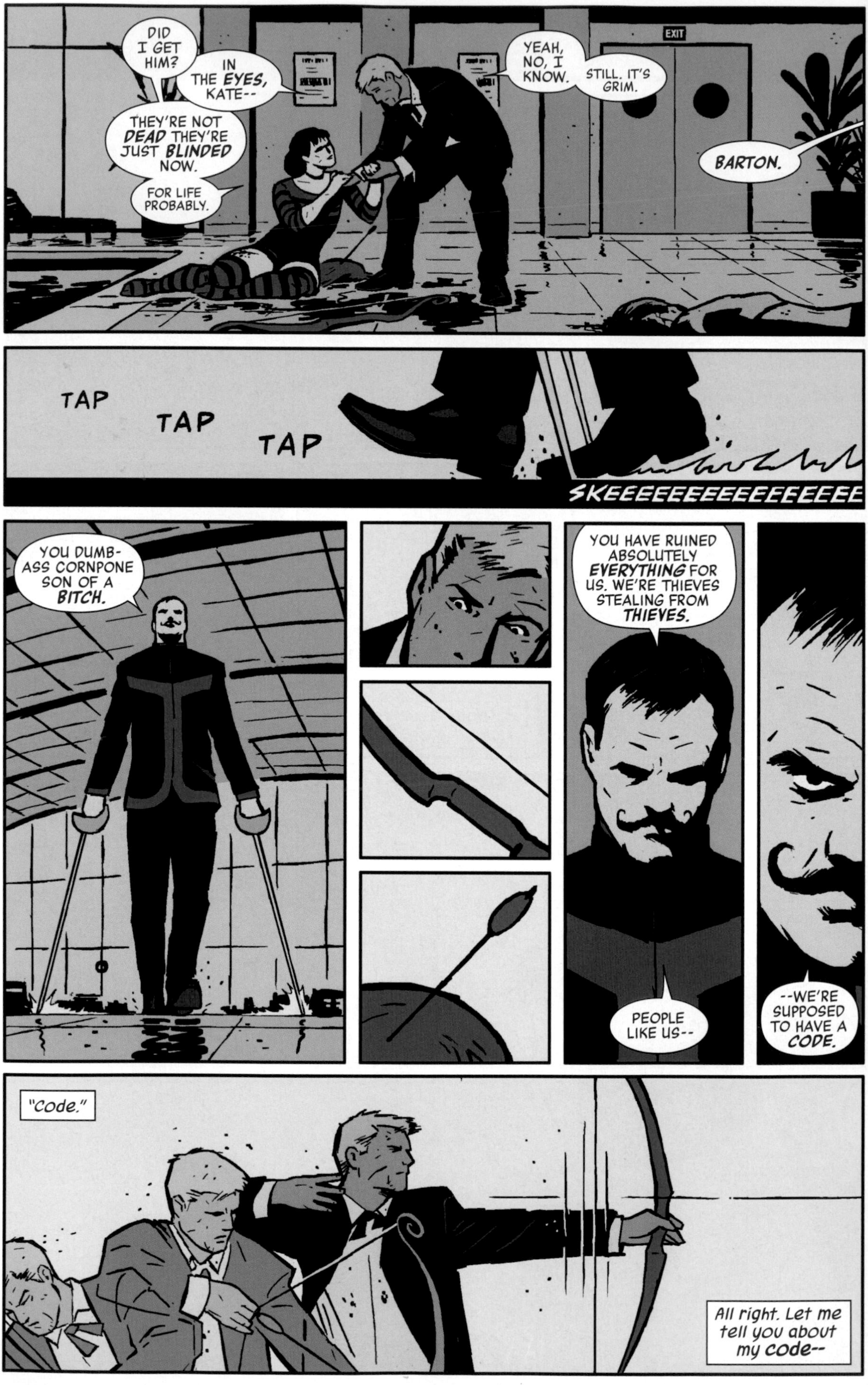
DID I GET HIM?
IN THE EYES, KATE--
THEY'RE NOT DEAD THEY'RE JUST BLINDED NOW.
FOR LIFE PROBABLY.
YEAH, NO, I KNOW.
STILL. IT'S GRIM.
EXIT
BARTON.
TAP
TAP
TAP
SKEEEEEEEEEEEEEEE
YOU DUMB-ASS CORNPONE SON OF A BITCH.
YOU HAVE RUINED ABSOLUTELY EVERYTHING FOR US. WE'RE THIEVES STEALING FROM THIEVES.
PEOPLE LIKE US--
--WE'RE SUPPOSED TO HAVE A CODE.
"Code."
All right. Let me tell you about my code--

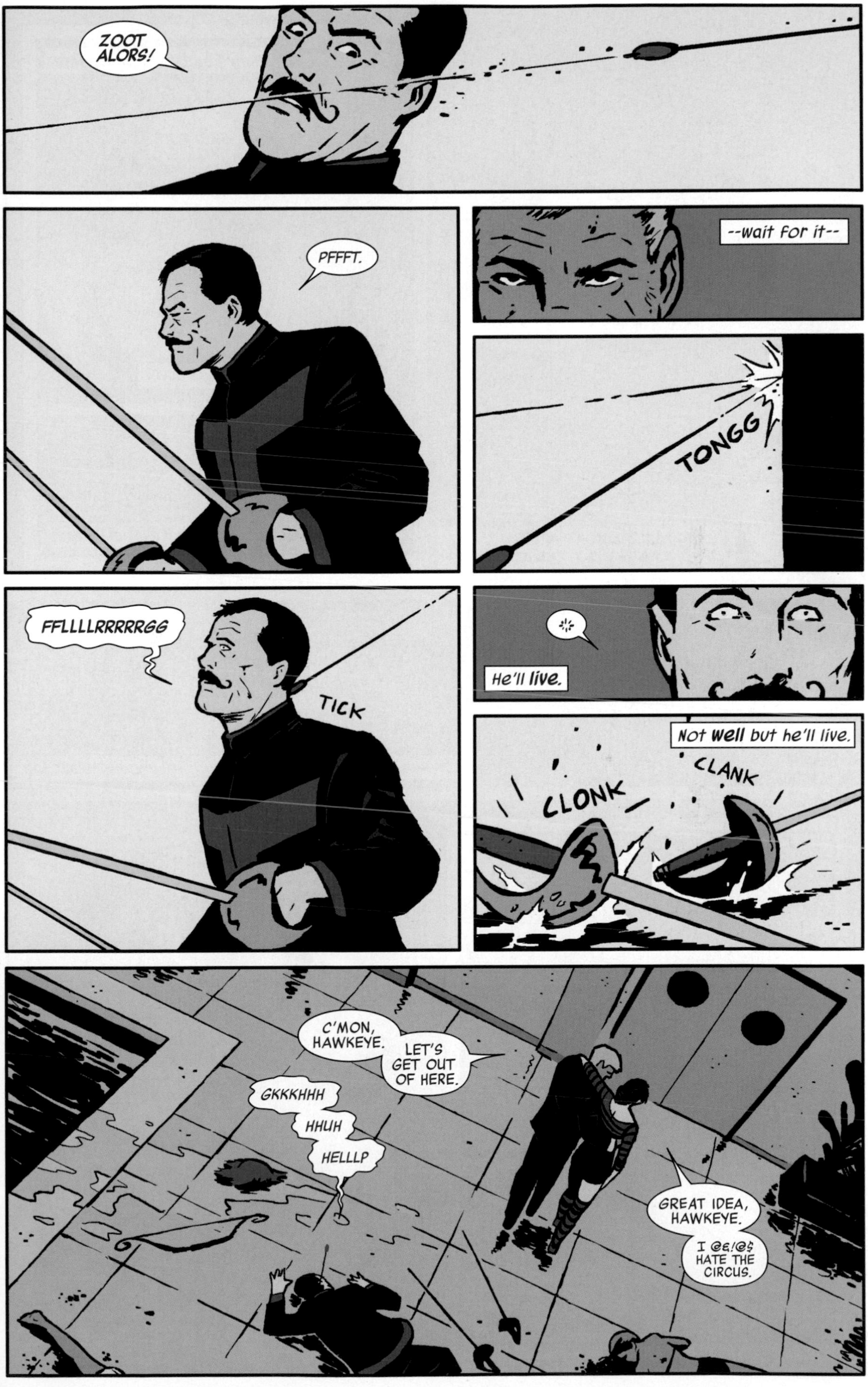
ZOOT ALORS!
PFFFT.
--wait for it--
TONGG
FFLLLLRRRRRGG
TICK
He'll live.
Not well but he'll live.
CLONK
CLANK
C'MON, HAWKEYE.
LET'S GET OUT OF HERE.
GKKKHHH
HHUH
HELLLP
GREAT IDEA, HAWKEYE.
I @&!@$ HATE THE CIRCUS.

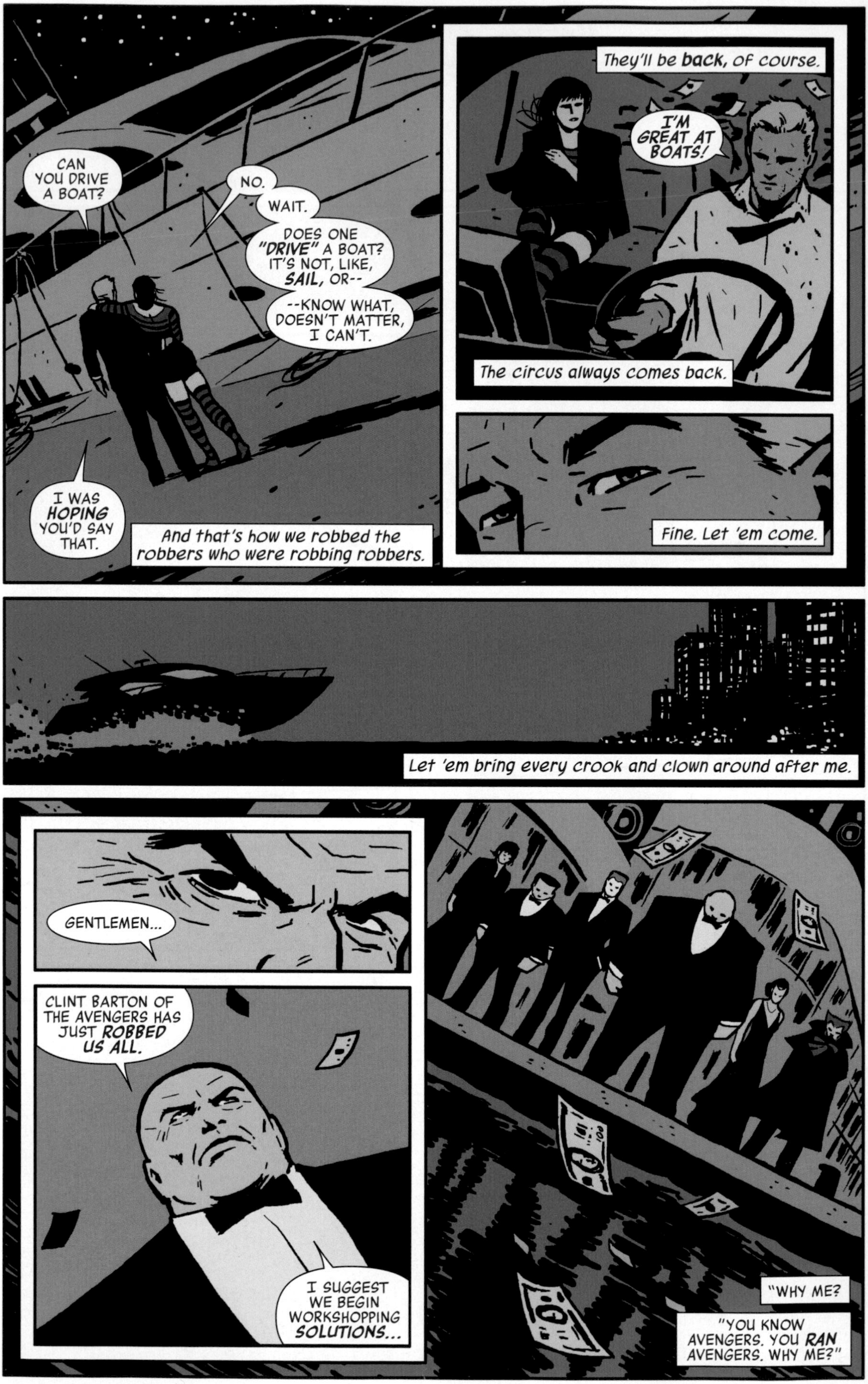

CAN YOU DRIVE A BOAT?
NO.
WAIT.
DOES ONE "DRIVE" A BOAT? IT'S NOT, LIKE, SAIL, OR--
--KNOW WHAT, DOESN'T MATTER, I CAN'T.
I WAS HOPING YOU'D SAY THAT.
And that's how we robbed the robbers who were robbing robbers.
They'll be back, of course.
I'M GREAT AT BOATS!
The circus always comes back.
Fine. Let 'em come.
Let 'em bring every crook and clown around after me.
GENTLEMEN...
CLINT BARTON OF THE AVENGERS HAS JUST ROBBED US ALL.
I SUGGEST WE BEGIN WORKSHOPPING SOLUTIONS...
"WHY ME?
"YOU KNOW AVENGERS. YOU RAN AVENGERS. WHY ME?"

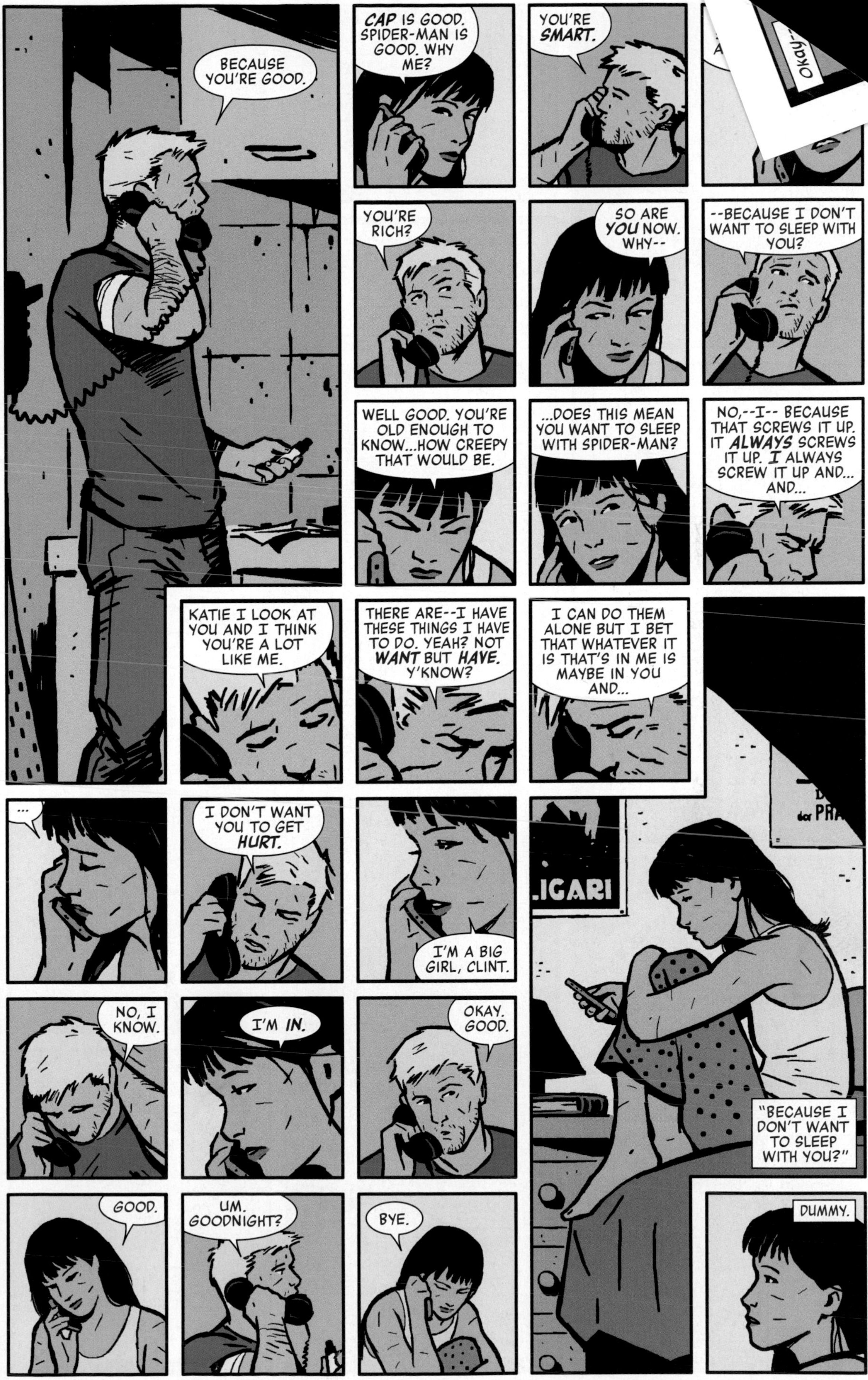
BECAUSE YOU'RE GOOD.
CAP IS GOOD. SPIDER-MAN IS GOOD. WHY ME?
YOU'RE SMART.
YOU'RE RICH?
SO ARE YOU NOW. WHY--
--BECAUSE I DON'T WANT TO SLEEP WITH YOU?
WELL GOOD. YOU'RE OLD ENOUGH TO KNOW...HOW CREEPY THAT WOULD BE.
...DOES THIS MEAN YOU WANT TO SLEEP WITH SPIDER-MAN?
NO,--I-- BECAUSE THAT SCREWS IT UP. IT ALWAYS SCREWS IT UP. I ALWAYS SCREW IT UP AND... AND...
KATIE I LOOK AT YOU AND I THINK YOU'RE A LOT LIKE ME.
THERE ARE--I HAVE THESE THINGS I HAVE TO DO. YEAH? NOT WANT BUT HAVE. Y'KNOW?
I CAN DO THEM ALONE BUT I BET THAT WHATEVER IT IS THAT'S IN ME IS MAYBE IN YOU AND...
...
I DON'T WANT YOU TO GET HURT.
I'M A BIG GIRL, CLINT.
NO, I KNOW.
I'M IN.
OKAY. GOOD.
"BECAUSE I DON'T WANT TO SLEEP WITH YOU?"
GOOD.
UM. GOODNIGHT?
BYE.
DUMMY.

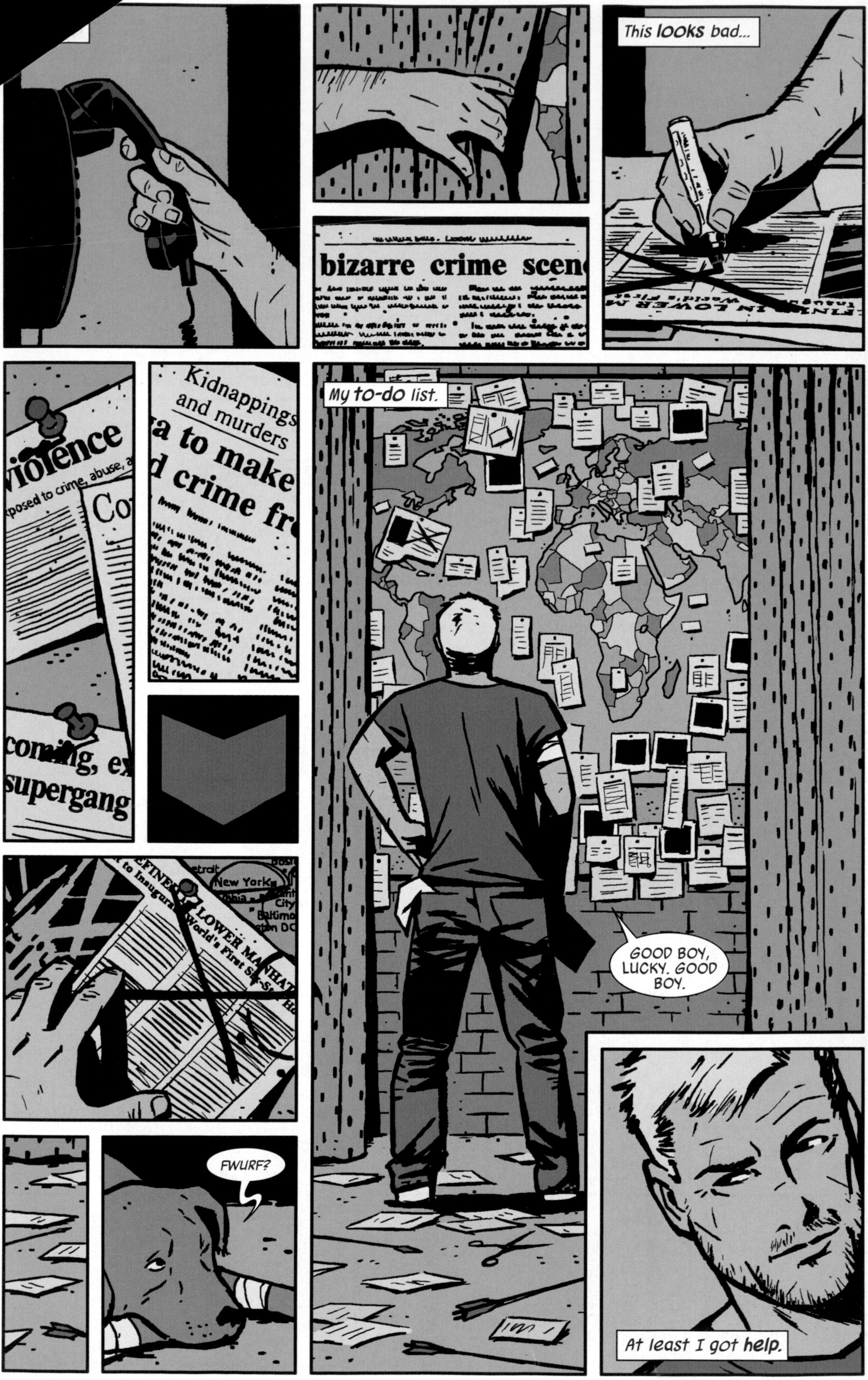

This looks bad...
bizarre crime scen
violence
exposed to crime, abuse, a
Kidnappings and murders
a to make
d crime fr
coming, ex
supergang
New York
My to-do list.
GOOD BOY, LUCKY. GOOD BOY.
FWURF?
At least I got help.

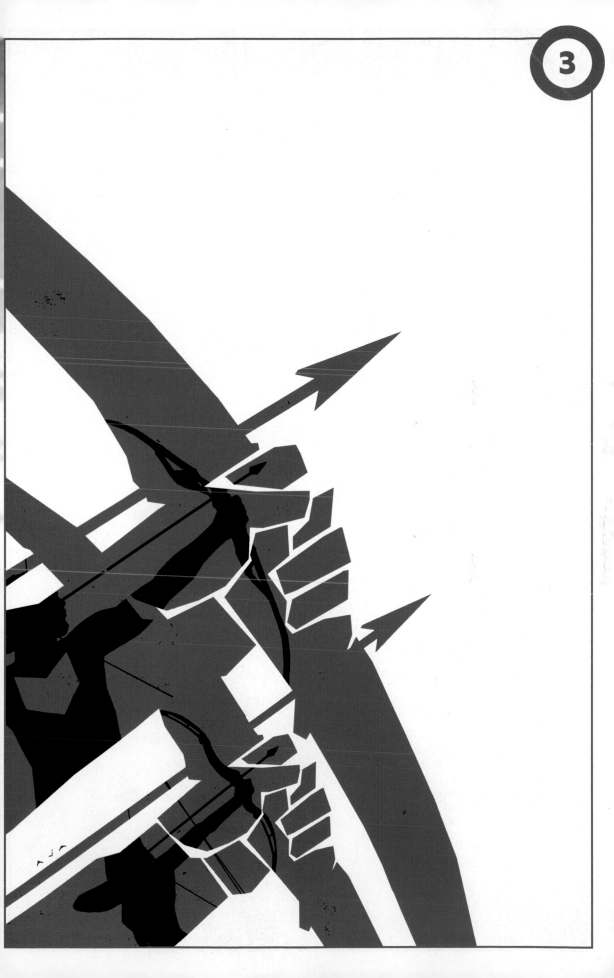

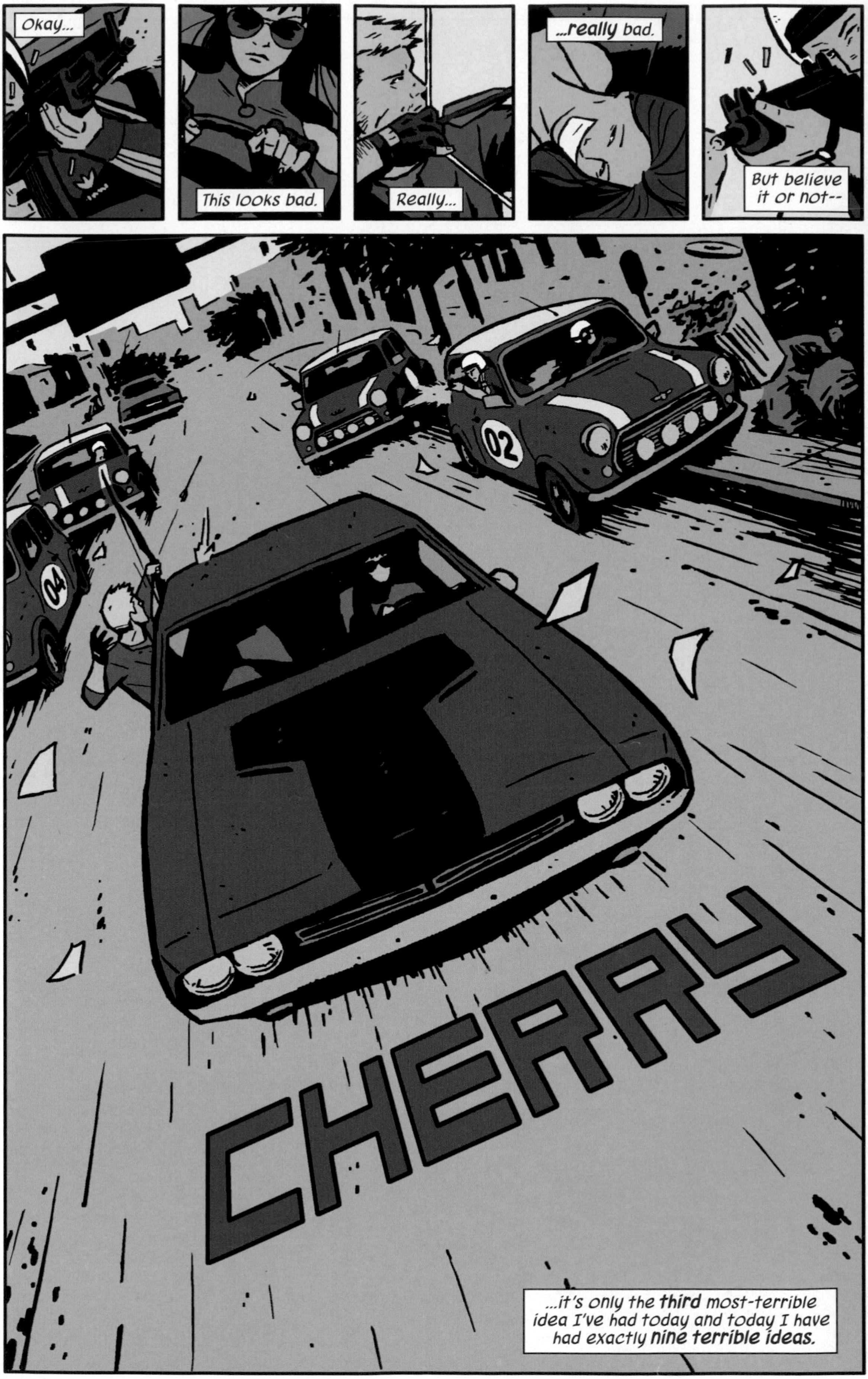
Okay...
This looks bad.
Really...
...really bad.
But believe it or not--
CHERRY
...it's only the **third** most-terrible idea I've had today and today I have had exactly **nine terrible ideas.**

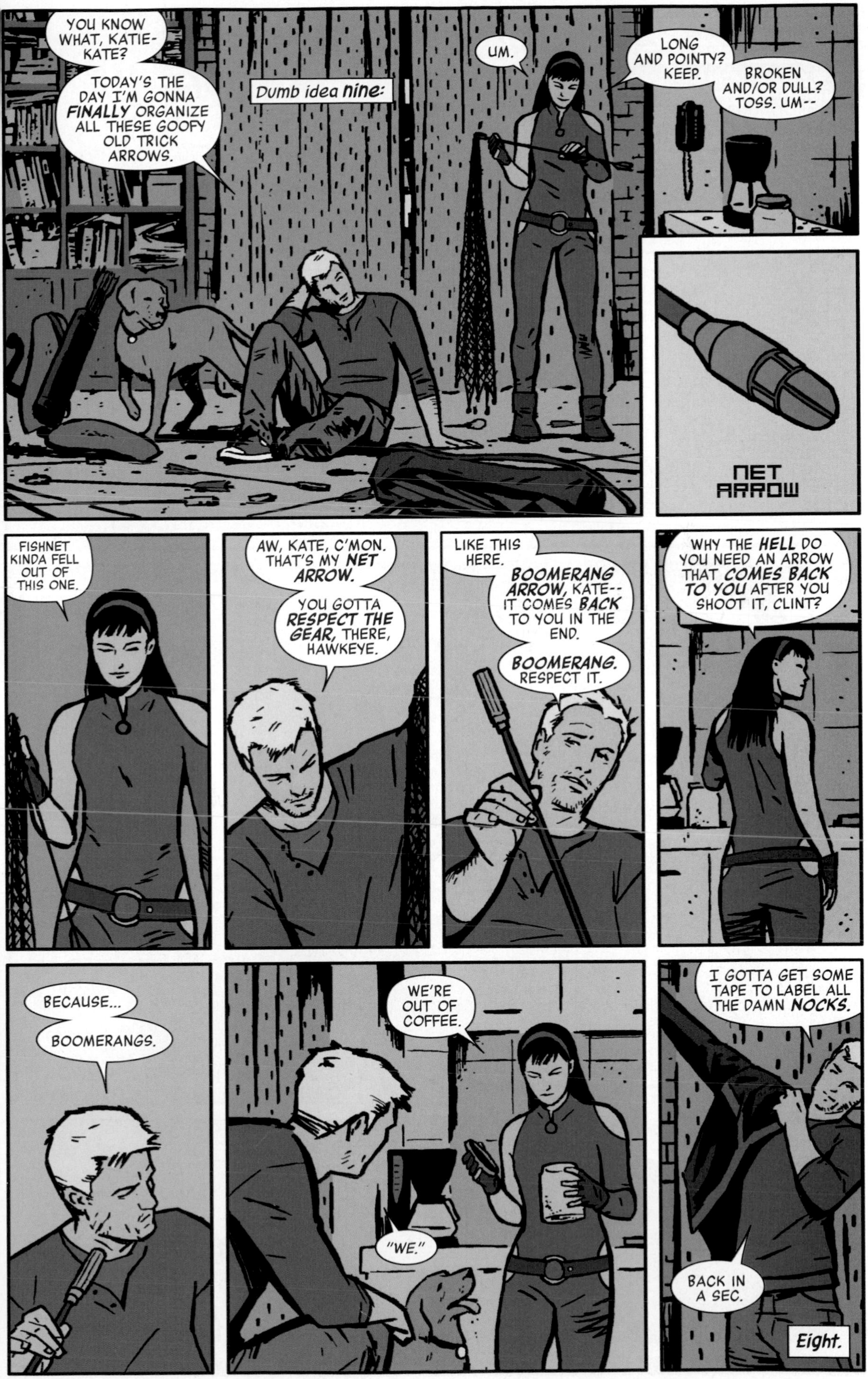
YOU KNOW WHAT, KATIE-KATE?
TODAY'S THE DAY I'M GONNA FINALLY ORGANIZE ALL THESE GOOFY OLD TRICK ARROWS.
Dumb idea nine:
UM.
LONG AND POINTY? KEEP.
BROKEN AND/OR DULL? TOSS. UM--
NET ARROW
FISHNET KINDA FELL OUT OF THIS ONE.
AW, KATE, C'MON. THAT'S MY NET ARROW.
YOU GOTTA RESPECT THE GEAR, THERE, HAWKEYE.
LIKE THIS HERE.
BOOMERANG ARROW, KATE--IT COMES BACK TO YOU IN THE END.
BOOMERANG. RESPECT IT.
WHY THE HELL DO YOU NEED AN ARROW THAT COMES BACK TO YOU AFTER YOU SHOOT IT, CLINT?
BECAUSE...
BOOMERANGS.
WE'RE OUT OF COFFEE.
"WE."
I GOTTA GET SOME TAPE TO LABEL ALL THE DAMN NOCKS.
BACK IN A SEC.
Eight.

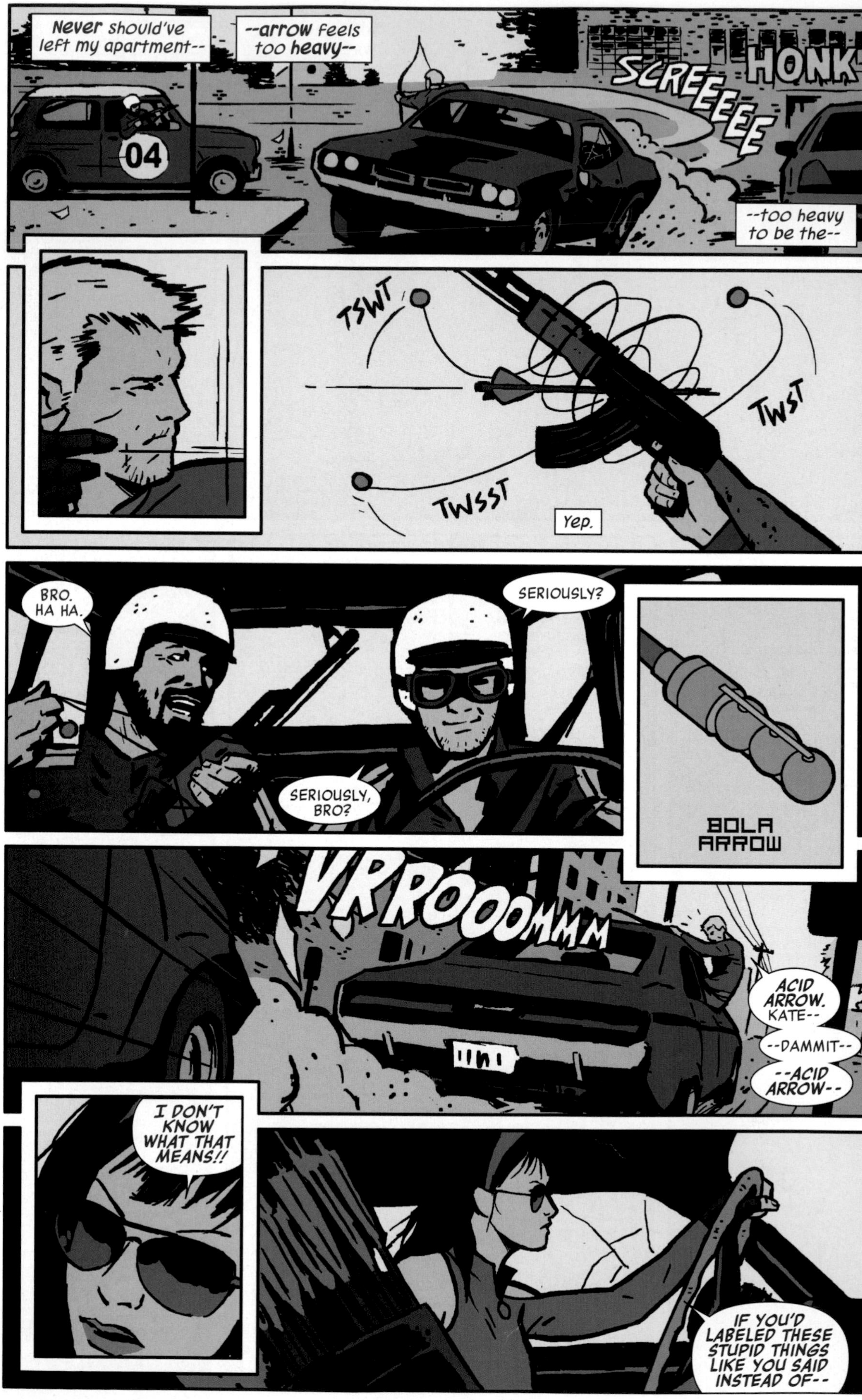
Never should've left my apartment--
--arrow feels too heavy--
SCREEEEEE
HONK
04
--too heavy to be the--
TSWT
TWST
TWSST
Yep.
BRO. HA HA.
SERIOUSLY?
SERIOUSLY, BRO?
BOLA ARROW
VRROOOMMM
ACID ARROW. KATE--
--DAMMIT--
--ACID ARROW--
I DON'T KNOW WHAT THAT MEANS!!
IF YOU'D LABELED THESE STUPID THINGS LIKE YOU SAID INSTEAD OF--

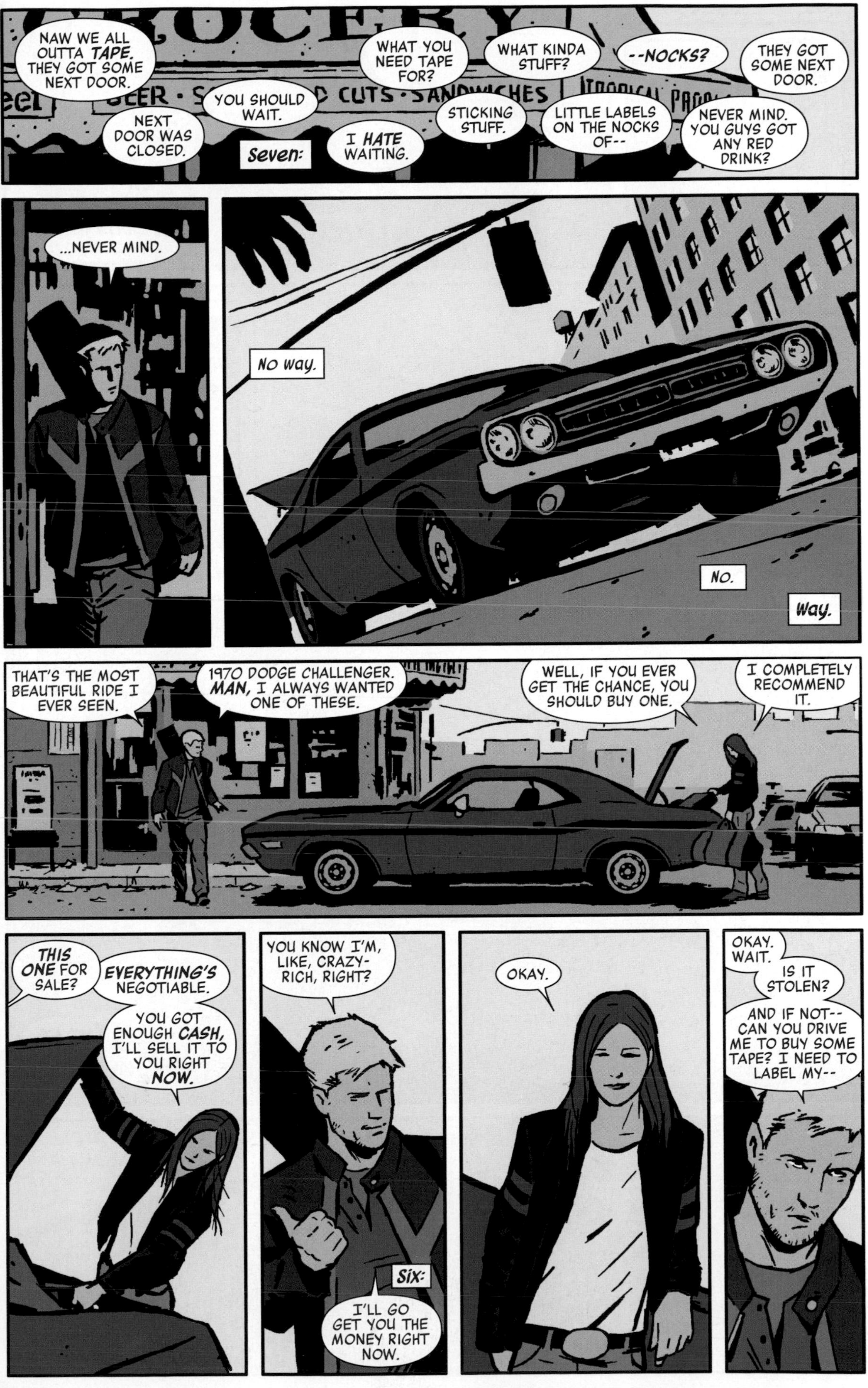
NAW WE ALL OUTTA TAPE. THEY GOT SOME NEXT DOOR.
NEXT DOOR WAS CLOSED.
YOU SHOULD WAIT.
Seven:
I HATE WAITING.
WHAT YOU NEED TAPE FOR?
STICKING STUFF.
WHAT KINDA STUFF?
LITTLE LABELS ON THE NOCKS OF--
--NOCKS?
THEY GOT SOME NEXT DOOR.
NEVER MIND. YOU GUYS GOT ANY RED DRINK?
...NEVER MIND.
No way.
No.
Way.
THAT'S THE MOST BEAUTIFUL RIDE I EVER SEEN.
1970 DODGE CHALLENGER. MAN, I ALWAYS WANTED ONE OF THESE.
WELL, IF YOU EVER GET THE CHANCE, YOU SHOULD BUY ONE.
I COMPLETELY RECOMMEND IT.
THIS ONE FOR SALE?
EVERYTHING'S NEGOTIABLE.
YOU GOT ENOUGH CASH, I'LL SELL IT TO YOU RIGHT NOW.
YOU KNOW I'M, LIKE, CRAZY-RICH, RIGHT?
Six:
I'LL GO GET YOU THE MONEY RIGHT NOW.
OKAY.
OKAY. WAIT.
IS IT STOLEN?
AND IF NOT--CAN YOU DRIVE ME TO BUY SOME TAPE? I NEED TO LABEL MY--

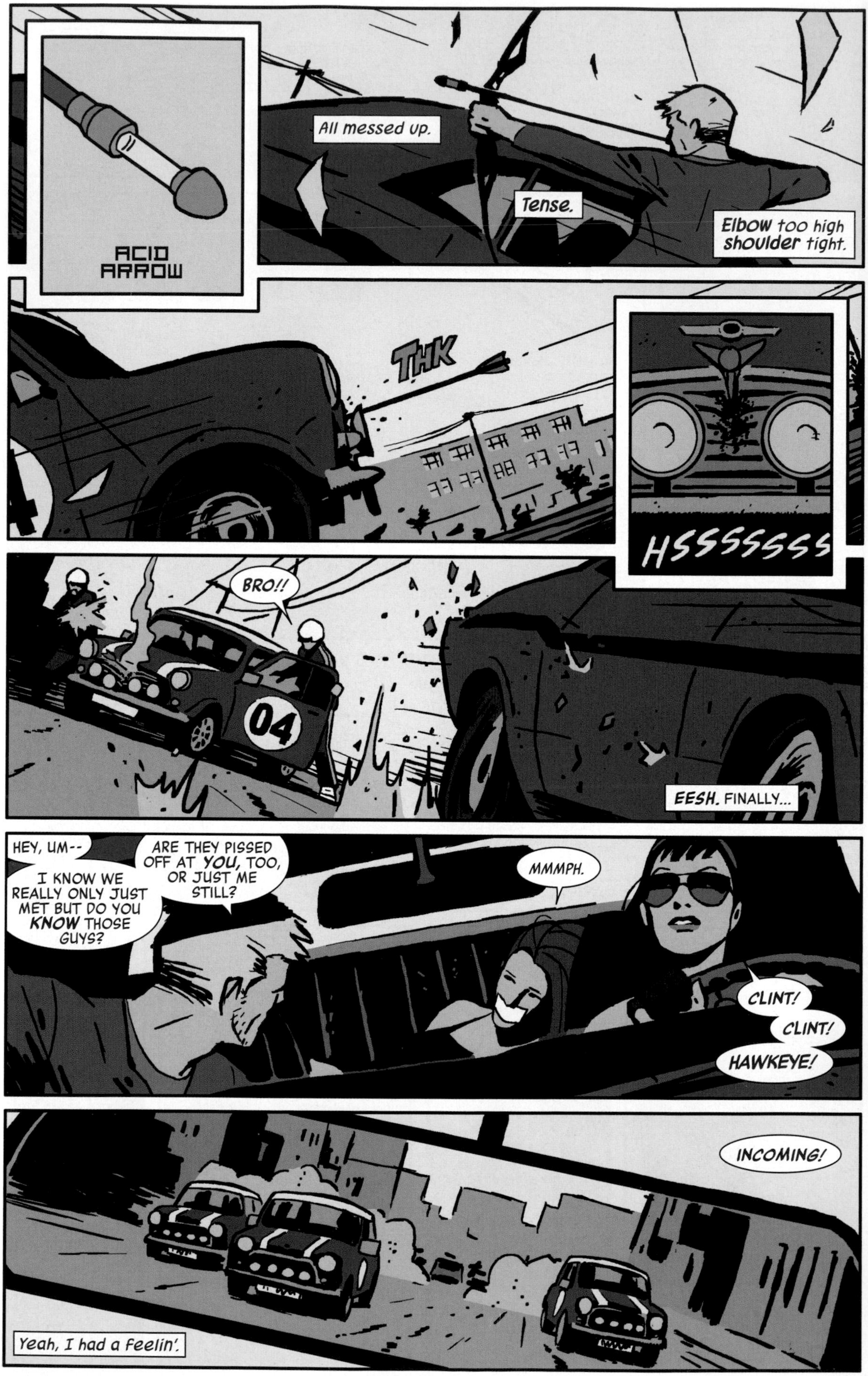
ACID ARROW
All messed up.
Tense.
Elbow too high shoulder tight.
THK
HSSSSSSS
BRO!!
EESH. FINALLY...
HEY, UM--
I KNOW WE REALLY ONLY JUST MET BUT DO YOU KNOW THOSE GUYS?
ARE THEY PISSED OFF AT YOU, TOO, OR JUST ME STILL?
MMMPH.
CLINT!
CLINT!
HAWKEYE!
INCOMING!
Yeah, I had a feelin'.

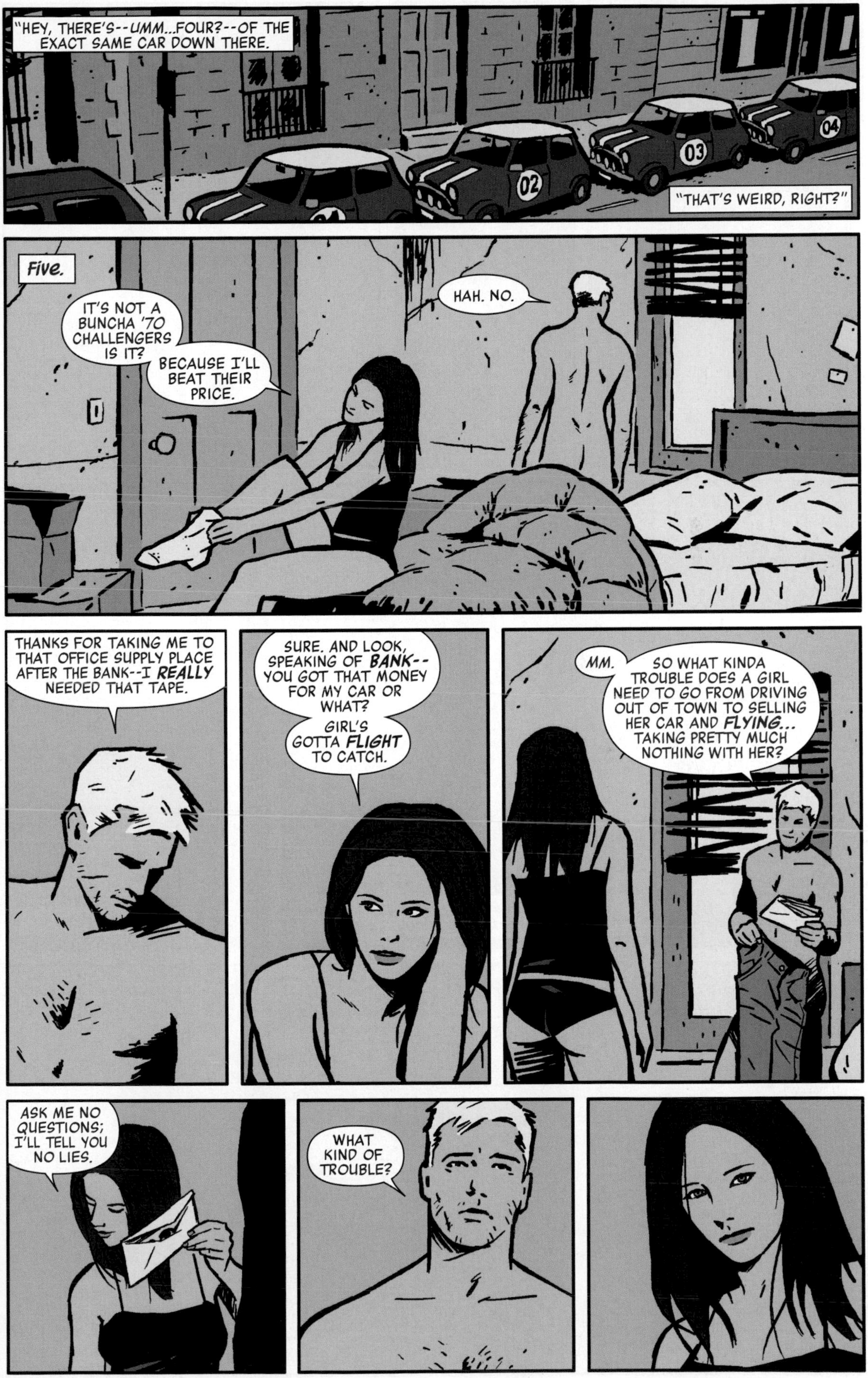
"HEY, THERE'S--UMM...FOUR?--OF THE EXACT SAME CAR DOWN THERE.
02
03
04
"THAT'S WEIRD, RIGHT?"
Five.
IT'S NOT A BUNCHA '70 CHALLENGERS IS IT?
BECAUSE I'LL BEAT THEIR PRICE.
HAH. NO.
THANKS FOR TAKING ME TO THAT OFFICE SUPPLY PLACE AFTER THE BANK--I REALLY NEEDED THAT TAPE.
SURE. AND LOOK, SPEAKING OF BANK--YOU GOT THAT MONEY FOR MY CAR OR WHAT?
GIRL'S GOTTA FLIGHT TO CATCH.
MM.
SO WHAT KINDA TROUBLE DOES A GIRL NEED TO GO FROM DRIVING OUT OF TOWN TO SELLING HER CAR AND FLYING... TAKING PRETTY MUCH NOTHING WITH HER?
ASK ME NO QUESTIONS; I'LL TELL YOU NO LIES.
WHAT KIND OF TROUBLE?

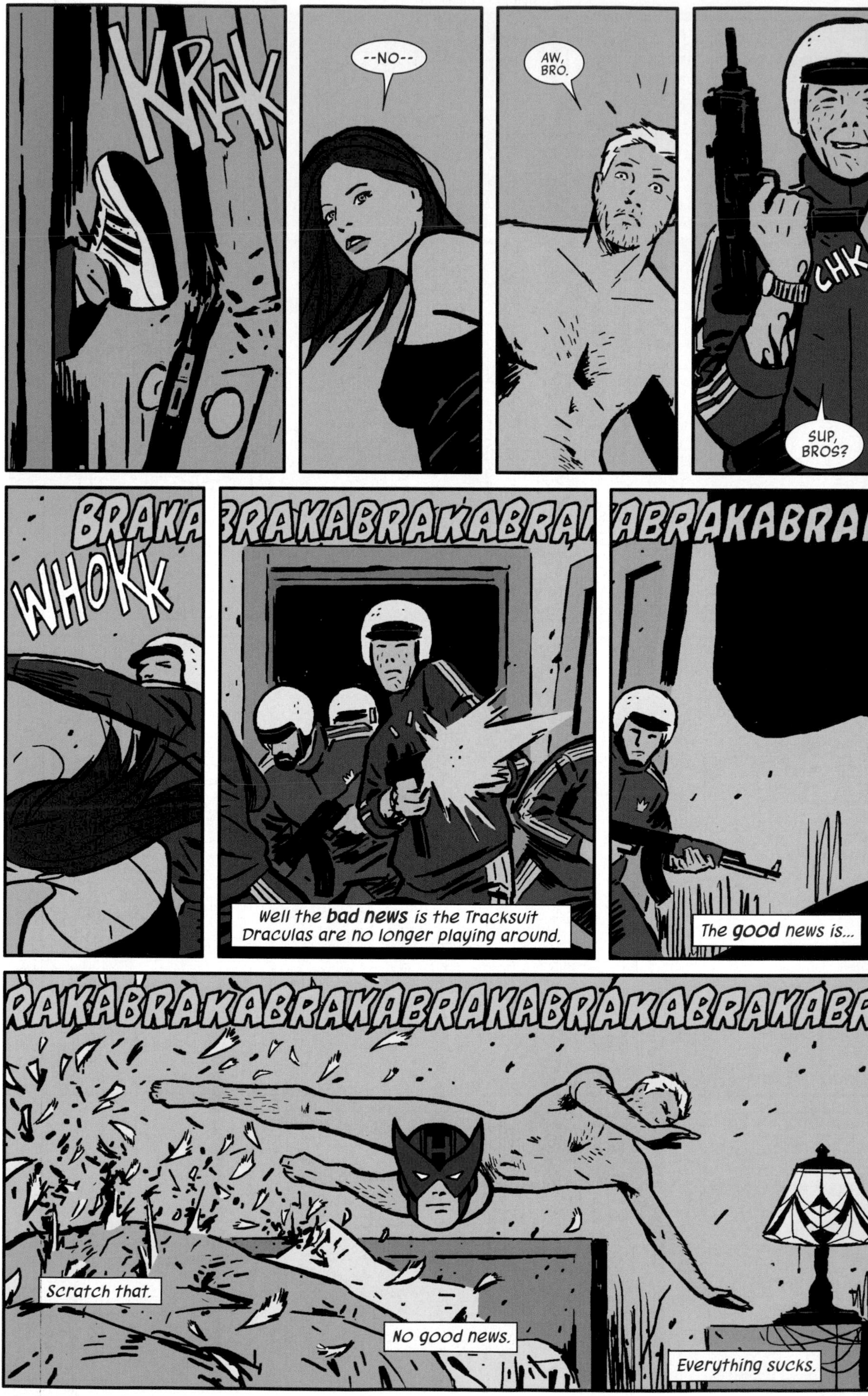
KRAK
--NO--
AW, BRO.
CHK
SUP, BROS?
BRAKABRAKABRAKABRAKABRAKABRA
WHOKK
Well the bad news is the Tracksuit Draculas are no longer playing around.
The good news is...
RAKABRAKABRAKABRAKABRAKABR
Scratch that.
No good news.
Everything sucks.

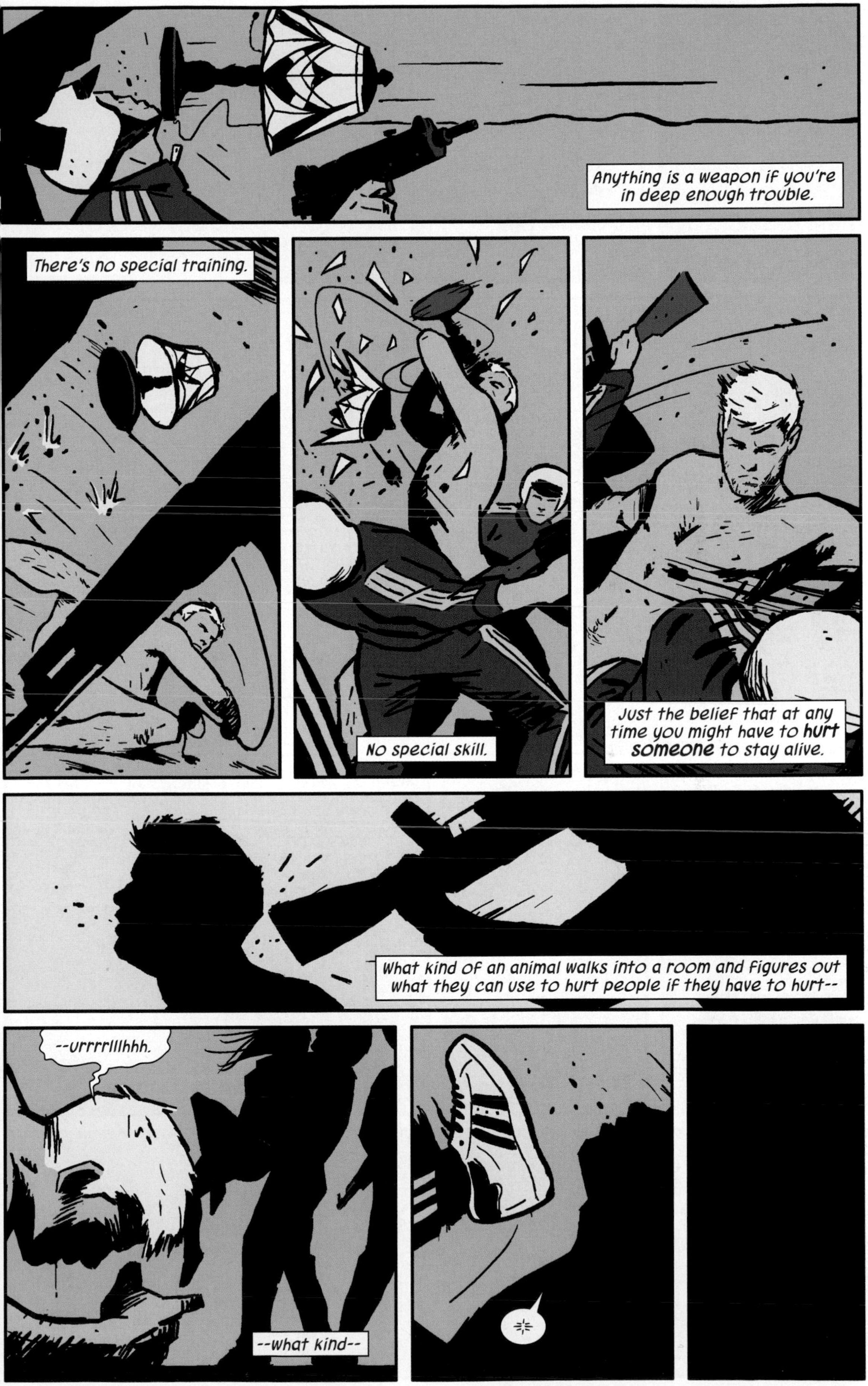

Anything is a weapon if you're in deep enough trouble.
There's no special training.
No special skill.
Just the belief that at any time you might have to **hurt someone** to stay alive.
What kind of an animal walks into a room and figures out what they can use to hurt people if they have to hurt--
--urrrrlllhhh.
--what kind--

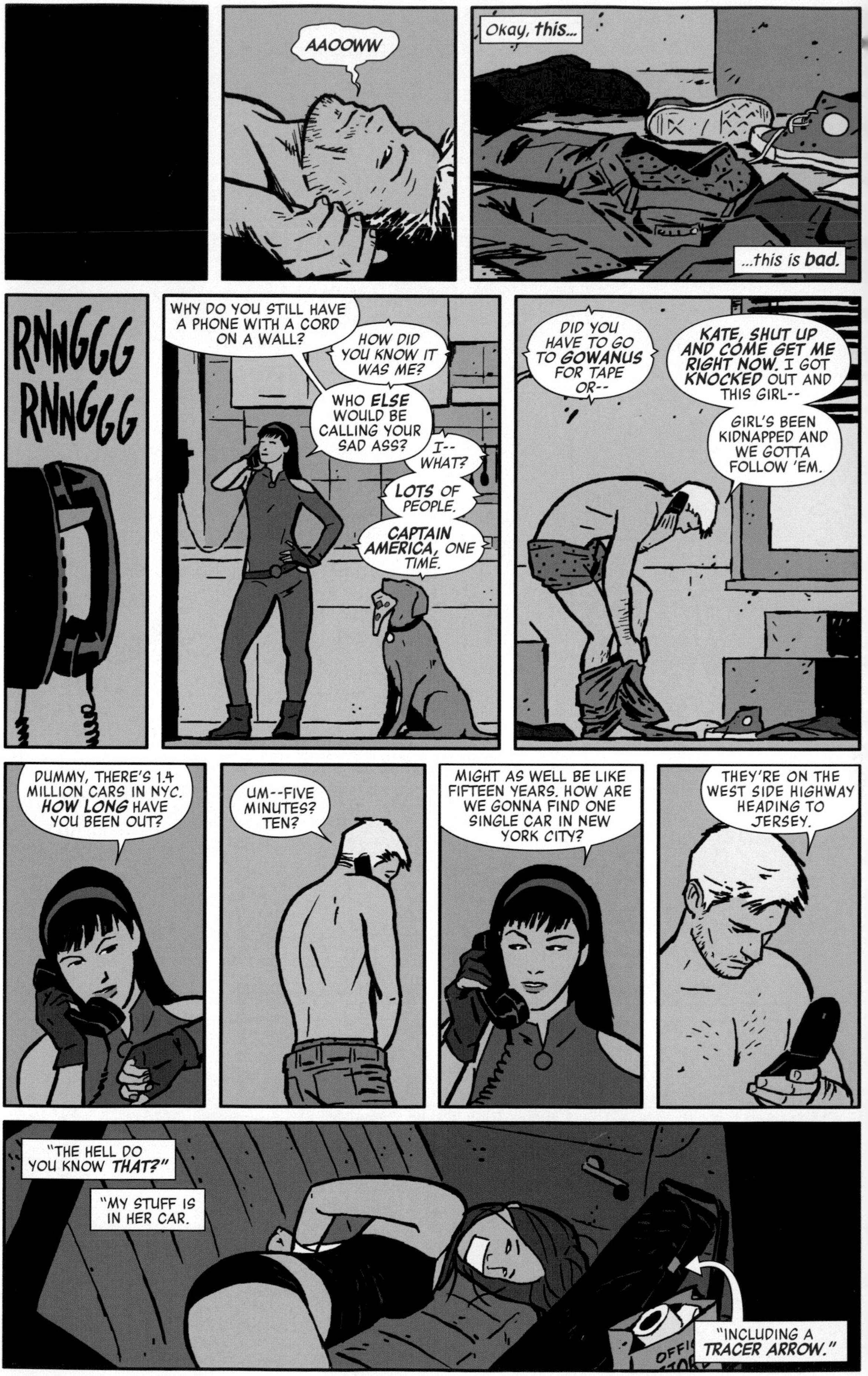
AAOOWW
Okay, this...
...this is bad.
RNNGGG RNNGGG
WHY DO YOU STILL HAVE A PHONE WITH A CORD ON A WALL?
HOW DID YOU KNOW IT WAS ME?
WHO ELSE WOULD BE CALLING YOUR SAD ASS?
I-- WHAT?
LOTS OF PEOPLE.
CAPTAIN AMERICA, ONE TIME.
DID YOU HAVE TO GO TO GOWANUS FOR TAPE OR--
KATE, SHUT UP AND COME GET ME RIGHT NOW. I GOT KNOCKED OUT AND THIS GIRL--
GIRL'S BEEN KIDNAPPED AND WE GOTTA FOLLOW 'EM.
DUMMY, THERE'S 1.4 MILLION CARS IN NYC. HOW LONG HAVE YOU BEEN OUT?
UM--FIVE MINUTES? TEN?
MIGHT AS WELL BE LIKE FIFTEEN YEARS. HOW ARE WE GONNA FIND ONE SINGLE CAR IN NEW YORK CITY?
THEY'RE ON THE WEST SIDE HIGHWAY HEADING TO JERSEY.
"THE HELL DO YOU KNOW THAT?"
"MY STUFF IS IN HER CAR.
"INCLUDING A TRACER ARROW."

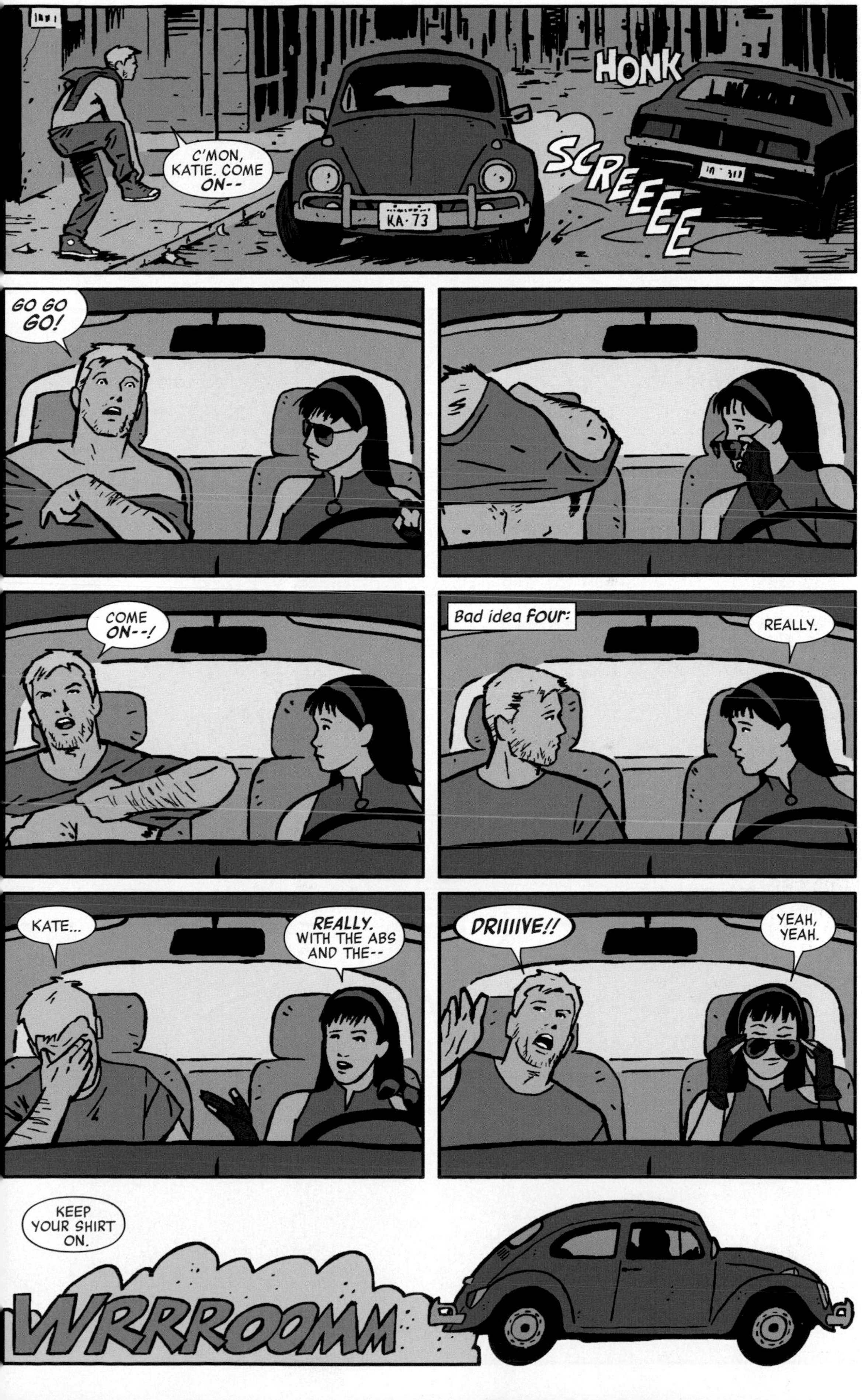

C'MON, KATIE. COME ON--
HONK
SCREEEEE
KA-73
GO GO GO!
COME ON--!
Bad idea four:
REALLY.
KATE...
REALLY. WITH THE ABS AND THE--
DRIIIIVE!!
YEAH, YEAH.
KEEP YOUR SHIRT ON.
WRRROOMM

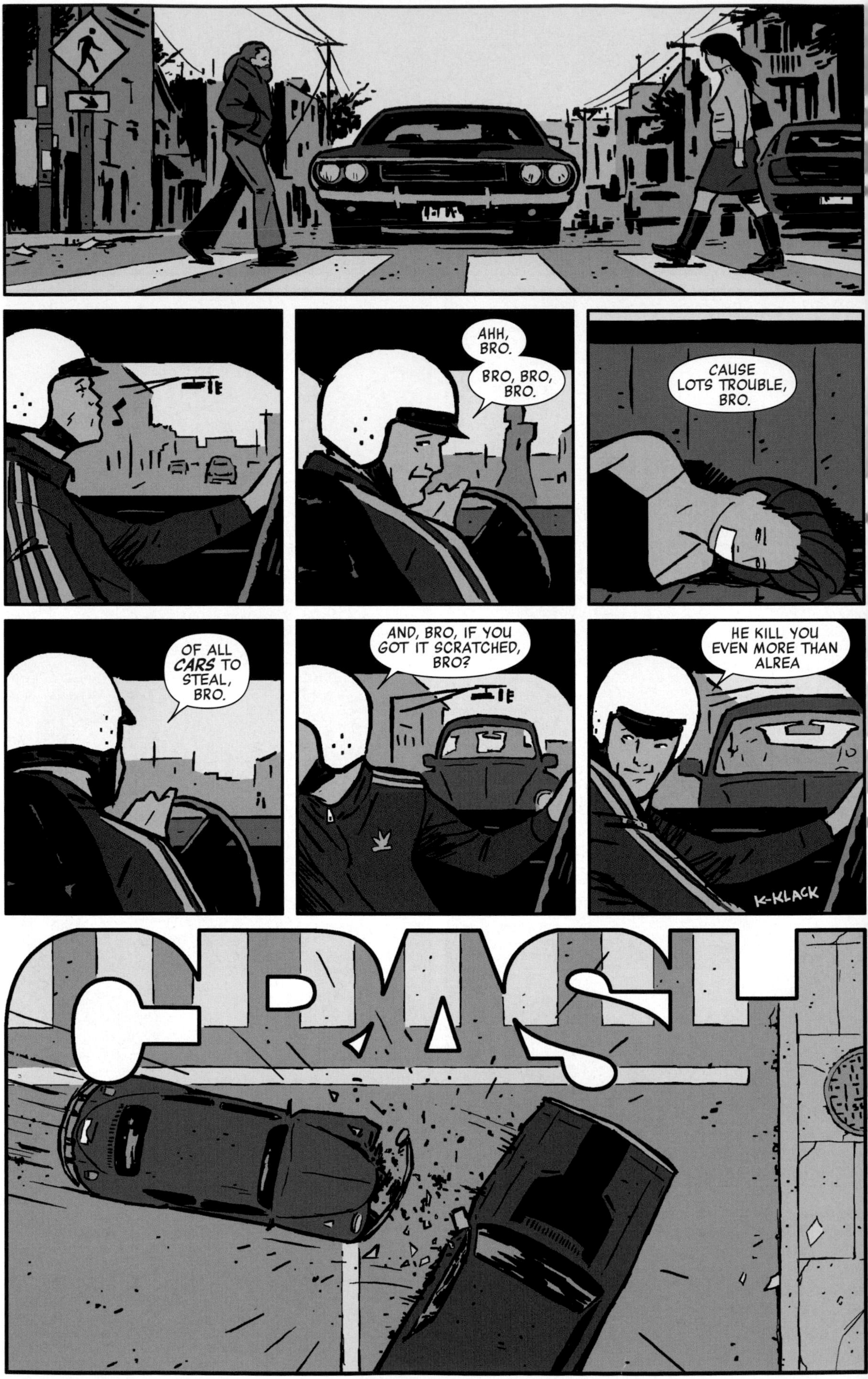
AHH, BRO.
BRO, BRO, BRO.
CAUSE LOTS TROUBLE, BRO.
OF ALL CARS TO STEAL, BRO.
AND, BRO, IF YOU GOT IT SCRATCHED, BRO?
HE KILL YOU EVEN MORE THAN ALREA
K-KLACK
CRASH

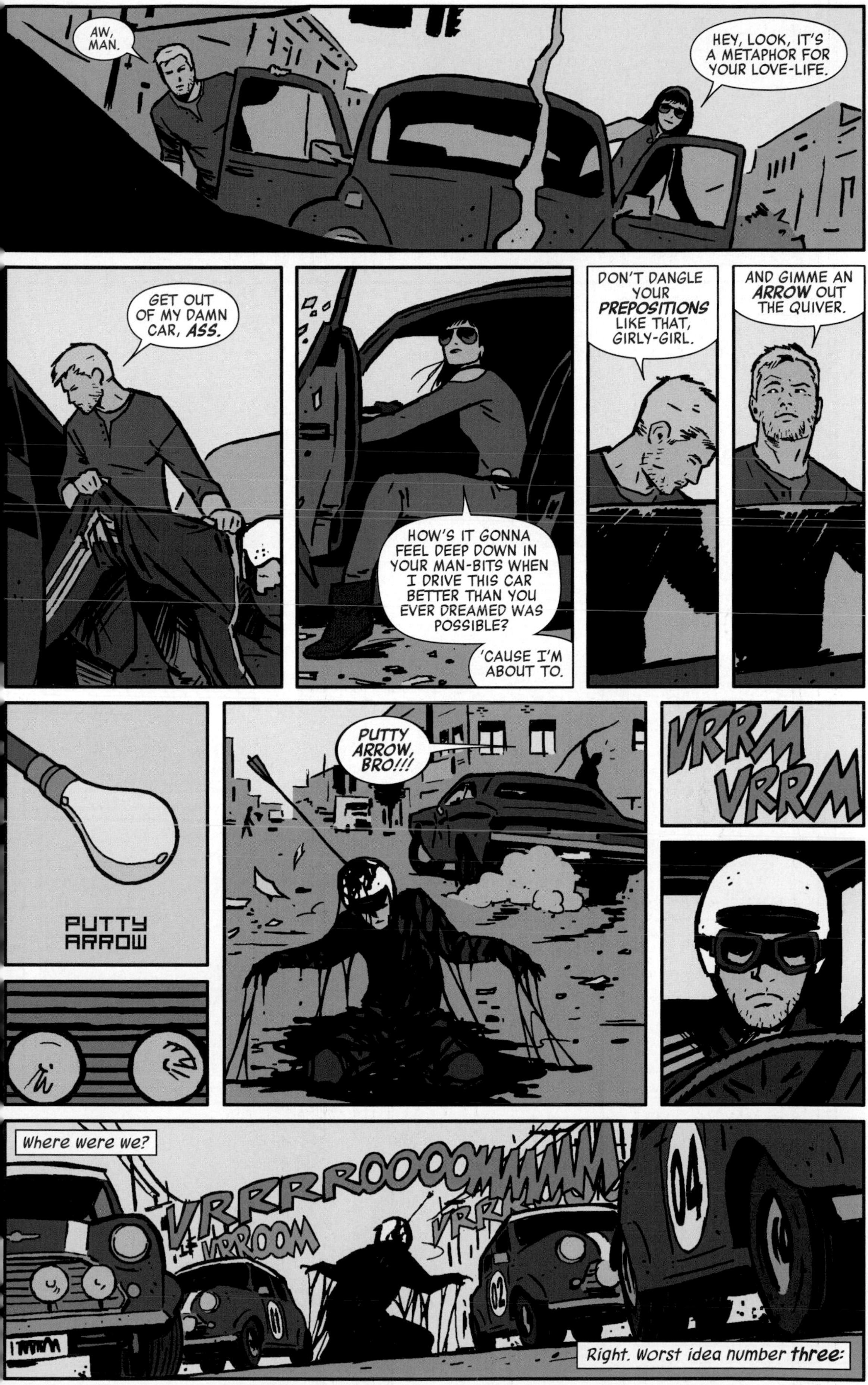
AW, MAN.
HEY, LOOK, IT'S A METAPHOR FOR YOUR LOVE-LIFE.
GET OUT OF MY DAMN CAR, ASS.
HOW'S IT GONNA FEEL DEEP DOWN IN YOUR MAN-BITS WHEN I DRIVE THIS CAR BETTER THAN YOU EVER DREAMED WAS POSSIBLE?
'CAUSE I'M ABOUT TO.
DON'T DANGLE YOUR PREPOSITIONS LIKE THAT, GIRLY-GIRL.
AND GIMME AN ARROW OUT THE QUIVER.
PUTTY ARROW
PUTTY ARROW, BRO!!!
VRRM VRRM
Where were we?
VRRRROOOOMMMM
VRRROOM
Right. Worst idea number three:

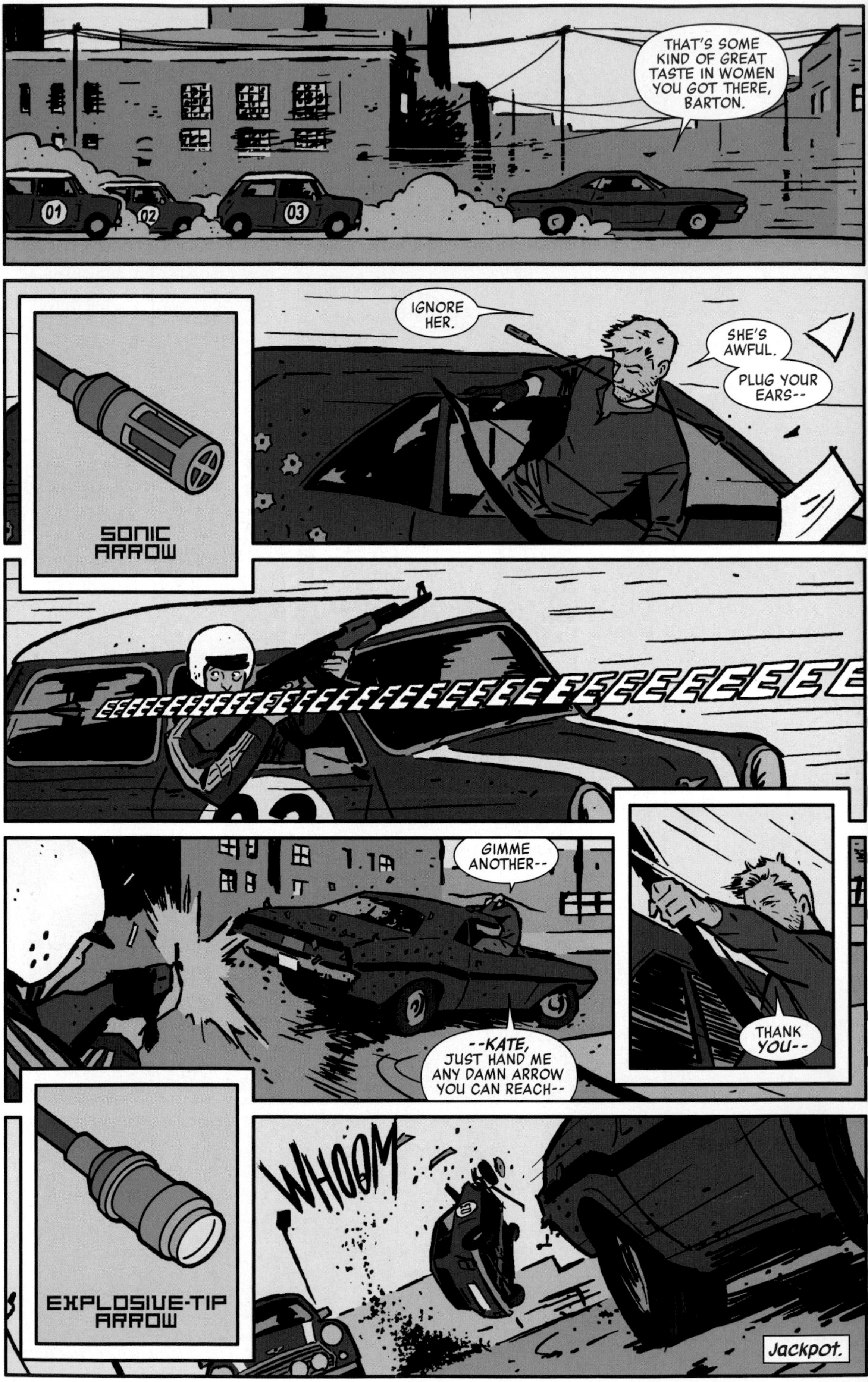

THAT'S SOME KIND OF GREAT TASTE IN WOMEN YOU GOT THERE, BARTON.
01
02
03
IGNORE HER.
SHE'S AWFUL.
PLUG YOUR EARS--
SONIC ARROW
EEEEEEEEEEEEEEEEEEEEEEEEEEEEEEEEEEEEEEEE
GIMME ANOTHER--
--KATE, JUST HAND ME ANY DAMN ARROW YOU CAN REACH--
THANK YOU--
EXPLOSIVE-TIP ARROW
WHOOM
Jackpot.

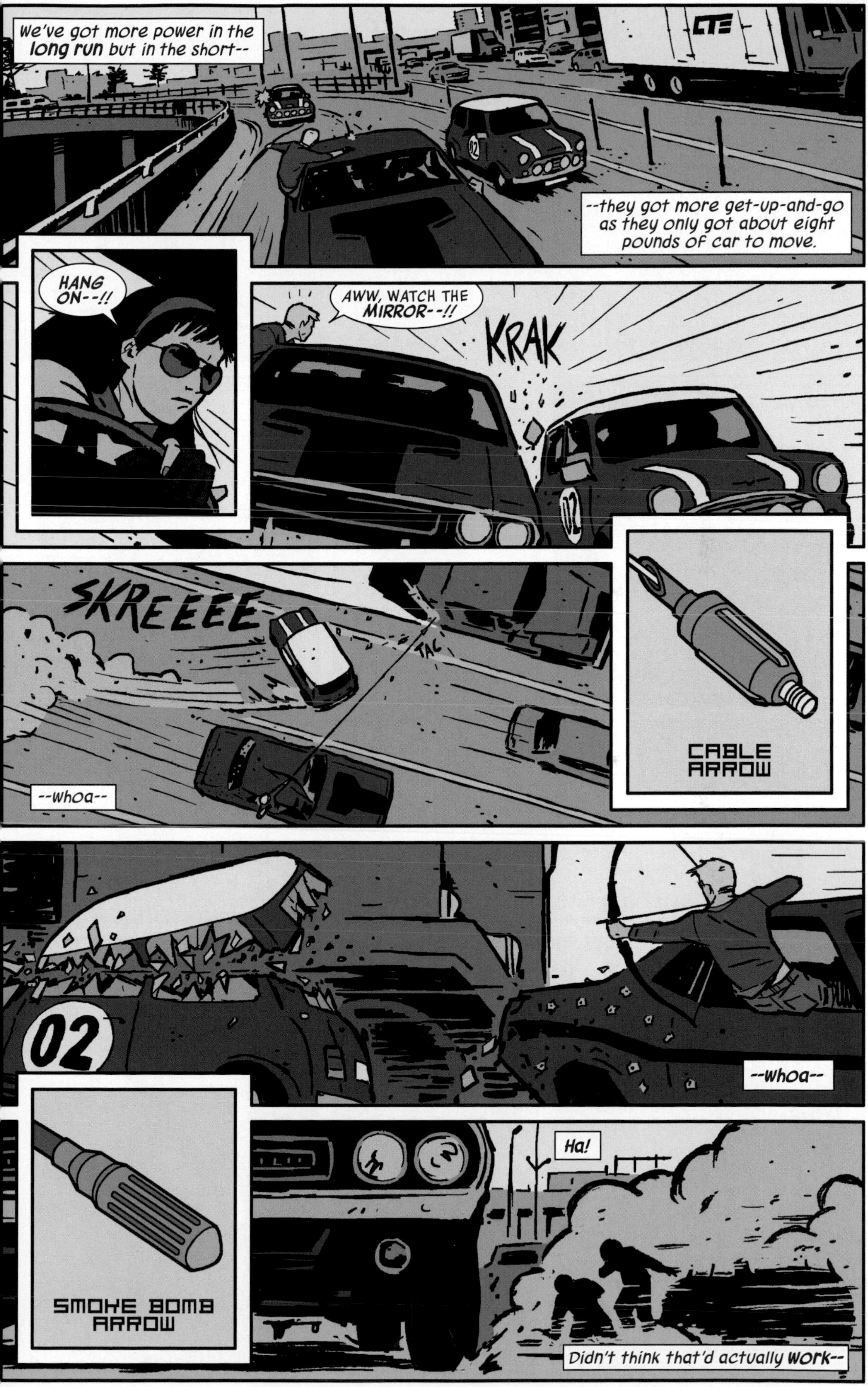

We've got more power in the long run but in the short--
--they got more get-up-and-go as they only got about eight pounds of car to move.
HANG ON--!!
AWW, WATCH THE MIRROR--!!
KRAK
SKREEEEE
TAC
--whoa--
CABLE ARROW
--whoa--
SMOKE BOMB ARROW
Ha!
Didn't think that'd actually work--

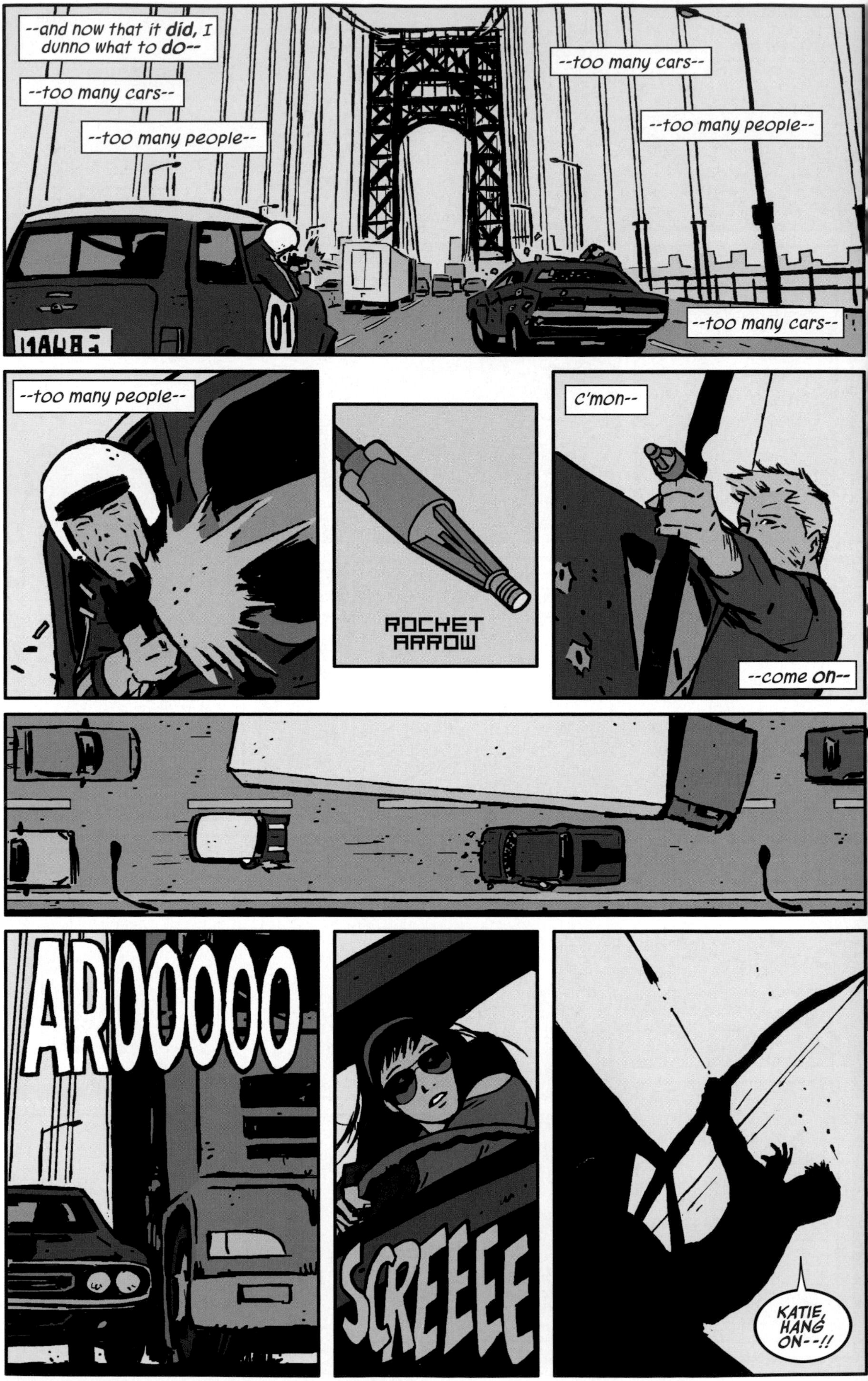
--and now that it did, I dunno what to do--
--too many cars--
--too many people--
--too many cars--
--too many people--
--too many cars--
--too many people--
ROCKET ARROW
C'mon--
--come on--
AROOOOO
SCREEEE
KATIE, HANG ON--!!

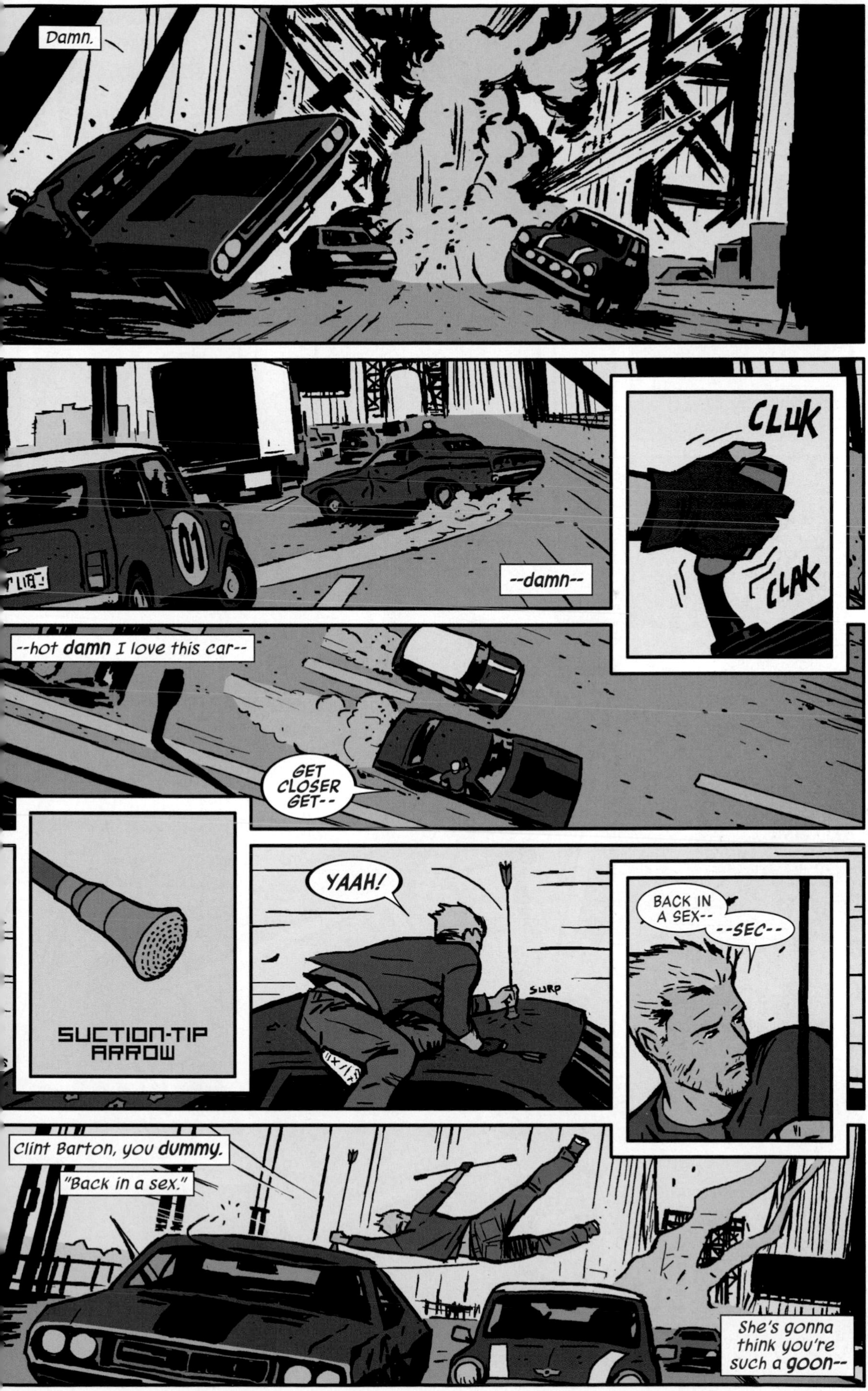

Damn.
--damn--
CLUK
CLAK
--hot damn I love this car--
GET CLOSER GET--
SUCTION-TIP ARROW
YAAH!
SURP
BACK IN A SEX--
--SEC--
Clint Barton, you dummy.
"Back in a sex."
She's gonna think you're such a goon--

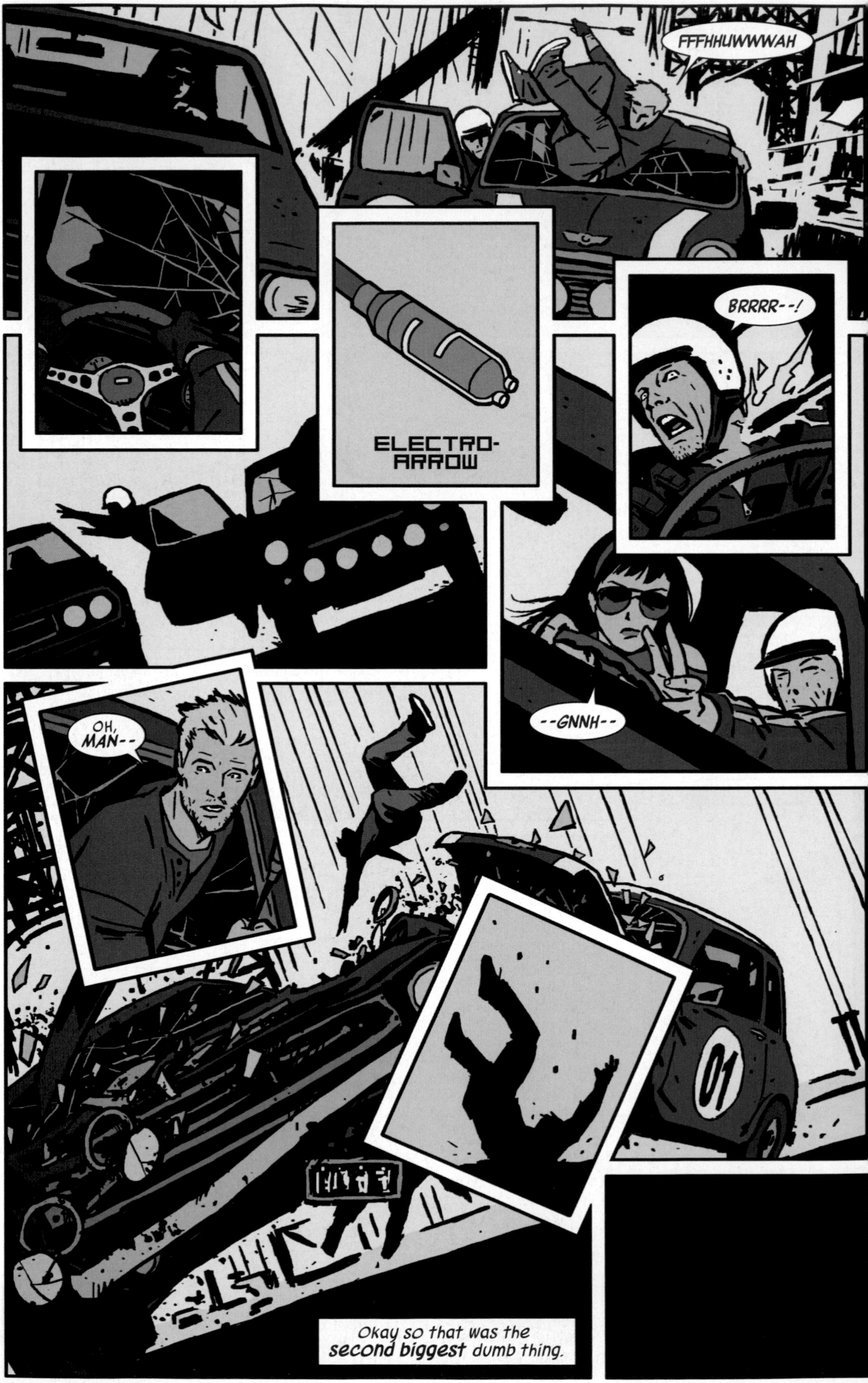
FFFHHUWWWAH
ELECTRO-ARROW
BRRRR--!
--GNNH--
OH, MAN--
Okay so that was the second biggest dumb thing.

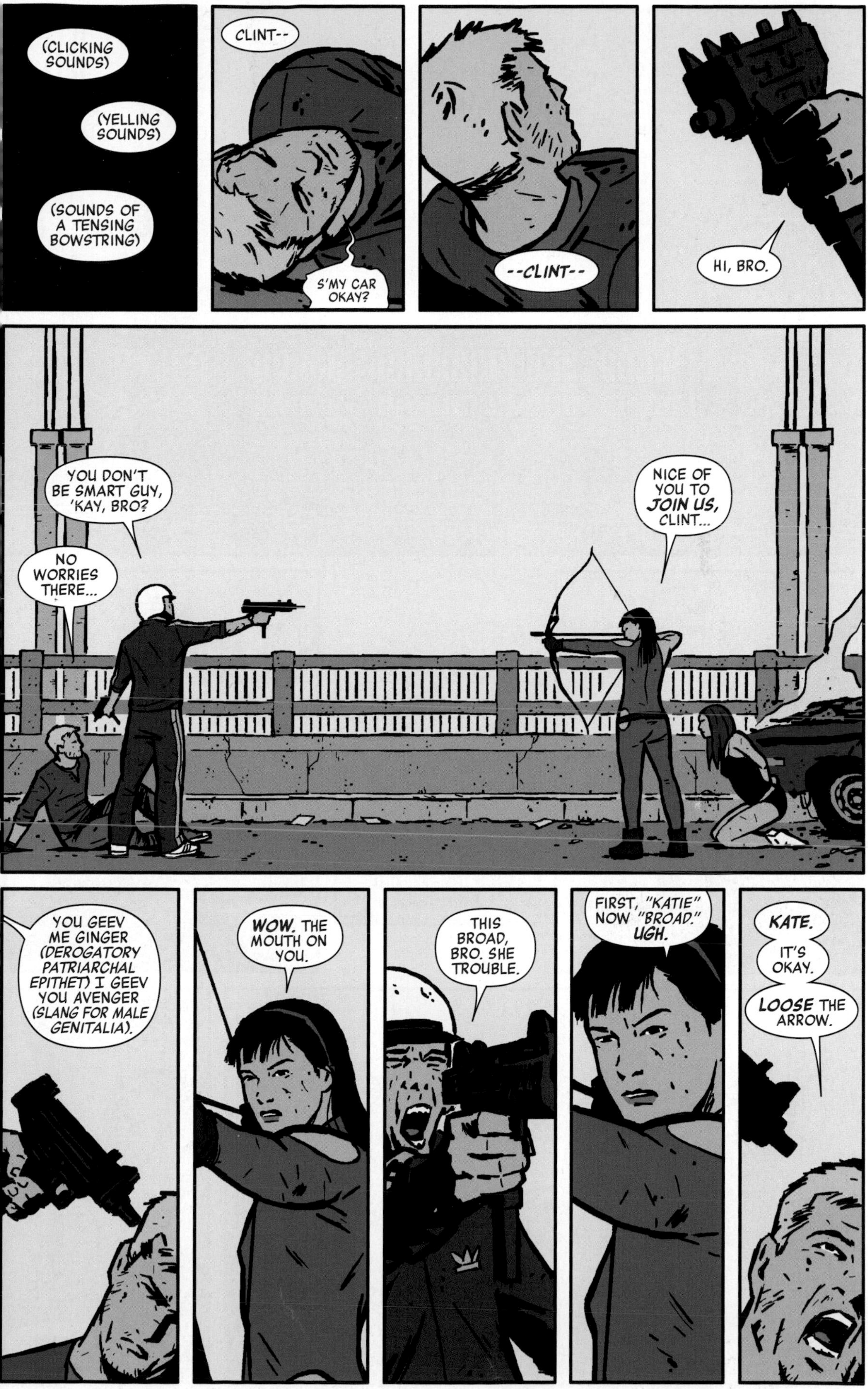
(CLICKING SOUNDS)
(YELLING SOUNDS)
(SOUNDS OF A TENSING BOWSTRING)
CLINT--
S'MY CAR OKAY?
--CLINT--
HI, BRO.
YOU DON'T BE SMART GUY, 'KAY, BRO?
NO WORRIES THERE...
NICE OF YOU TO JOIN US, CLINT...
YOU GEEV ME GINGER (DEROGATORY PATRIARCHAL EPITHET) I GEEV YOU AVENGER (SLANG FOR MALE GENITALIA).
WOW. THE MOUTH ON YOU.
THIS BROAD, BRO. SHE TROUBLE.
FIRST, "KATIE" NOW "BROAD." UGH.
KATE.
IT'S OKAY.
LOOSE THE ARROW.

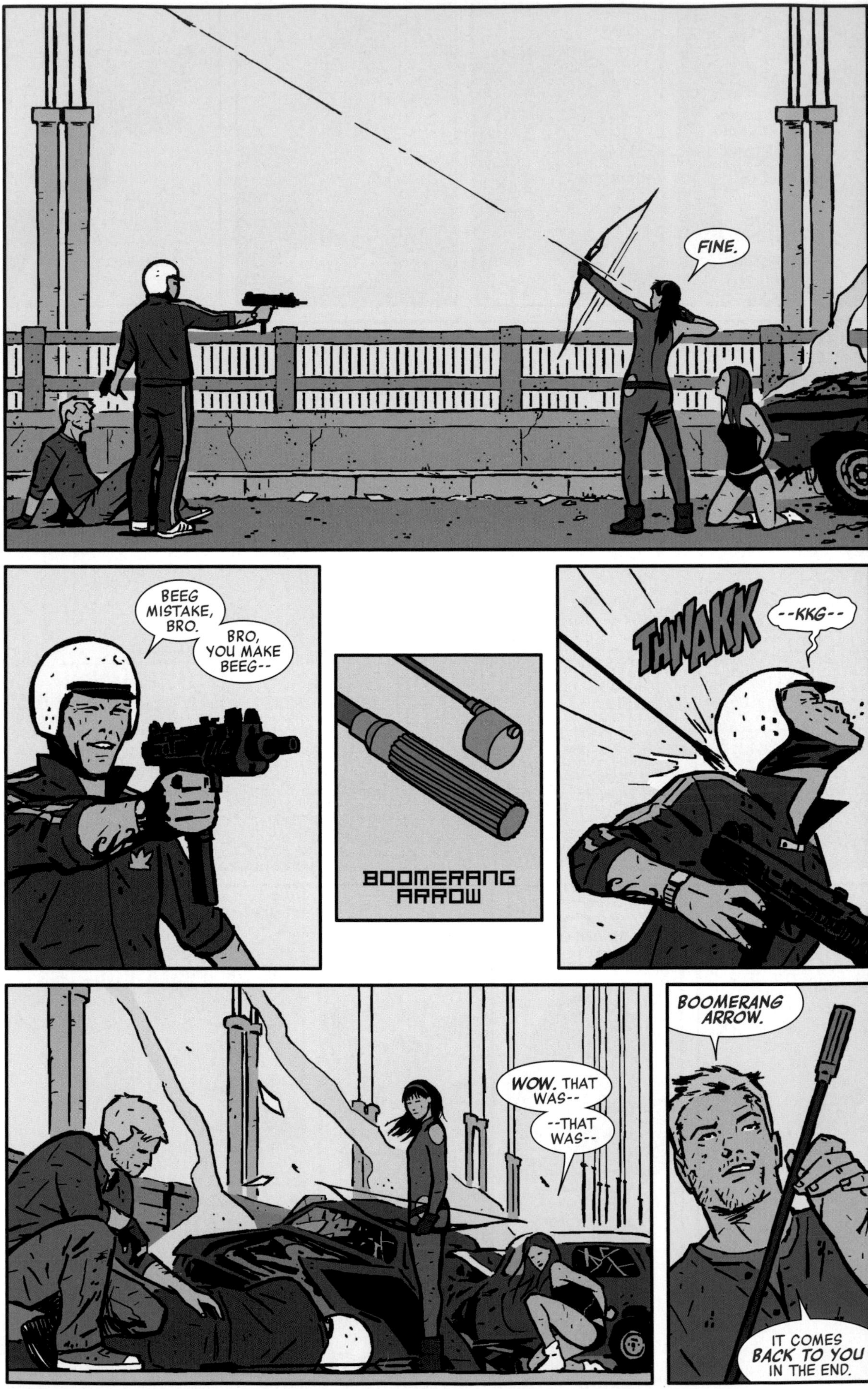
FINE.
BEEG MISTAKE, BRO.
BRO, YOU MAKE BEEG--
BOOMERANG ARROW
THWAKK
--KKG--
WOW. THAT WAS--
--THAT WAS--
BOOMERANG ARROW.
IT COMES BACK TO YOU IN THE END.

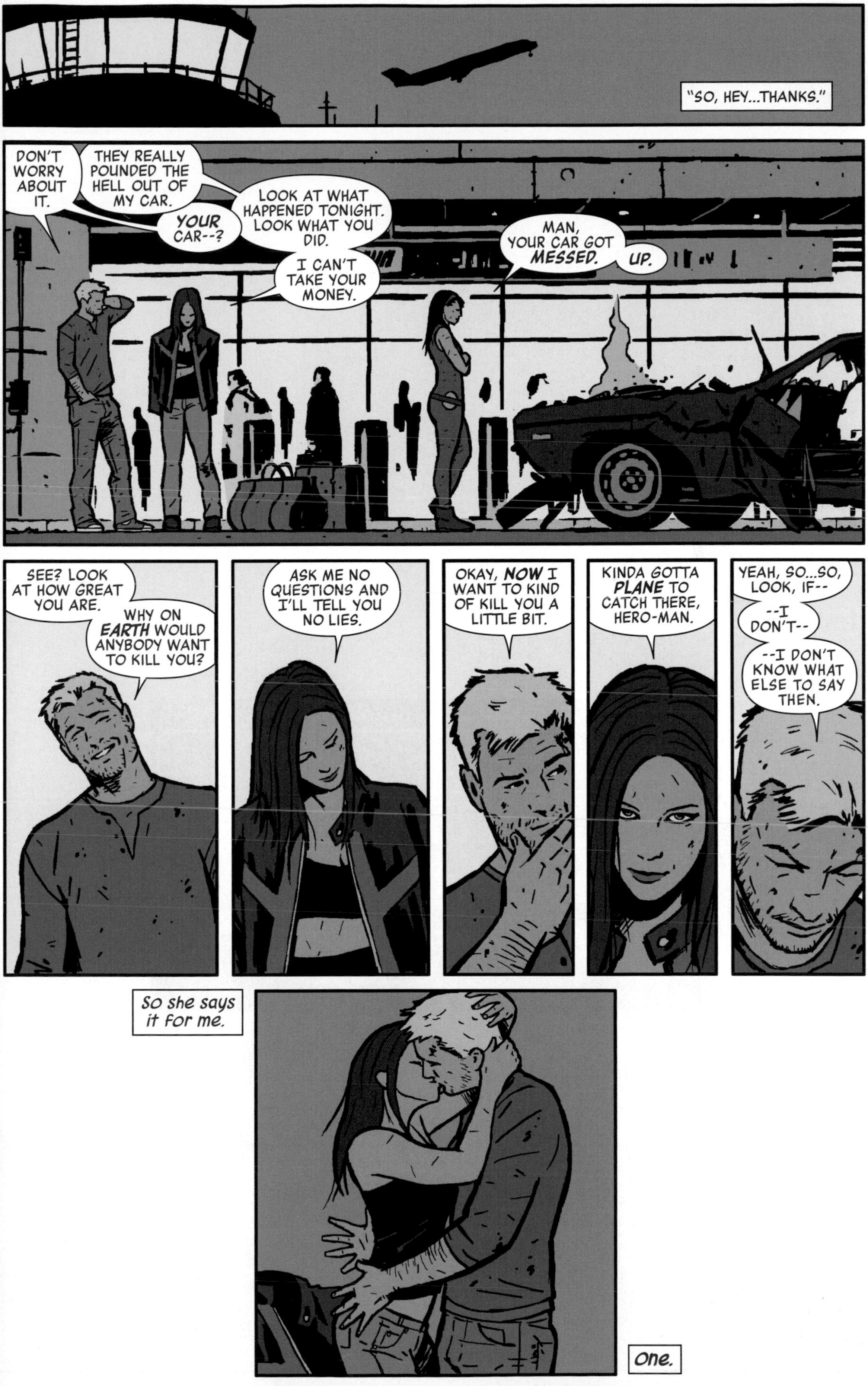
"SO, HEY...THANKS."
DON'T WORRY ABOUT IT.
THEY REALLY POUNDED THE HELL OUT OF MY CAR.
YOUR CAR--?
LOOK AT WHAT HAPPENED TONIGHT. LOOK WHAT YOU DID.
I CAN'T TAKE YOUR MONEY.
MAN, YOUR CAR GOT MESSED.
UP.
SEE? LOOK AT HOW GREAT YOU ARE.
WHY ON EARTH WOULD ANYBODY WANT TO KILL YOU?
ASK ME NO QUESTIONS AND I'LL TELL YOU NO LIES.
OKAY, NOW I WANT TO KIND OF KILL YOU A LITTLE BIT.
KINDA GOTTA PLANE TO CATCH THERE, HERO-MAN.
YEAH, SO...SO, LOOK, IF--
--I DON'T--
--I DON'T KNOW WHAT ELSE TO SAY THEN.
So she says it for me.
One.

4

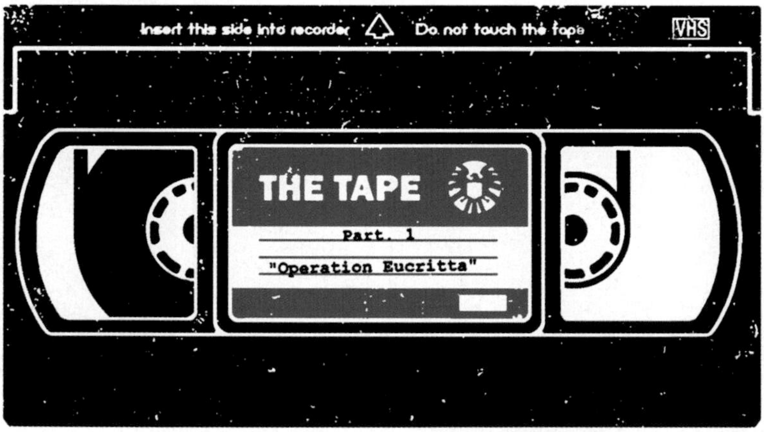
Insert this side into recorder
Do not touch the tape
VHS
THE TAPE
Part. 1
"Operation Eucritta"

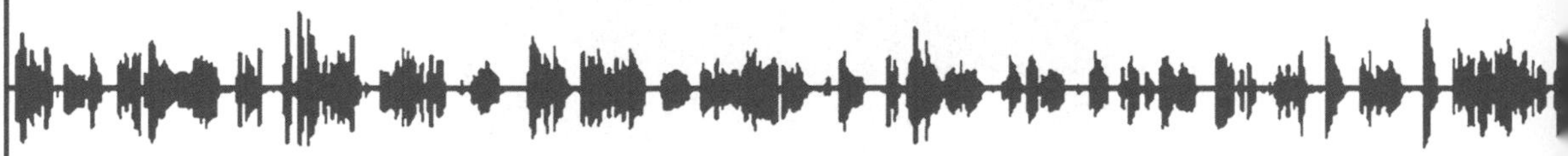

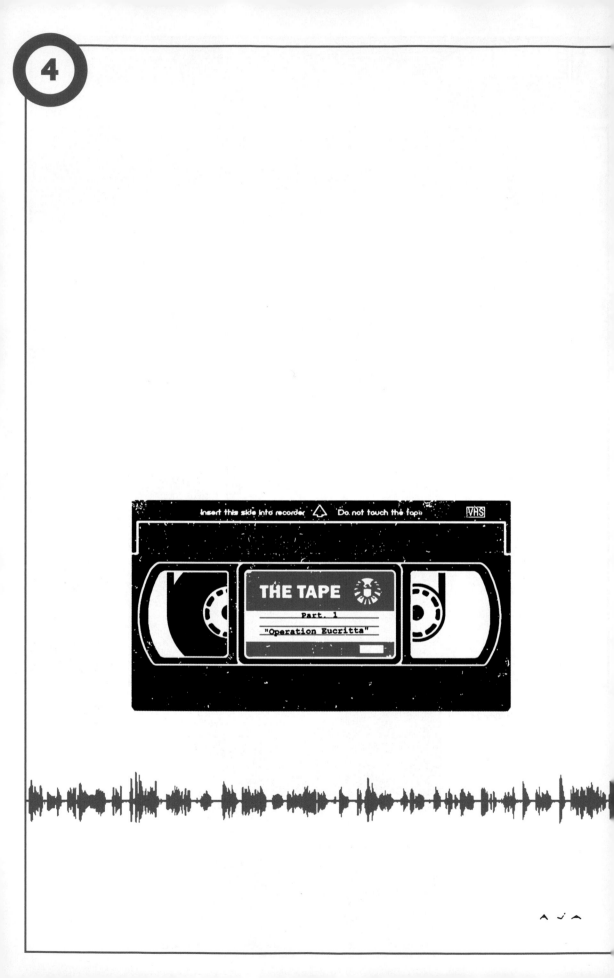

clint barton is
hawkeye
THE TAPE
1 OF 2

21:09:59:29

"YOU EVER KILL
ANYBODY, CLINT?"

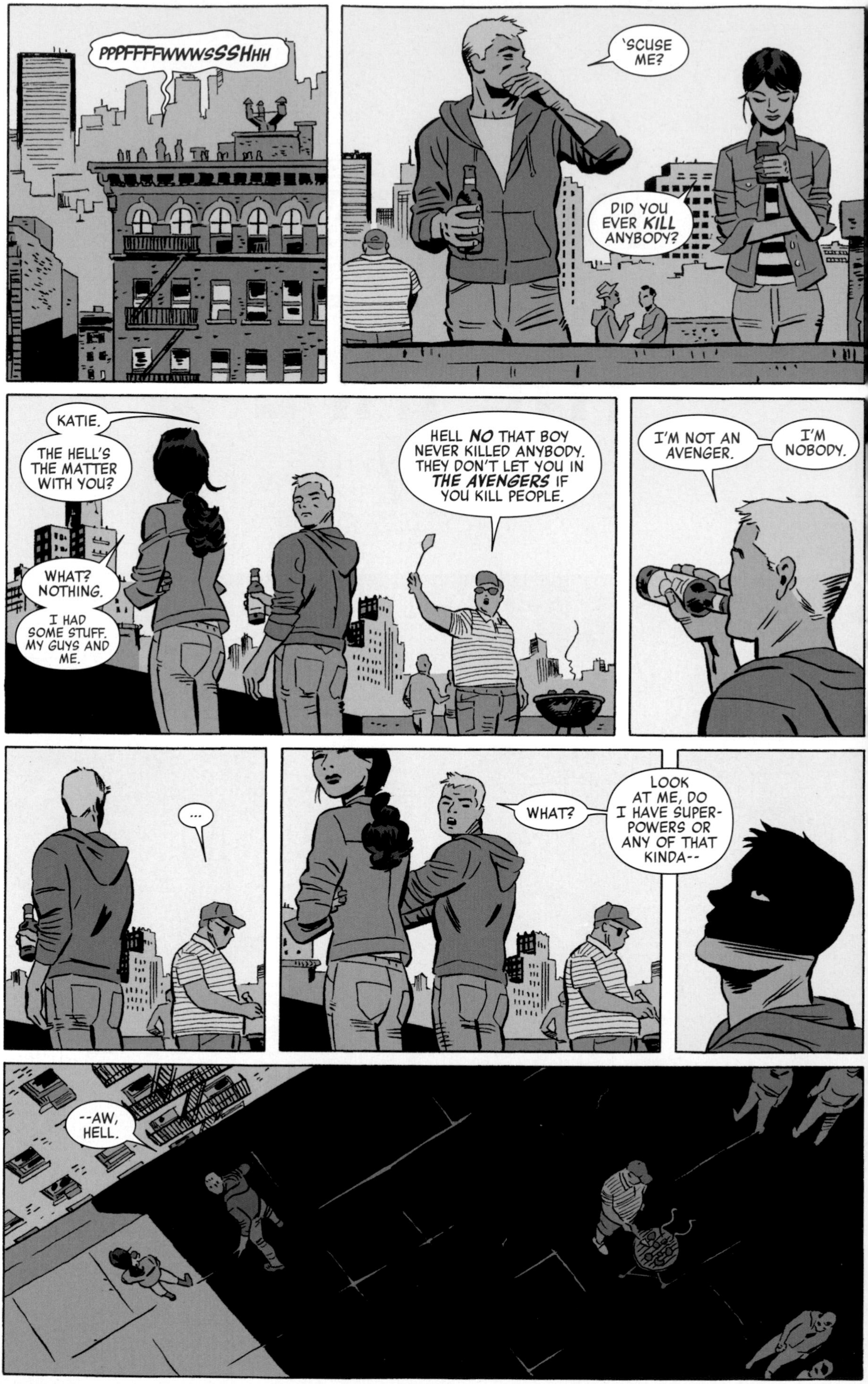
PPPFFFFWWWSSSHHH
'SCUSE ME?
DID YOU EVER KILL ANYBODY?
KATIE.
THE HELL'S THE MATTER WITH YOU?
WHAT? NOTHING.
I HAD SOME STUFF. MY GUYS AND ME.
HELL NO THAT BOY NEVER KILLED ANYBODY. THEY DON'T LET YOU IN THE AVENGERS IF YOU KILL PEOPLE.
I'M NOT AN AVENGER.
I'M NOBODY.
...
WHAT?
LOOK AT ME, DO I HAVE SUPER-POWERS OR ANY OF THAT KINDA--
--AW, HELL.

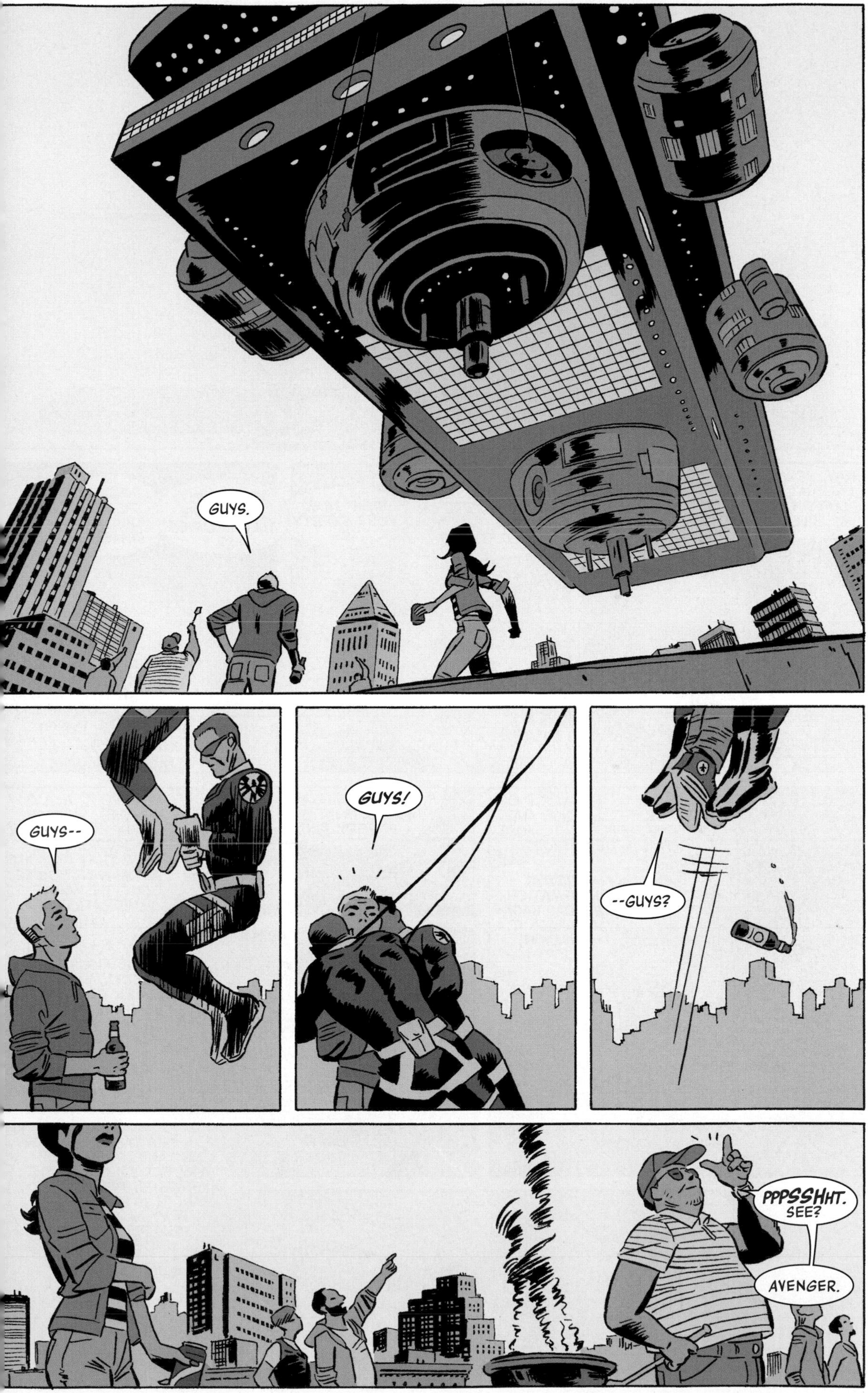
GUYS.
GUYS--
GUYS!
--GUYS?
PPPSSHHT.
SEE?
AVENGER.

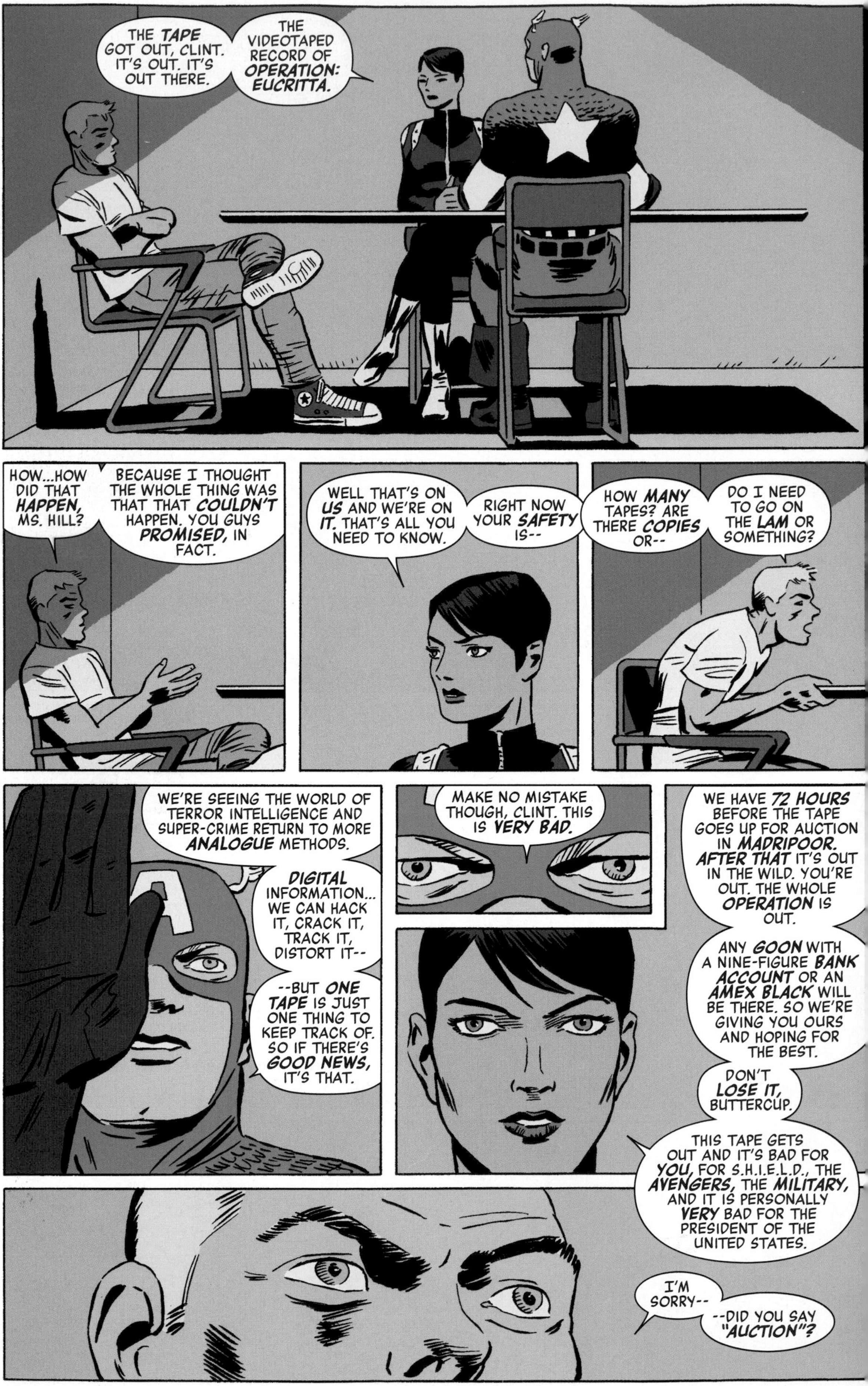
THE TAPE GOT OUT, CLINT. IT'S OUT. IT'S OUT THERE.
THE VIDEOTAPED RECORD OF OPERATION: EUCRITTA.
HOW...HOW DID THAT HAPPEN, MS. HILL?
BECAUSE I THOUGHT THE WHOLE THING WAS THAT THAT COULDN'T HAPPEN. YOU GUYS PROMISED, IN FACT.
WELL THAT'S ON US AND WE'RE ON IT. THAT'S ALL YOU NEED TO KNOW.
RIGHT NOW YOUR SAFETY IS--
HOW MANY TAPES? ARE THERE COPIES OR--
DO I NEED TO GO ON THE LAM OR SOMETHING?
WE'RE SEEING THE WORLD OF TERROR INTELLIGENCE AND SUPER-CRIME RETURN TO MORE ANALOGUE METHODS.
DIGITAL INFORMATION... WE CAN HACK IT, CRACK IT, TRACK IT, DISTORT IT--
--BUT ONE TAPE IS JUST ONE THING TO KEEP TRACK OF. SO IF THERE'S GOOD NEWS, IT'S THAT.
MAKE NO MISTAKE THOUGH, CLINT. THIS IS VERY BAD.
WE HAVE 72 HOURS BEFORE THE TAPE GOES UP FOR AUCTION IN MADRIPOOR. AFTER THAT IT'S OUT IN THE WILD. YOU'RE OUT. THE WHOLE OPERATION IS OUT.
ANY GOON WITH A NINE-FIGURE BANK ACCOUNT OR AN AMEX BLACK WILL BE THERE. SO WE'RE GIVING YOU OURS AND HOPING FOR THE BEST.
DON'T LOSE IT, BUTTERCUP.
THIS TAPE GETS OUT AND IT'S BAD FOR YOU, FOR S.H.I.E.L.D., THE AVENGERS, THE MILITARY, AND IT IS PERSONALLY VERY BAD FOR THE PRESIDENT OF THE UNITED STATES.
I'M SORRY--
--DID YOU SAY "AUCTION"?

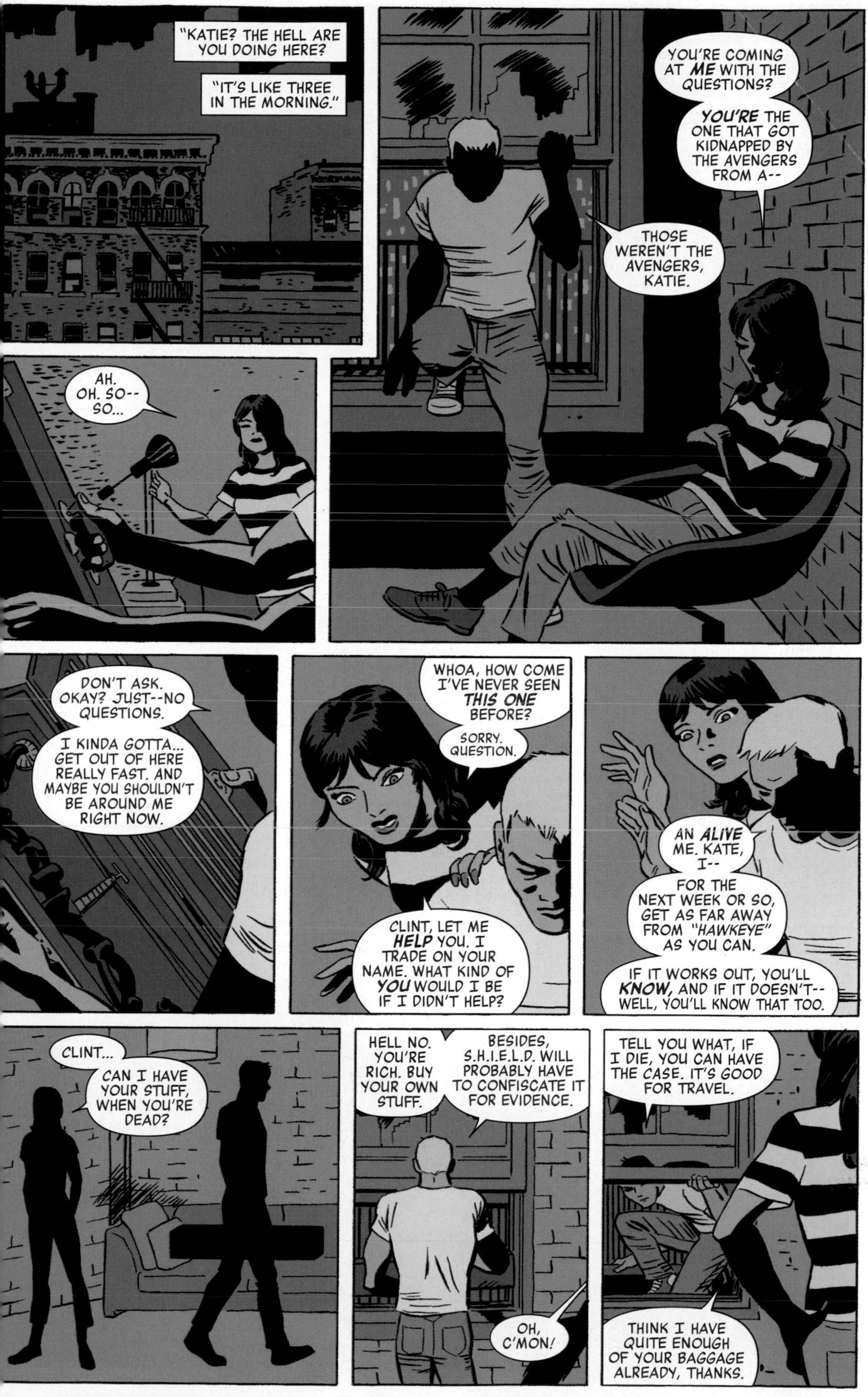
"KATIE? THE HELL ARE YOU DOING HERE?
"IT'S LIKE THREE IN THE MORNING."
YOU'RE COMING AT ME WITH THE QUESTIONS?
YOU'RE THE ONE THAT GOT KIDNAPPED BY THE AVENGERS FROM A--
THOSE WEREN'T THE AVENGERS, KATIE.
AH. OH. SO-- SO...
DON'T ASK. OKAY? JUST--NO QUESTIONS.
I KINDA GOTTA... GET OUT OF HERE REALLY FAST. AND MAYBE YOU SHOULDN'T BE AROUND ME RIGHT NOW.
WHOA, HOW COME I'VE NEVER SEEN THIS ONE BEFORE?
SORRY. QUESTION.
CLINT, LET ME HELP YOU. I TRADE ON YOUR NAME. WHAT KIND OF YOU WOULD I BE IF I DIDN'T HELP?
AN ALIVE ME. KATE, I--
FOR THE NEXT WEEK OR SO, GET AS FAR AWAY FROM "HAWKEYE" AS YOU CAN.
IF IT WORKS OUT, YOU'LL KNOW, AND IF IT DOESN'T-- WELL, YOU'LL KNOW THAT TOO.
CLINT...
CAN I HAVE YOUR STUFF, WHEN YOU'RE DEAD?
HELL NO. YOU'RE RICH. BUY YOUR OWN STUFF.
BESIDES, S.H.I.E.L.D. WILL PROBABLY HAVE TO CONFISCATE IT FOR EVIDENCE.
OH, C'MON!
TELL YOU WHAT, IF I DIE, YOU CAN HAVE THE CASE. IT'S GOOD FOR TRAVEL.
THINK I HAVE QUITE ENOUGH OF YOUR BAGGAGE ALREADY, THANKS.

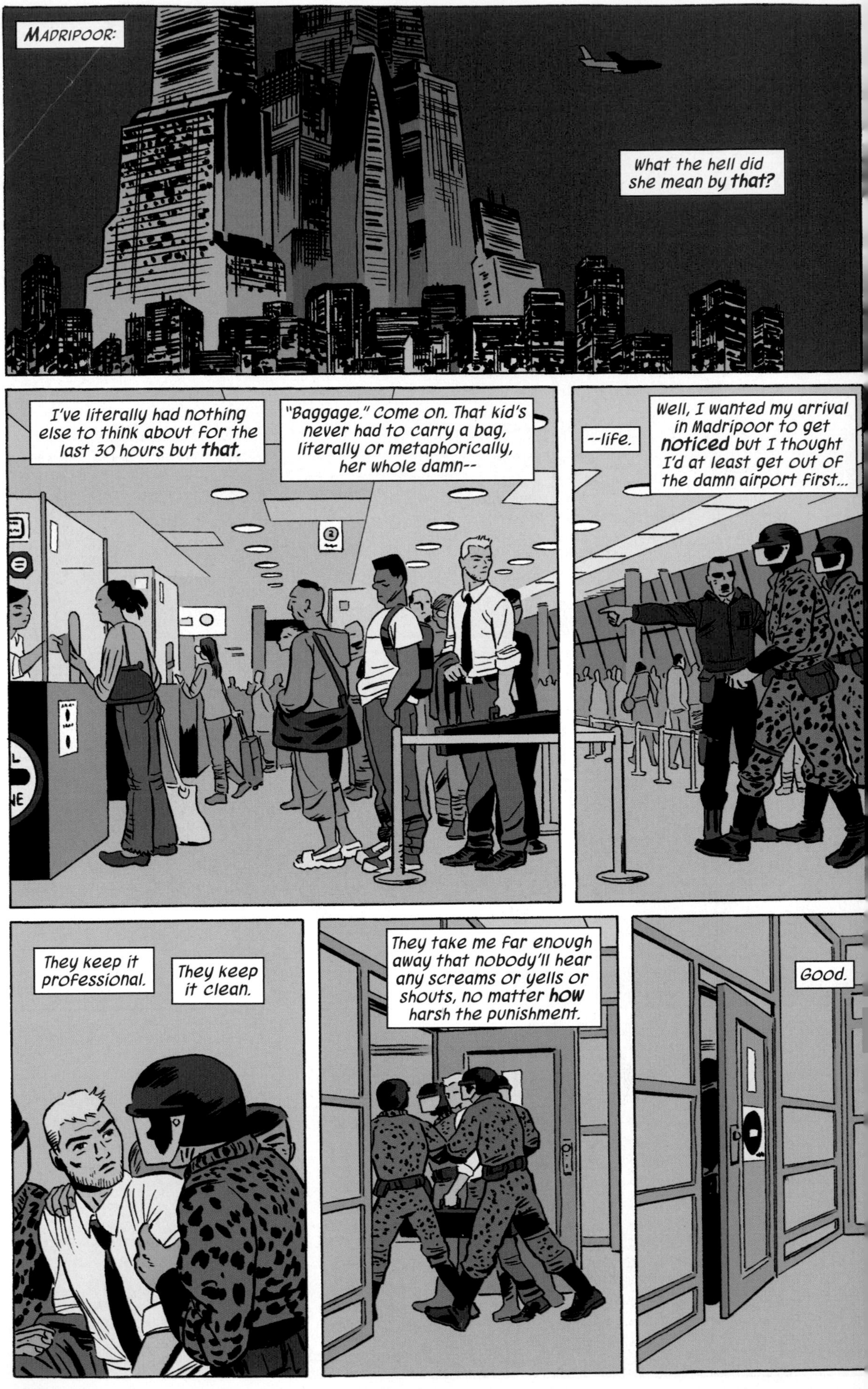
MADRIPOOR:
What the hell did she mean by that?
I've literally had nothing else to think about for the last 30 hours but that.
"Baggage." Come on. That kid's never had to carry a bag, literally or metaphorically, her whole damn--
--life.
Well, I wanted my arrival in Madripoor to get noticed but I thought I'd at least get out of the damn airport first...
They keep it professional.
They keep it clean.
They take me far enough away that nobody'll hear any screams or yells or shouts, no matter how harsh the punishment.
Good.

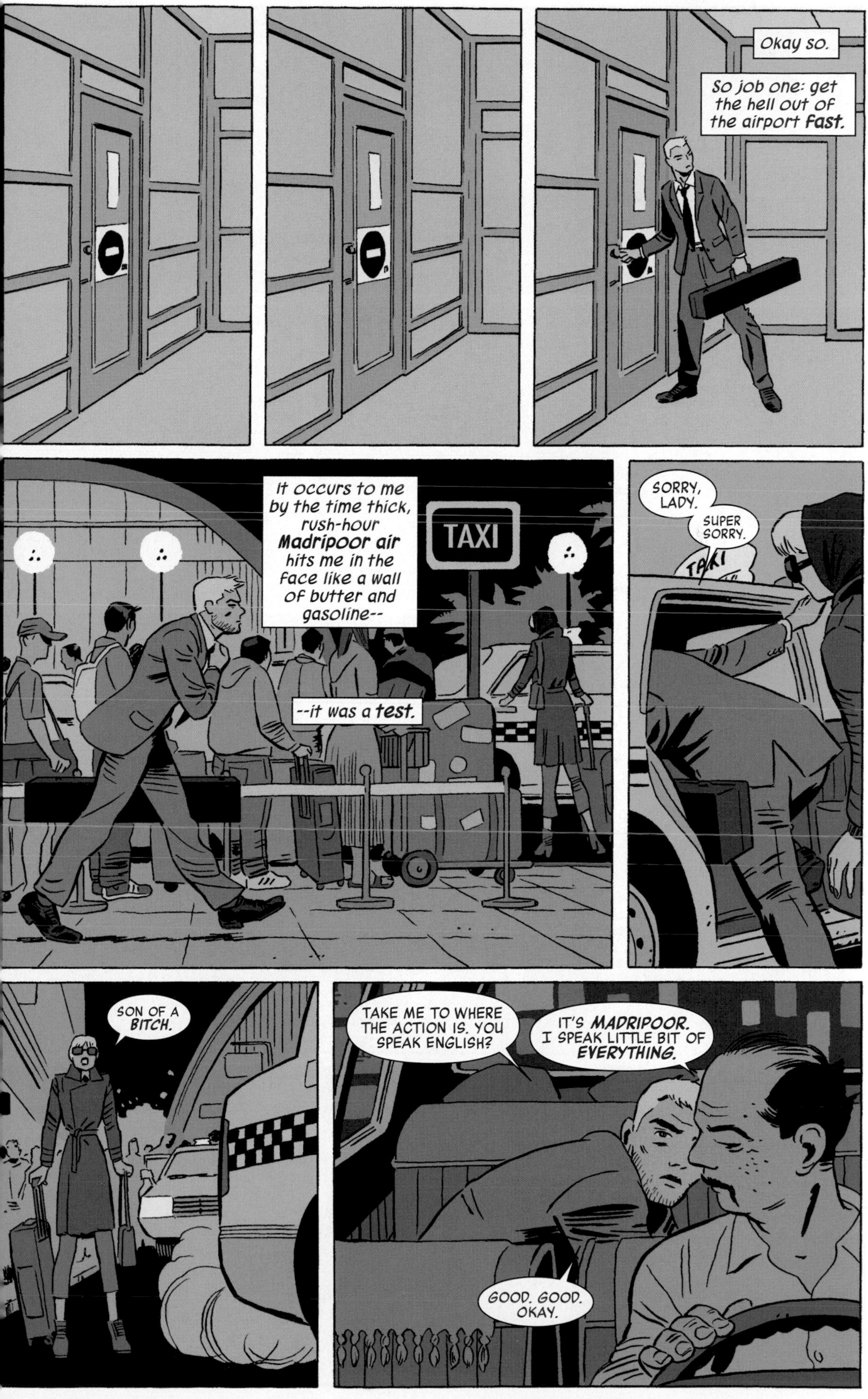
Okay so.
So job one: get the hell out of the airport **fast.**
It occurs to me by the time thick, rush-hour **Madripoor air** hits me in the face like a wall of butter and gasoline--
TAXI
--it was a **test.**
SORRY, LADY.
SUPER SORRY.
SON OF A **BITCH.**
TAKE ME TO WHERE THE ACTION IS. YOU SPEAK ENGLISH?
IT'S **MADRIPOOR.** I SPEAK LITTLE BIT OF **EVERYTHING.**
GOOD. GOOD. OKAY.

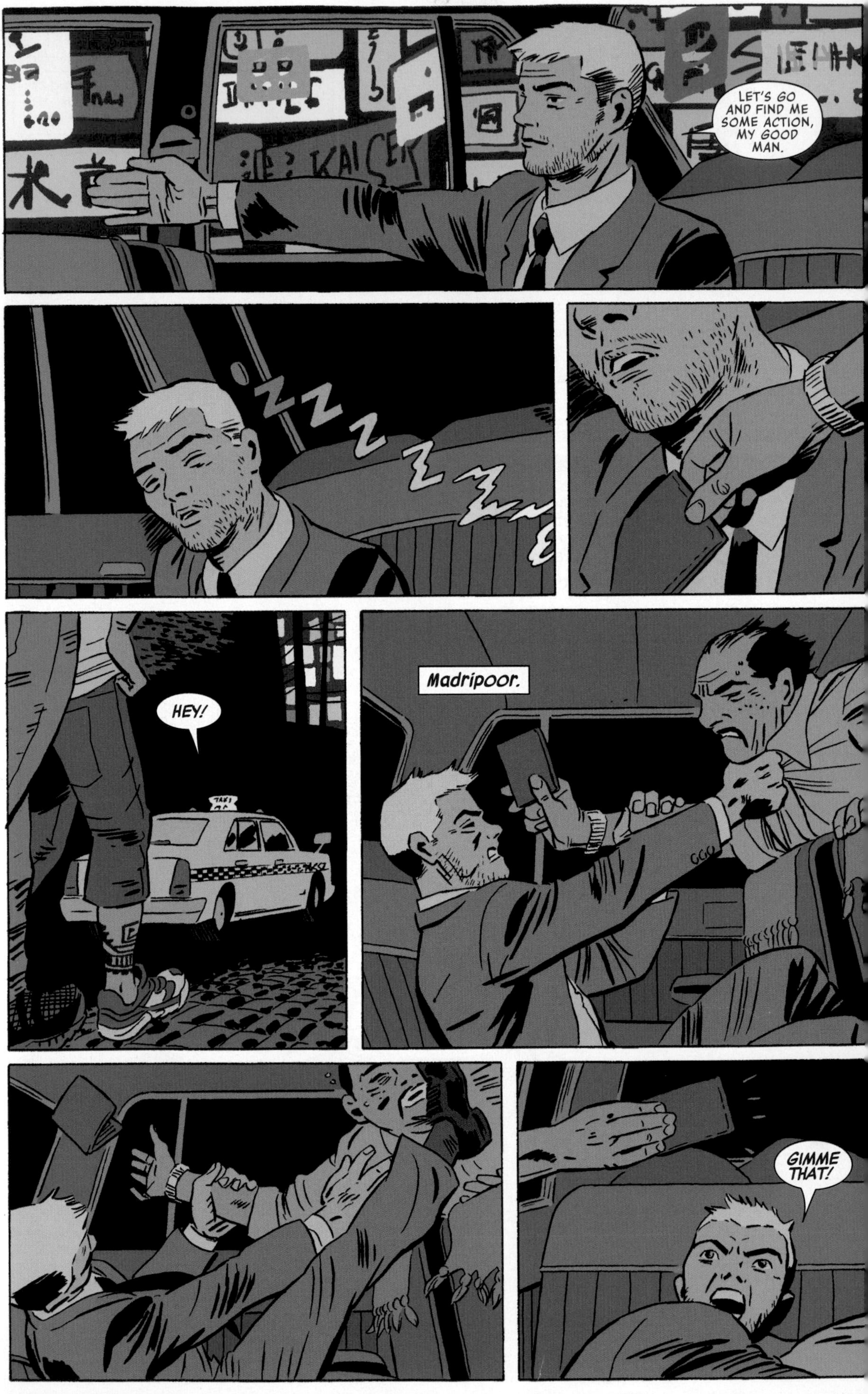
LET'S GO AND FIND ME SOME ACTION, MY GOOD MAN.
HEY!
Madripoor.
GIMME THAT!

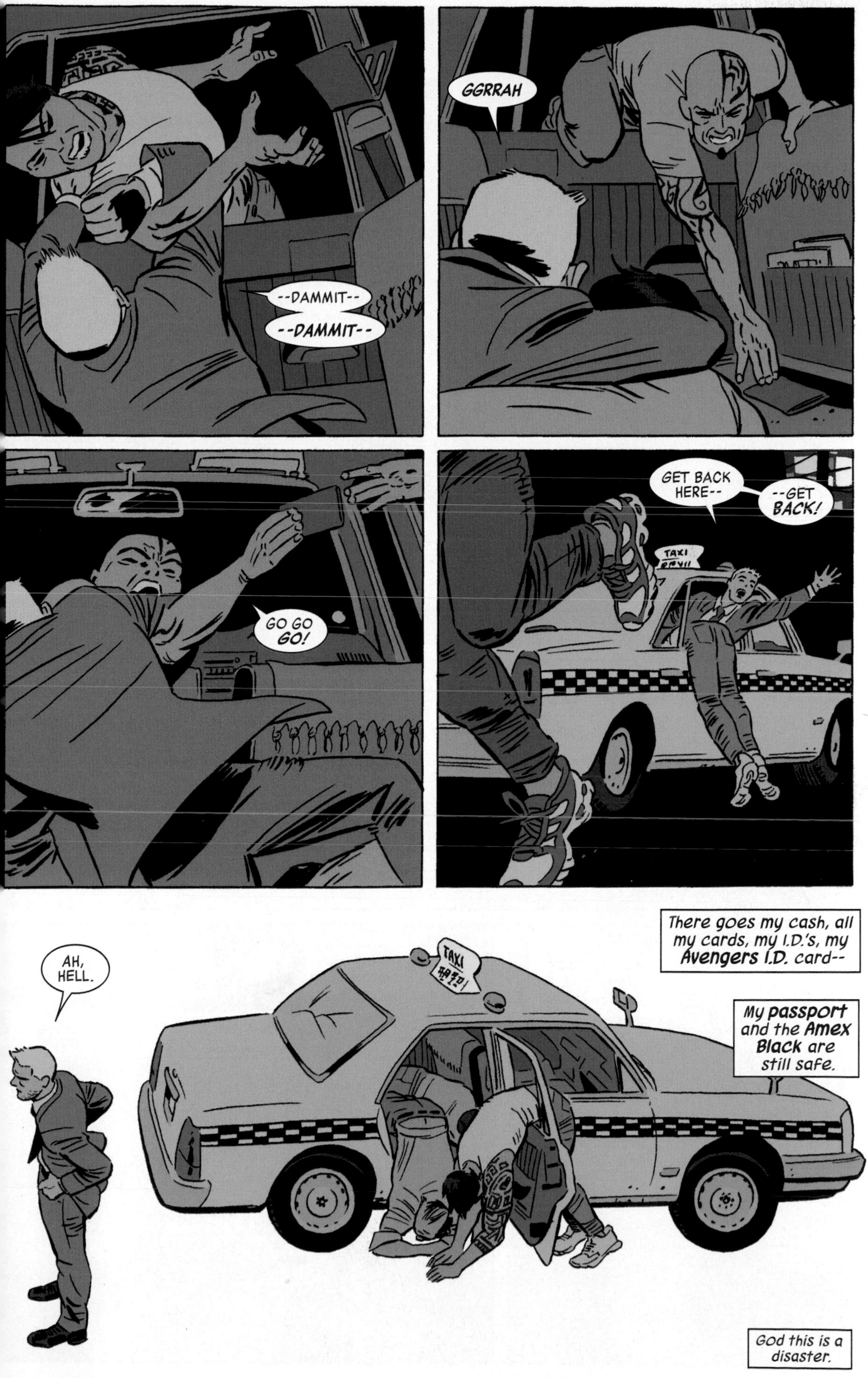
--DAMMIT--
--DAMMIT--
GGRRAH
GO GO GO!
GET BACK HERE--
--GET BACK!
TAXI
AH, HELL.
There goes my cash, all my cards, my I.D.'s, my Avengers I.D. card--
My passport and the Amex Black are still safe.
God this is a disaster.

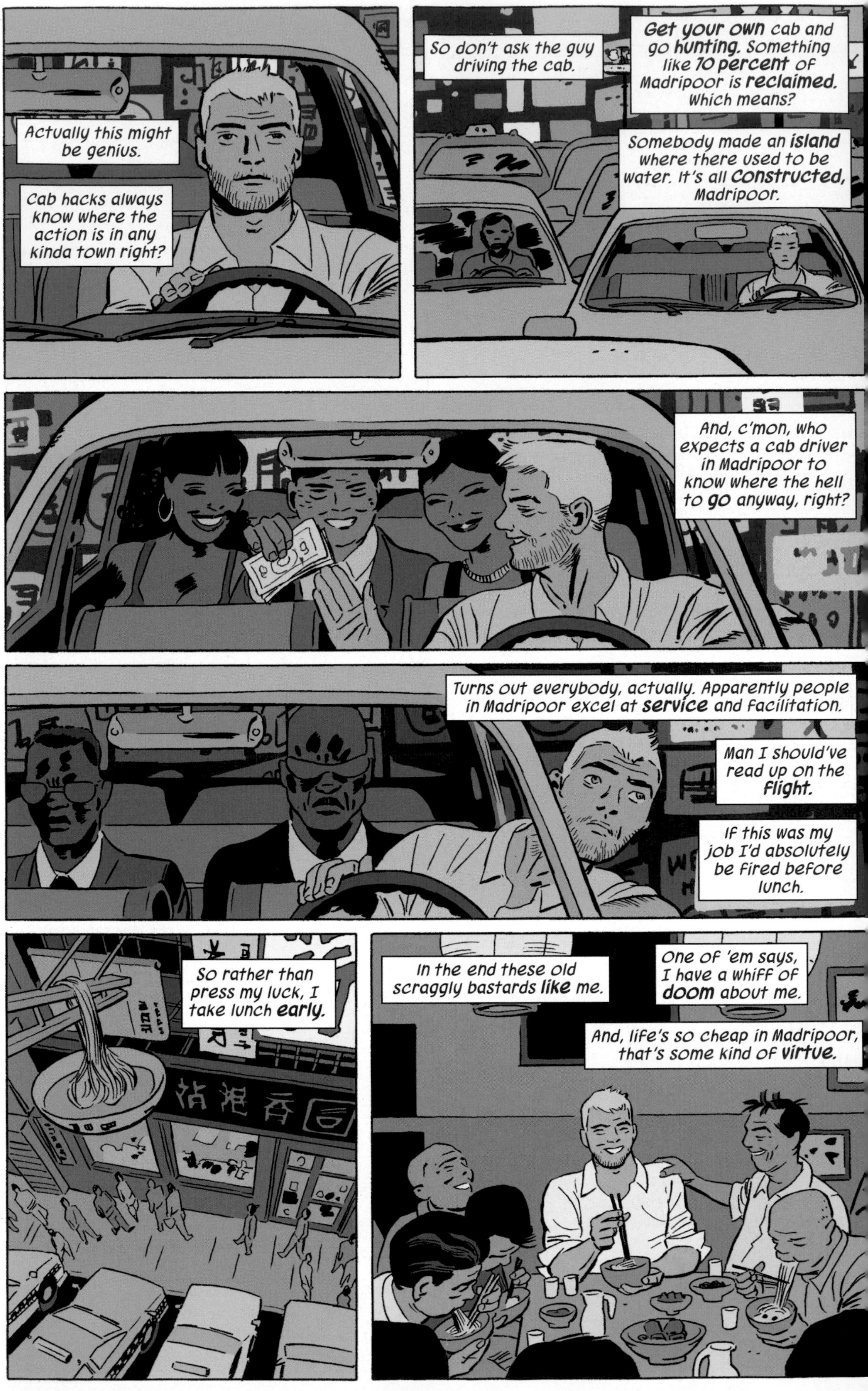
Actually this might be genius.
Cab hacks always know where the action is in any kinda town right?
So don't ask the guy driving the cab.
Get your own cab and go hunting. Something like 70 percent of Madripoor is reclaimed. Which means?
Somebody made an island where there used to be water. It's all constructed, Madripoor.
And, c'mon, who expects a cab driver in Madripoor to know where the hell to go anyway, right?
Turns out everybody, actually. Apparently people in Madripoor excel at service and facilitation.
Man I should've read up on the flight.
If this was my job I'd absolutely be fired before lunch.
So rather than press my luck, I take lunch early.
In the end these old scraggly bastards like me.
One of 'em says, I have a whiff of doom about me.
And, life's so cheap in Madripoor, that's some kind of virtue.

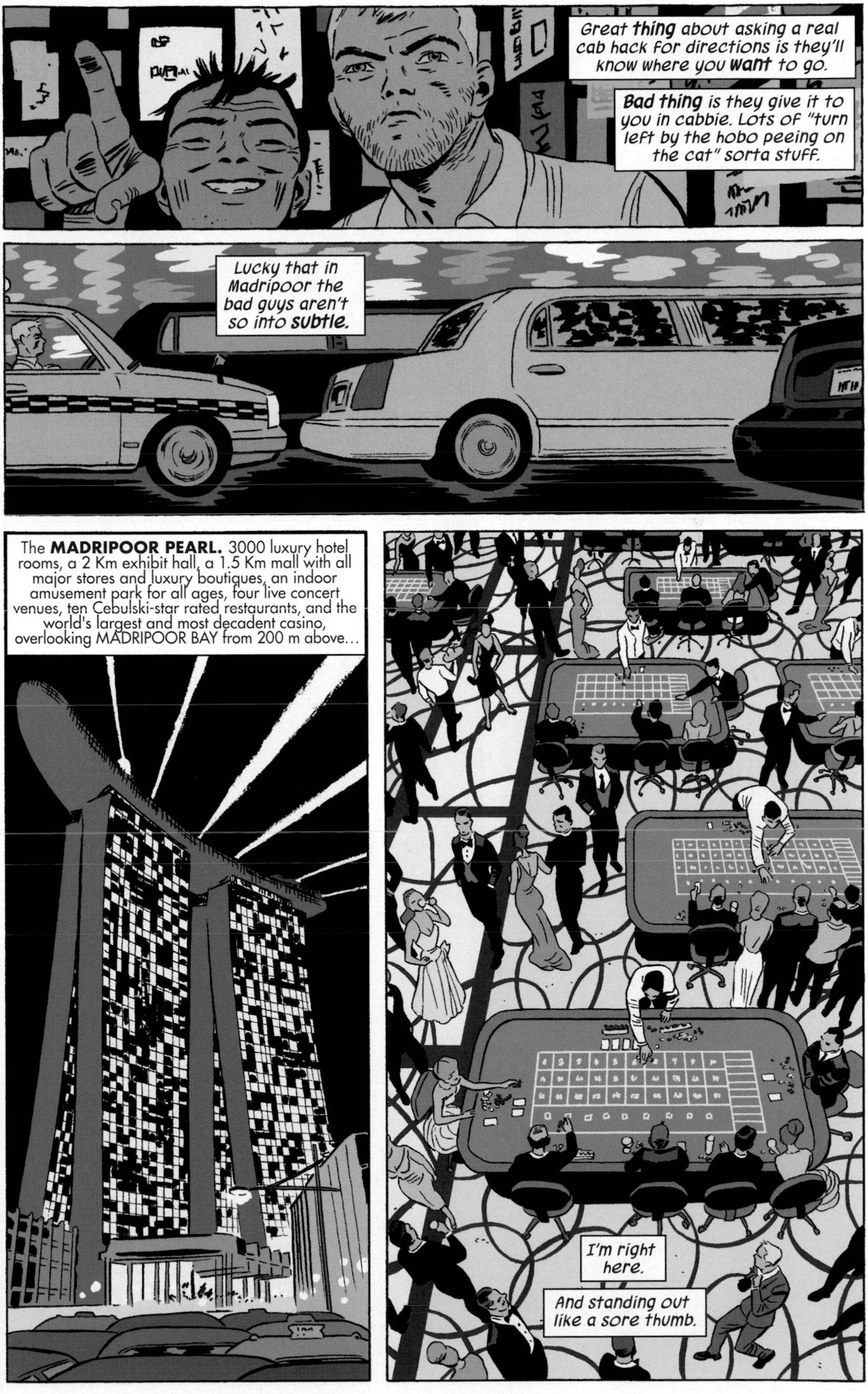
Great thing about asking a real cab hack for directions is they'll know where you want to go.
Bad thing is they give it to you in cabbie. Lots of "turn left by the hobo peeing on the cat" sorta stuff.
Lucky that in Madripoor the bad guys aren't so into subtle.
The MADRIPOOR PEARL. 3000 luxury hotel rooms, a 2 Km exhibit hall, a 1.5 Km mall with all major stores and luxury boutiques, an indoor amusement park for all ages, four live concert venues, ten Cebulski-star rated restaurants, and the world's largest and most decadent casino, overlooking MADRIPOOR BAY from 200 m above...
I'm right here.
And standing out like a sore thumb.

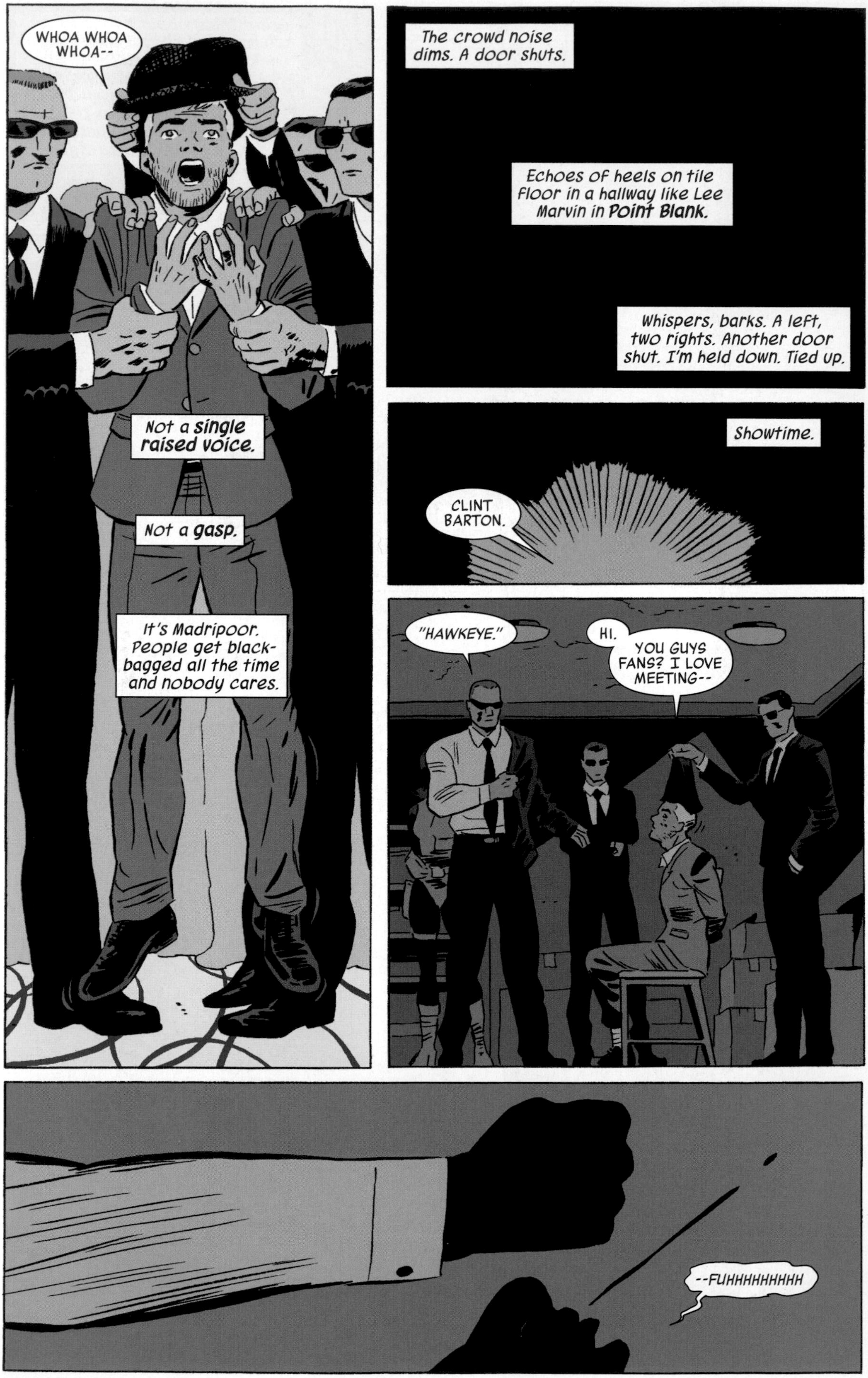
WHOA WHOA WHOA--
Not a single raised voice.
Not a gasp.
It's Madripoor. People get black-bagged all the time and nobody cares.
The crowd noise dims. A door shuts.
Echoes of heels on tile floor in a hallway like Lee Marvin in Point Blank.
Whispers, barks. A left, two rights. Another door shut. I'm held down. Tied up.
Showtime.
CLINT BARTON.
"HAWKEYE."
HI.
YOU GUYS FANS? I LOVE MEETING--
--FUHHHHHHHHHH

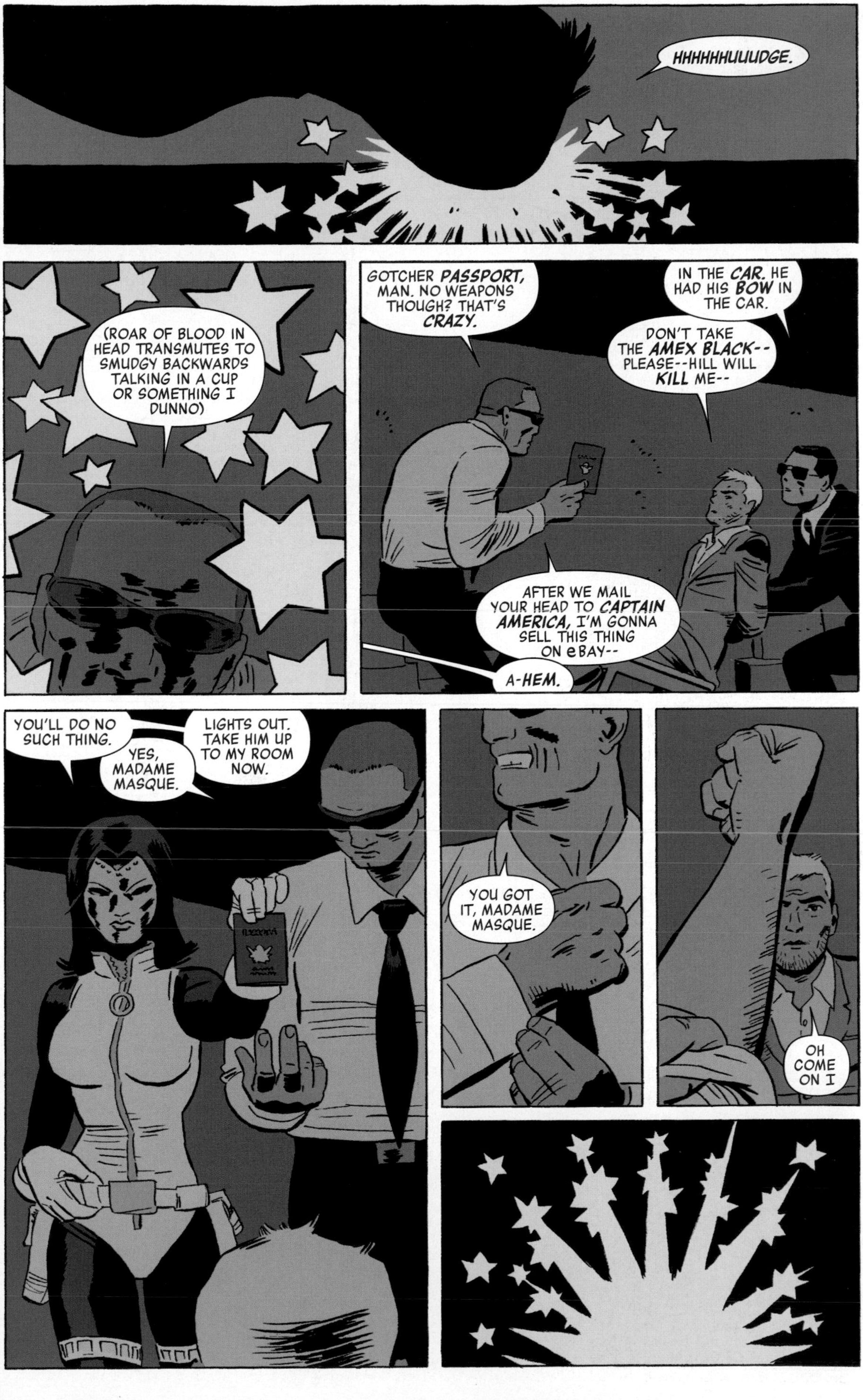
HHHHHHUUUDGE.
(ROAR OF BLOOD IN HEAD TRANSMUTES TO SMUDGY BACKWARDS TALKING IN A CUP OR SOMETHING I DUNNO)
GOTCHER PASSPORT, MAN. NO WEAPONS THOUGH? THAT'S CRAZY.
IN THE CAR. HE HAD HIS BOW IN THE CAR.
DON'T TAKE THE AMEX BLACK-- PLEASE--HILL WILL KILL ME--
AFTER WE MAIL YOUR HEAD TO CAPTAIN AMERICA, I'M GONNA SELL THIS THING ON eBAY--
A-HEM.
YOU'LL DO NO SUCH THING.
YES, MADAME MASQUE.
LIGHTS OUT. TAKE HIM UP TO MY ROOM NOW.
YOU GOT IT, MADAME MASQUE.
OH COME ON I

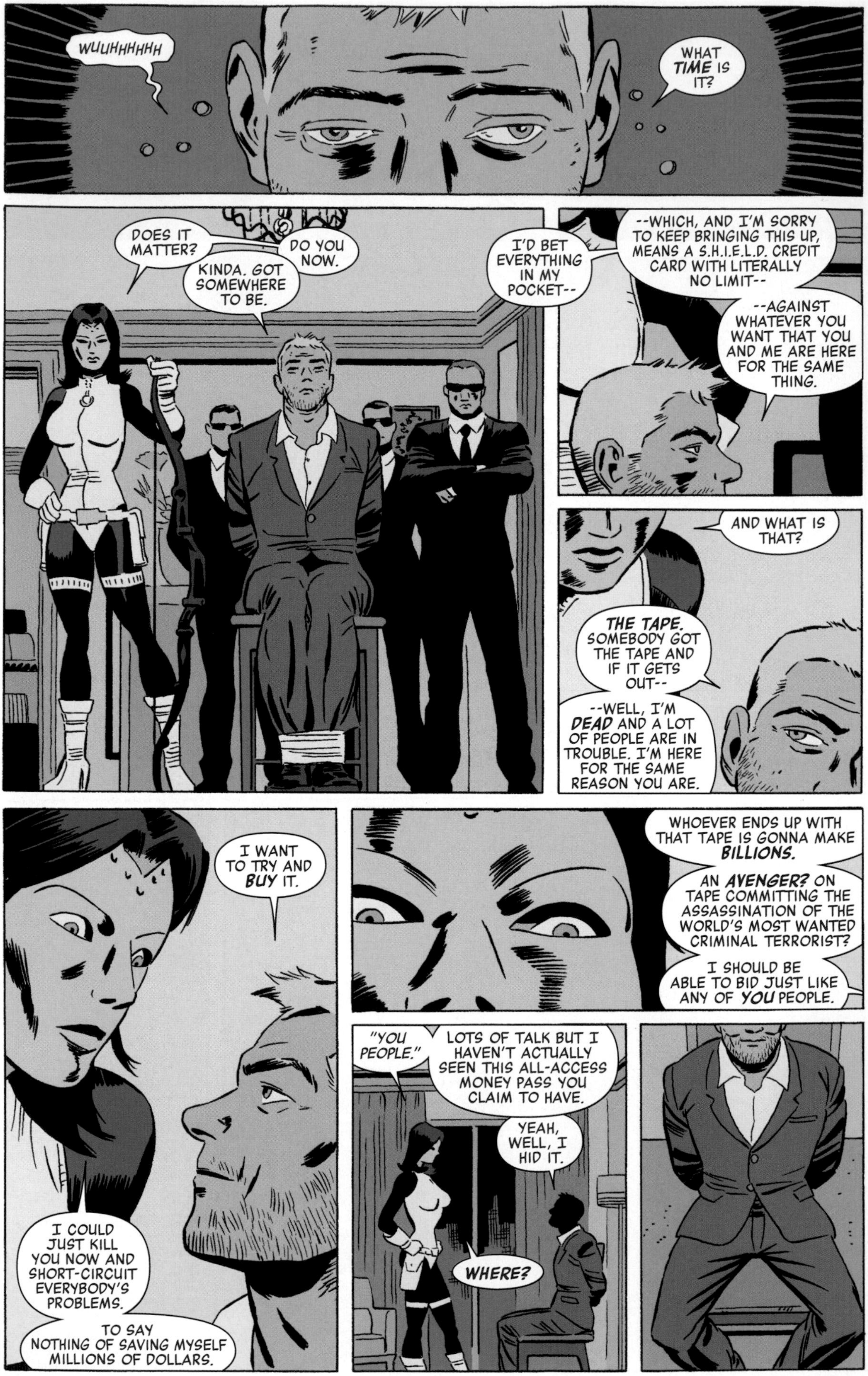
WUUHHHHHH
WHAT TIME IS IT?
DOES IT MATTER?
DO YOU NOW.
KINDA. GOT SOMEWHERE TO BE.
I'D BET EVERYTHING IN MY POCKET--
--WHICH, AND I'M SORRY TO KEEP BRINGING THIS UP, MEANS A S.H.I.E.L.D. CREDIT CARD WITH LITERALLY NO LIMIT--
--AGAINST WHATEVER YOU WANT THAT YOU AND ME ARE HERE FOR THE SAME THING.
AND WHAT IS THAT?
THE TAPE. SOMEBODY GOT THE TAPE AND IF IT GETS OUT--
--WELL, I'M DEAD AND A LOT OF PEOPLE ARE IN TROUBLE. I'M HERE FOR THE SAME REASON YOU ARE.
I WANT TO TRY AND BUY IT.
I COULD JUST KILL YOU NOW AND SHORT-CIRCUIT EVERYBODY'S PROBLEMS.
TO SAY NOTHING OF SAVING MYSELF MILLIONS OF DOLLARS.
WHOEVER ENDS UP WITH THAT TAPE IS GONNA MAKE BILLIONS.
AN AVENGER? ON TAPE COMMITTING THE ASSASSINATION OF THE WORLD'S MOST WANTED CRIMINAL TERRORIST?
I SHOULD BE ABLE TO BID JUST LIKE ANY OF YOU PEOPLE.
"YOU PEOPLE."
LOTS OF TALK BUT I HAVEN'T ACTUALLY SEEN THIS ALL-ACCESS MONEY PASS YOU CLAIM TO HAVE.
YEAH, WELL, I HID IT.
WHERE?

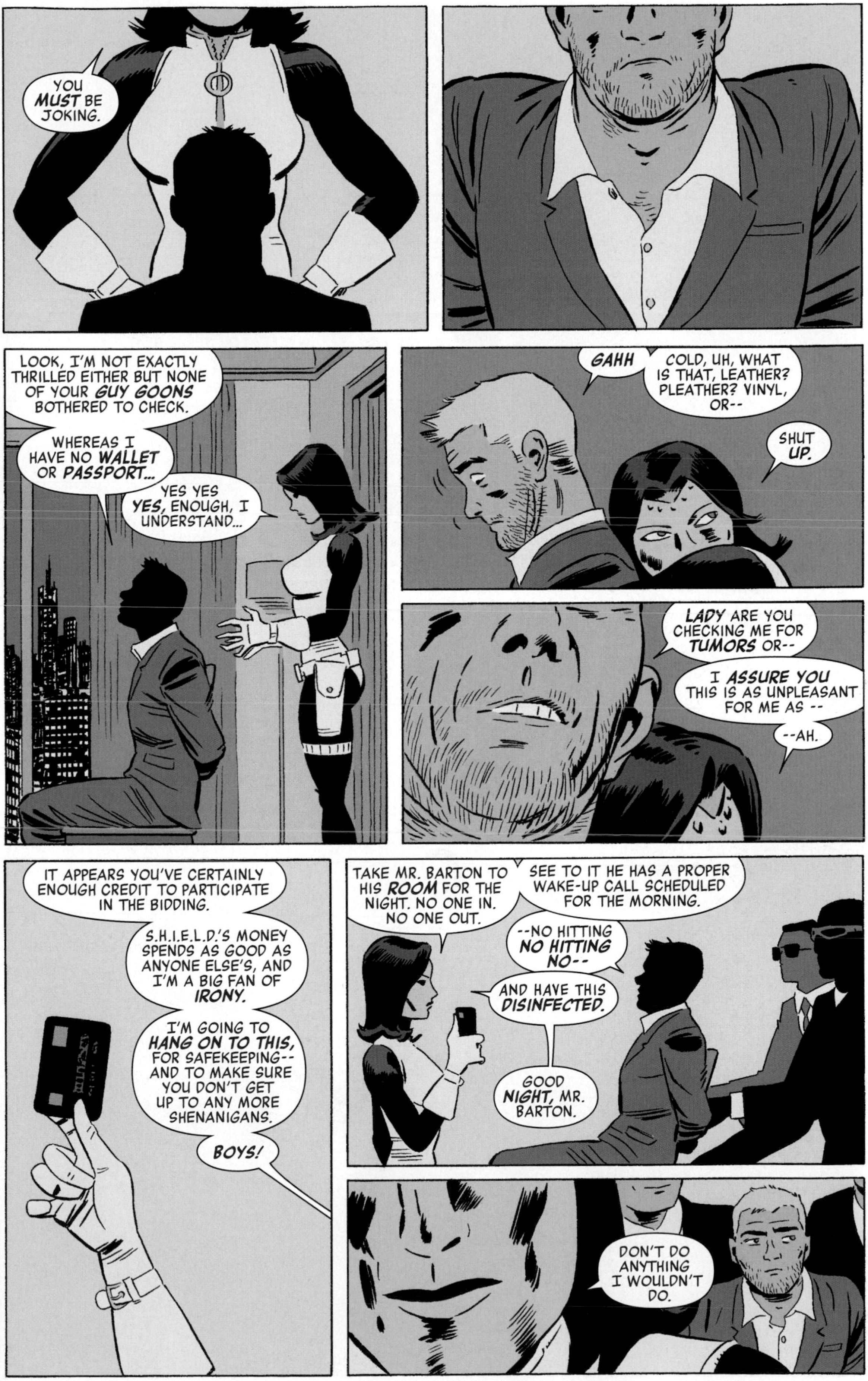
YOU MUST BE JOKING.
LOOK, I'M NOT EXACTLY THRILLED EITHER BUT NONE OF YOUR GUY GOONS BOTHERED TO CHECK.
WHEREAS I HAVE NO WALLET OR PASSPORT...
YES YES YES, ENOUGH, I UNDERSTAND...
GAHH
COLD, UH, WHAT IS THAT, LEATHER? PLEATHER? VINYL, OR--
SHUT UP.
LADY ARE YOU CHECKING ME FOR TUMORS OR--
I ASSURE YOU THIS IS AS UNPLEASANT FOR ME AS --
--AH.
IT APPEARS YOU'VE CERTAINLY ENOUGH CREDIT TO PARTICIPATE IN THE BIDDING.
S.H.I.E.L.D.'S MONEY SPENDS AS GOOD AS ANYONE ELSE'S, AND I'M A BIG FAN OF IRONY.
I'M GOING TO HANG ON TO THIS, FOR SAFEKEEPING-- AND TO MAKE SURE YOU DON'T GET UP TO ANY MORE SHENANIGANS.
BOYS!
TAKE MR. BARTON TO HIS ROOM FOR THE NIGHT. NO ONE IN. NO ONE OUT.
SEE TO IT HE HAS A PROPER WAKE-UP CALL SCHEDULED FOR THE MORNING.
--NO HITTING NO HITTING NO--
AND HAVE THIS DISINFECTED.
GOOD NIGHT, MR. BARTON.
DON'T DO ANYTHING I WOULDN'T DO.

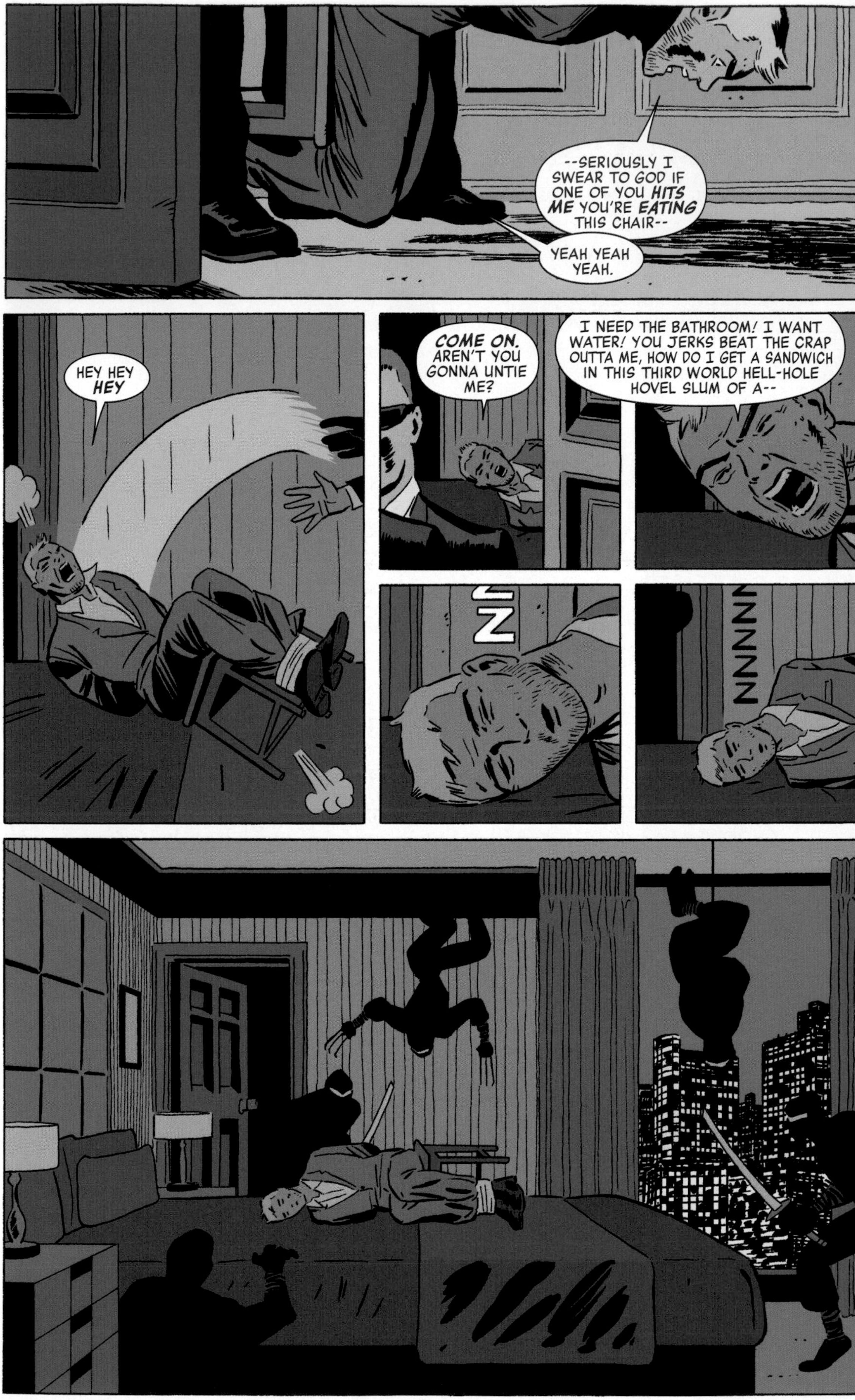
--SERIOUSLY I SWEAR TO GOD IF ONE OF YOU HITS ME YOU'RE EATING THIS CHAIR--
YEAH YEAH YEAH.
HEY HEY HEY
COME ON. AREN'T YOU GONNA UNTIE ME?
I NEED THE BATHROOM! I WANT WATER! YOU JERKS BEAT THE CRAP OUTTA ME, HOW DO I GET A SANDWICH IN THIS THIRD WORLD HELL-HOLE HOVEL SLUM OF A--
ZZ
NNNNNN

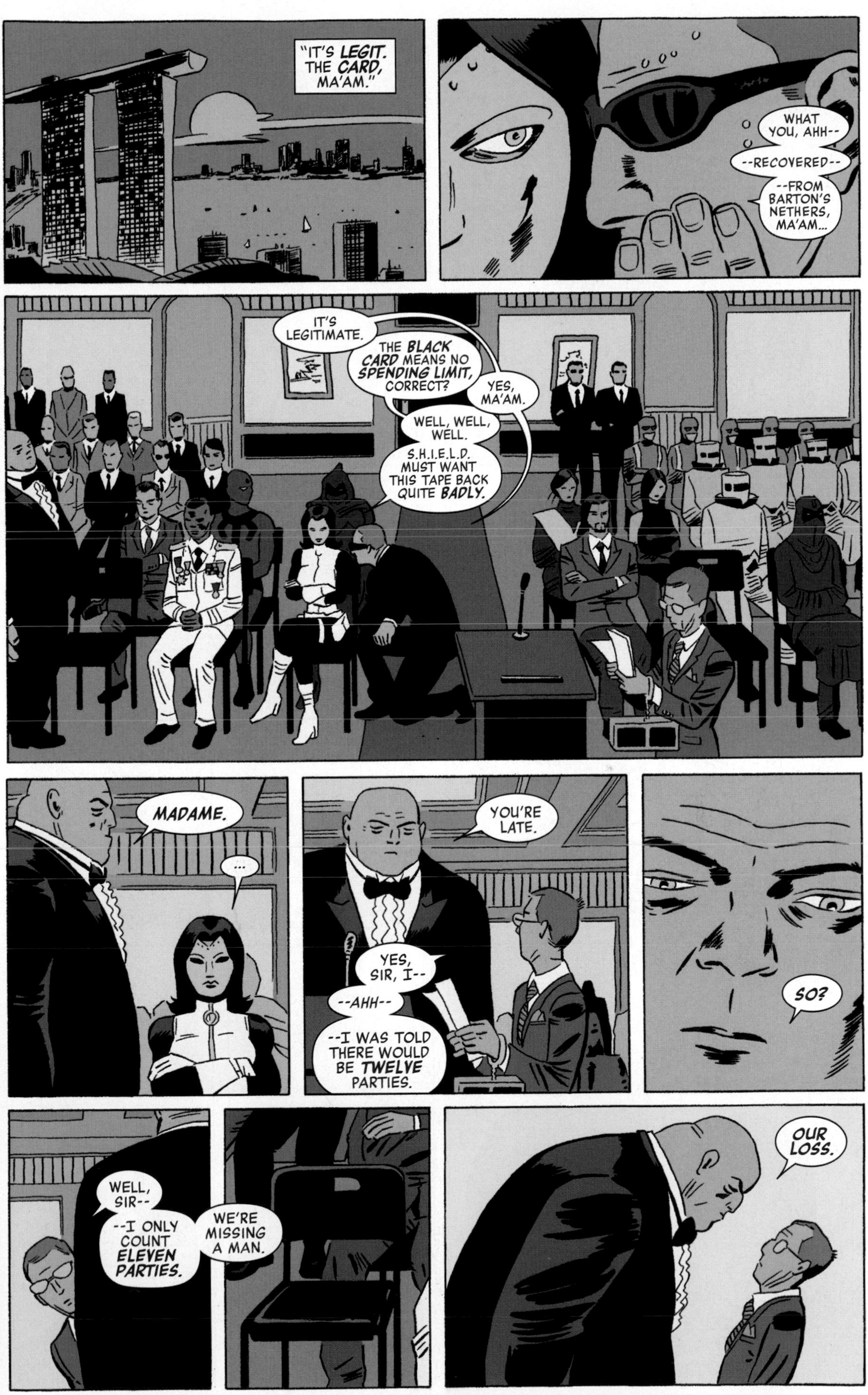
"IT'S LEGIT. THE CARD, MA'AM."
WHAT YOU, AHH--
--RECOVERED--
--FROM BARTON'S NETHERS, MA'AM...
IT'S LEGITIMATE.
THE BLACK CARD MEANS NO SPENDING LIMIT, CORRECT?
YES, MA'AM.
WELL, WELL, WELL.
S.H.I.E.L.D. MUST WANT THIS TAPE BACK QUITE BADLY.
MADAME.
...
YOU'RE LATE.
YES, SIR, I--
--AHH--
--I WAS TOLD THERE WOULD BE TWELVE PARTIES.
SO?
WELL, SIR--
--I ONLY COUNT ELEVEN PARTIES.
WE'RE MISSING A MAN.
OUR LOSS.

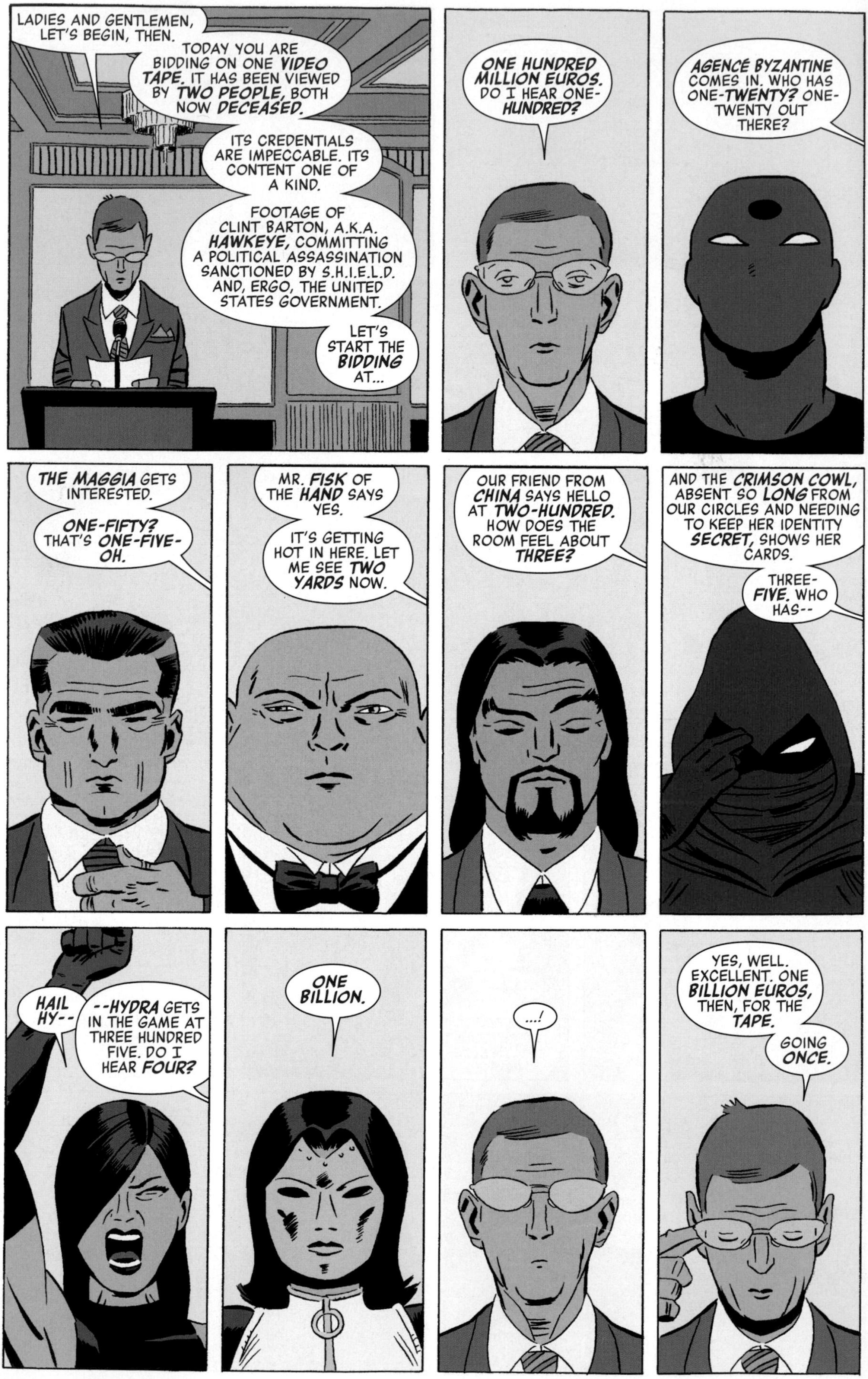

LADIES AND GENTLEMEN, LET'S BEGIN, THEN.
TODAY YOU ARE BIDDING ON ONE VIDEO TAPE. IT HAS BEEN VIEWED BY TWO PEOPLE, BOTH NOW DECEASED.
ITS CREDENTIALS ARE IMPECCABLE. ITS CONTENT ONE OF A KIND.
FOOTAGE OF CLINT BARTON, A.K.A. HAWKEYE, COMMITTING A POLITICAL ASSASSINATION SANCTIONED BY S.H.I.E.L.D. AND, ERGO, THE UNITED STATES GOVERNMENT.
LET'S START THE BIDDING AT...
ONE HUNDRED MILLION EUROS. DO I HEAR ONE-HUNDRED?
AGENCE BYZANTINE COMES IN. WHO HAS ONE-TWENTY? ONE-TWENTY OUT THERE?
THE MAGGIA GETS INTERESTED.
ONE-FIFTY? THAT'S ONE-FIVE-OH.
MR. FISK OF THE HAND SAYS YES.
IT'S GETTING HOT IN HERE. LET ME SEE TWO YARDS NOW.
OUR FRIEND FROM CHINA SAYS HELLO AT TWO-HUNDRED. HOW DOES THE ROOM FEEL ABOUT THREE?
AND THE CRIMSON COWL, ABSENT SO LONG FROM OUR CIRCLES AND NEEDING TO KEEP HER IDENTITY SECRET, SHOWS HER CARDS.
THREE-FIVE. WHO HAS--
HAIL HY--
--HYDRA GETS IN THE GAME AT THREE HUNDRED FIVE. DO I HEAR FOUR?
ONE BILLION.
...!
YES, WELL. EXCELLENT. ONE BILLION EUROS, THEN, FOR THE TAPE.
GOING ONCE.

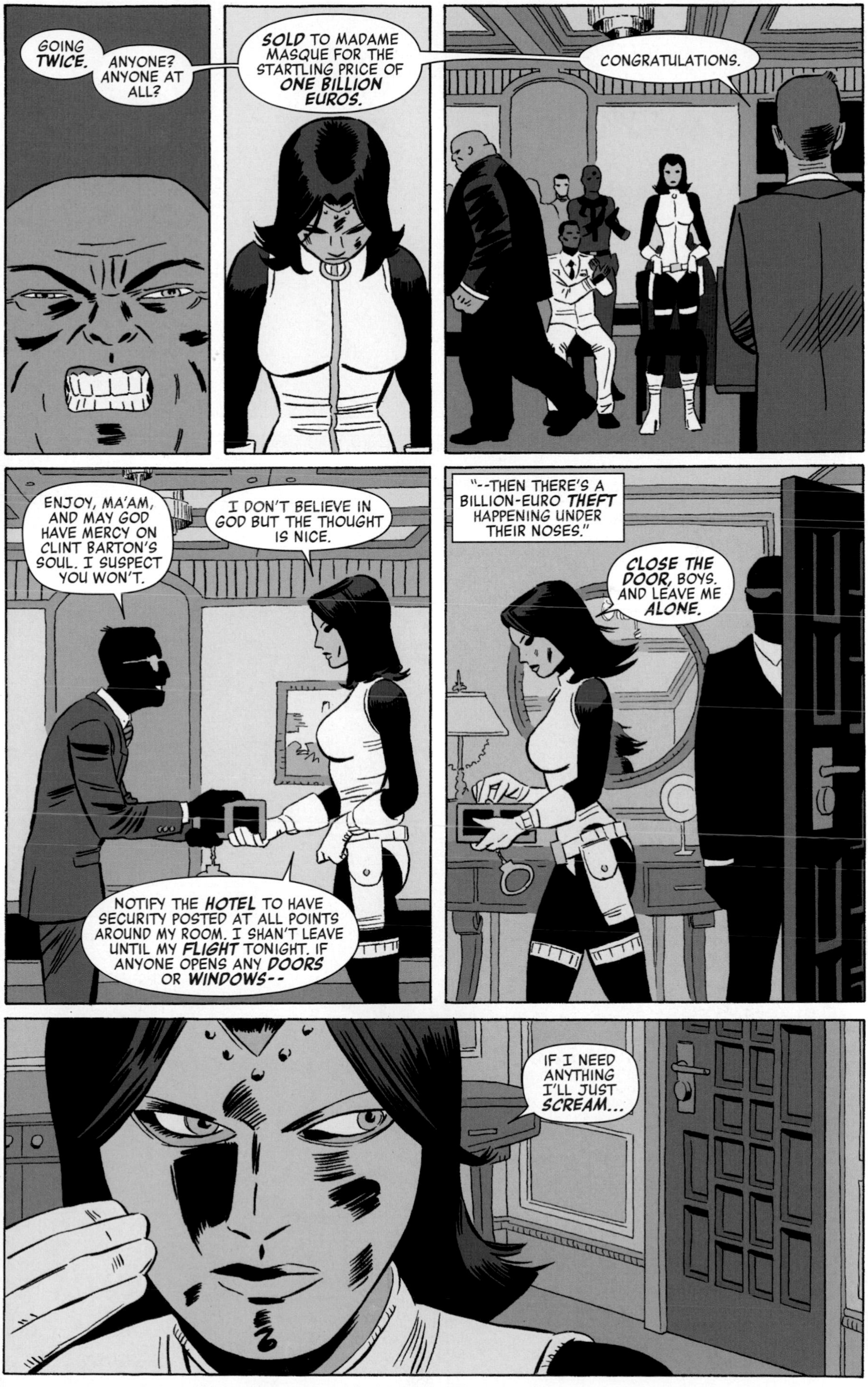
GOING TWICE.
ANYONE? ANYONE AT ALL?
SOLD TO MADAME MASQUE FOR THE STARTLING PRICE OF ONE BILLION EUROS.
CONGRATULATIONS.
ENJOY, MA'AM, AND MAY GOD HAVE MERCY ON CLINT BARTON'S SOUL. I SUSPECT YOU WON'T.
I DON'T BELIEVE IN GOD BUT THE THOUGHT IS NICE.
NOTIFY THE HOTEL TO HAVE SECURITY POSTED AT ALL POINTS AROUND MY ROOM. I SHAN'T LEAVE UNTIL MY FLIGHT TONIGHT. IF ANYONE OPENS ANY DOORS OR WINDOWS--
"--THEN THERE'S A BILLION-EURO THEFT HAPPENING UNDER THEIR NOSES."
CLOSE THE DOOR, BOYS. AND LEAVE ME ALONE.
IF I NEED ANYTHING I'LL JUST SCREAM...

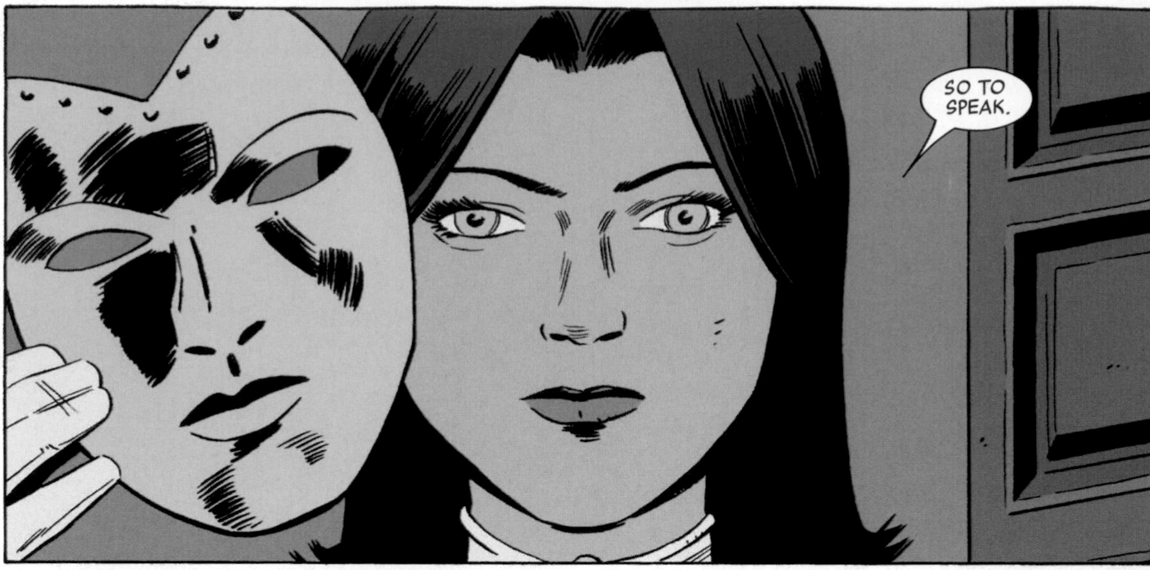
SO TO SPEAK.

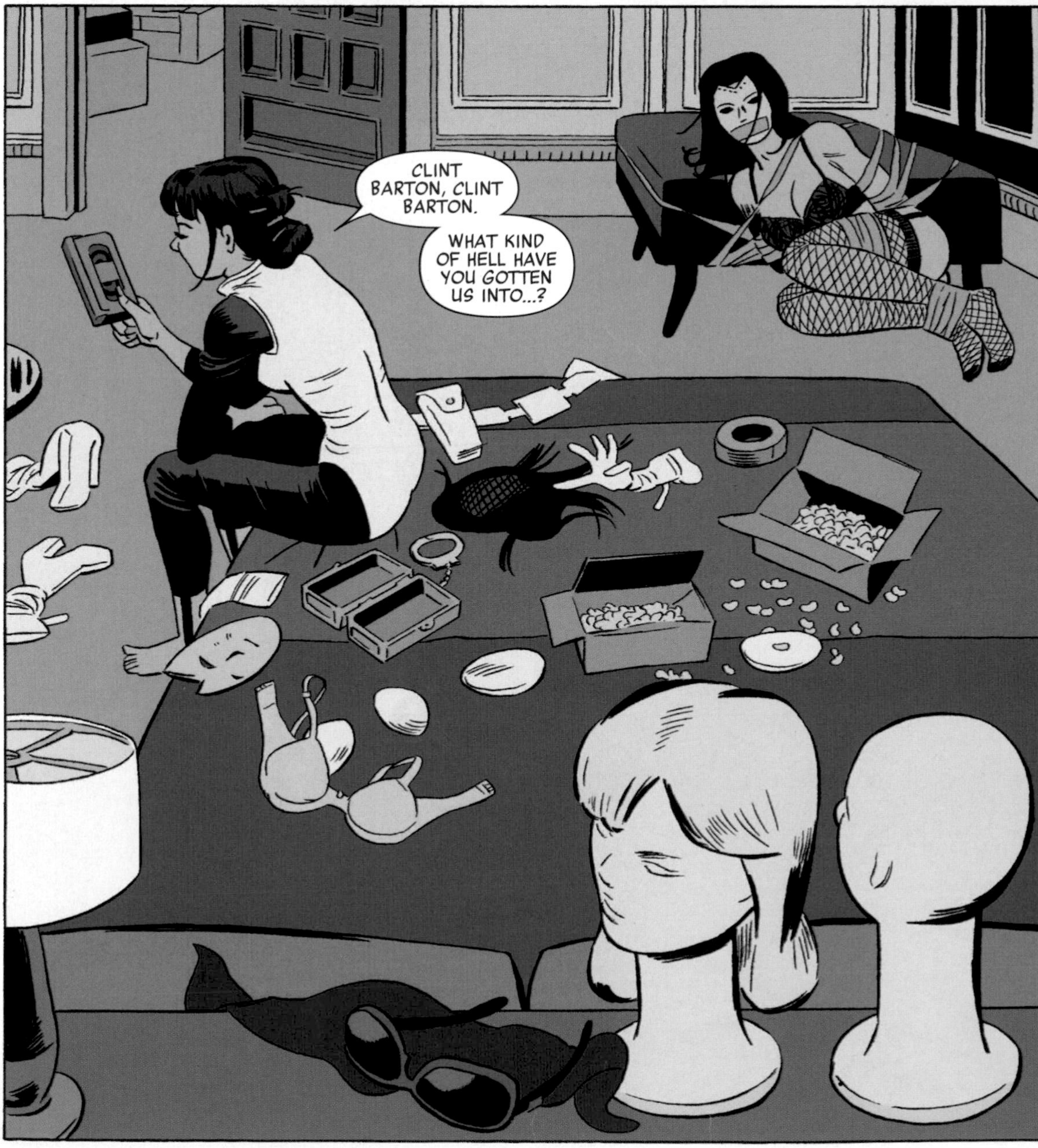
CLINT BARTON, CLINT BARTON.
WHAT KIND OF HELL HAVE YOU GOTTEN US INTO...?

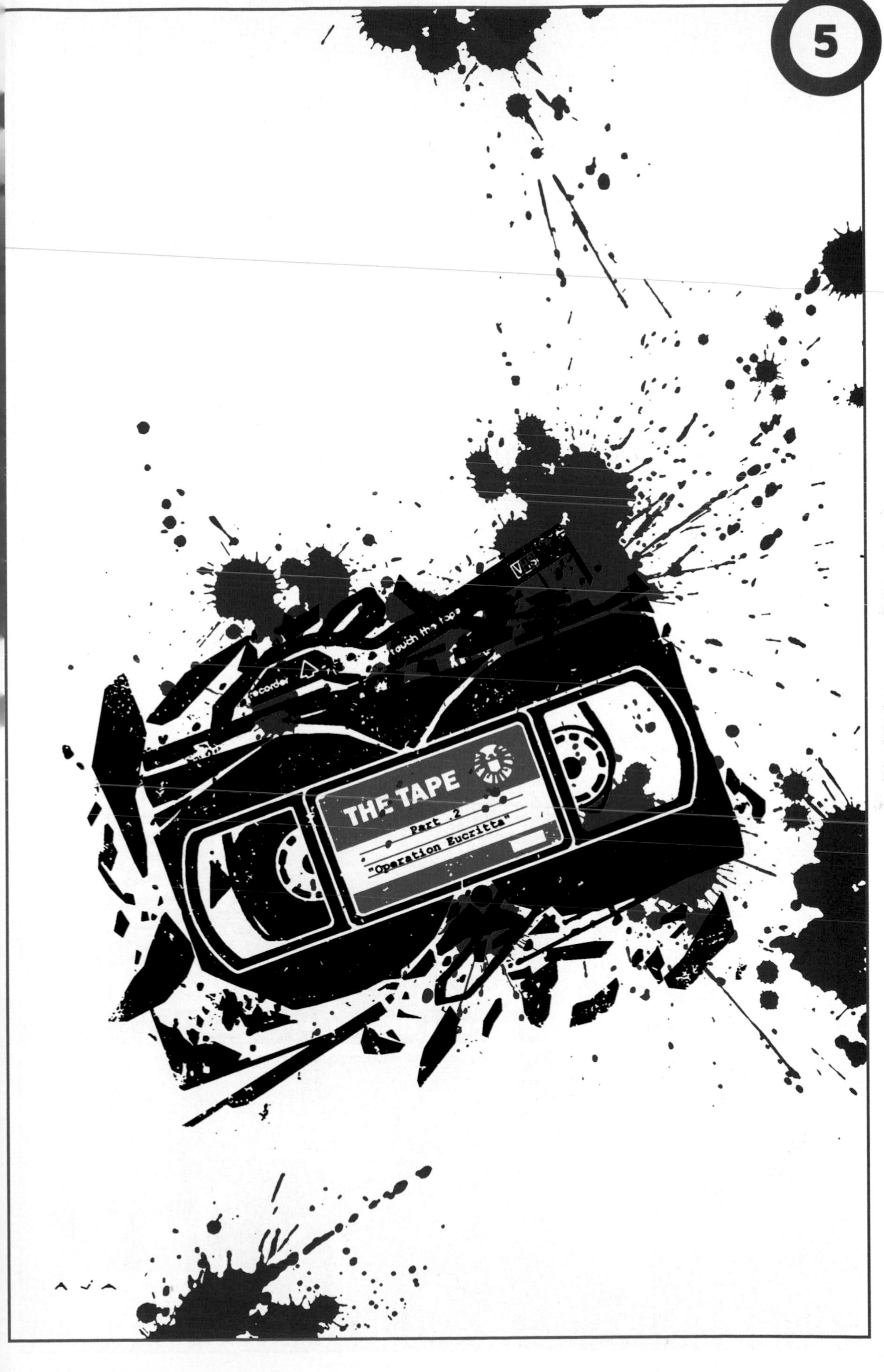
5
VHS
touch the tape
recorder
THE TAPE
Part .2
"Operation Eucritta"

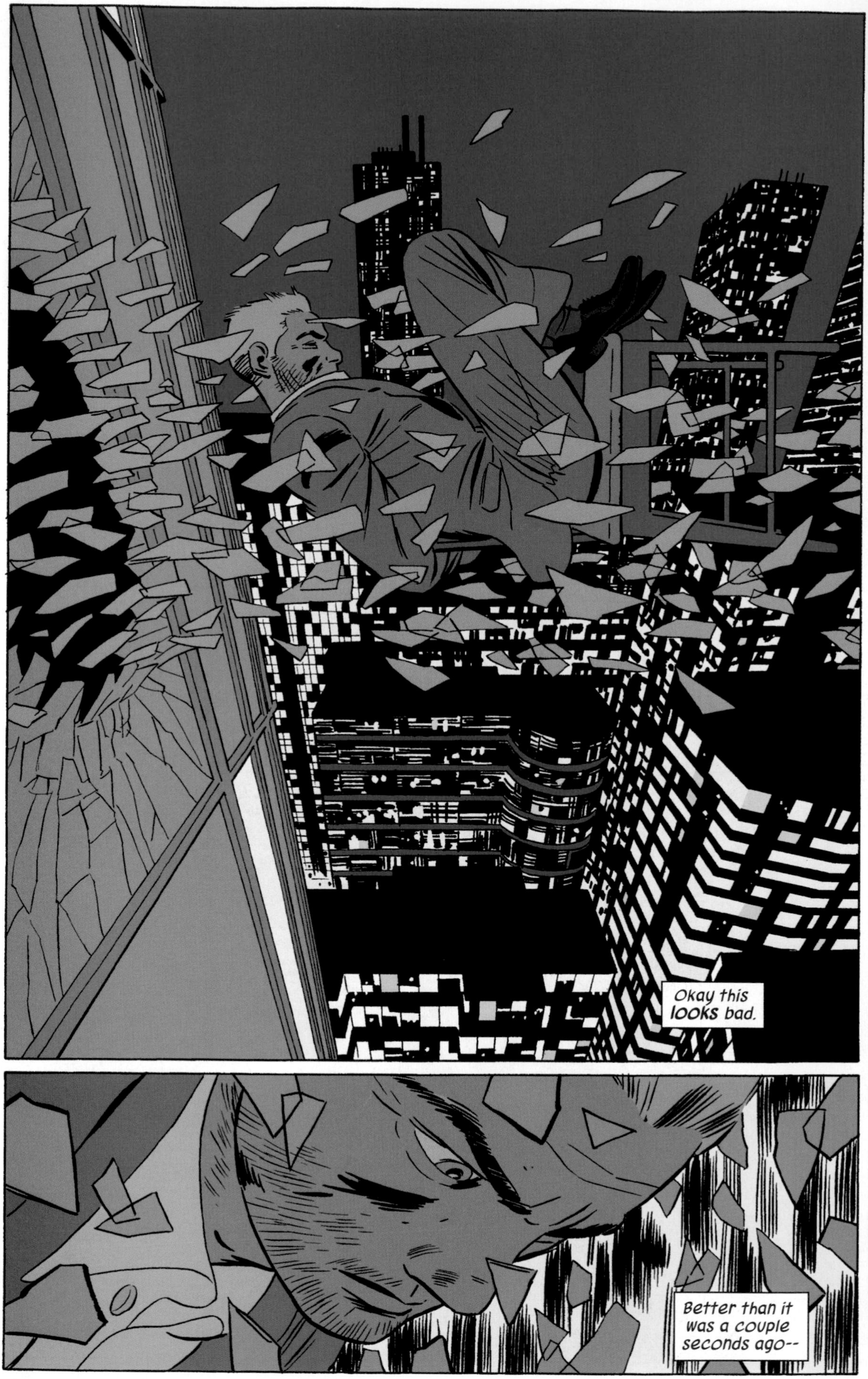
Okay this LOOKS bad.
Better than it was a couple seconds ago--

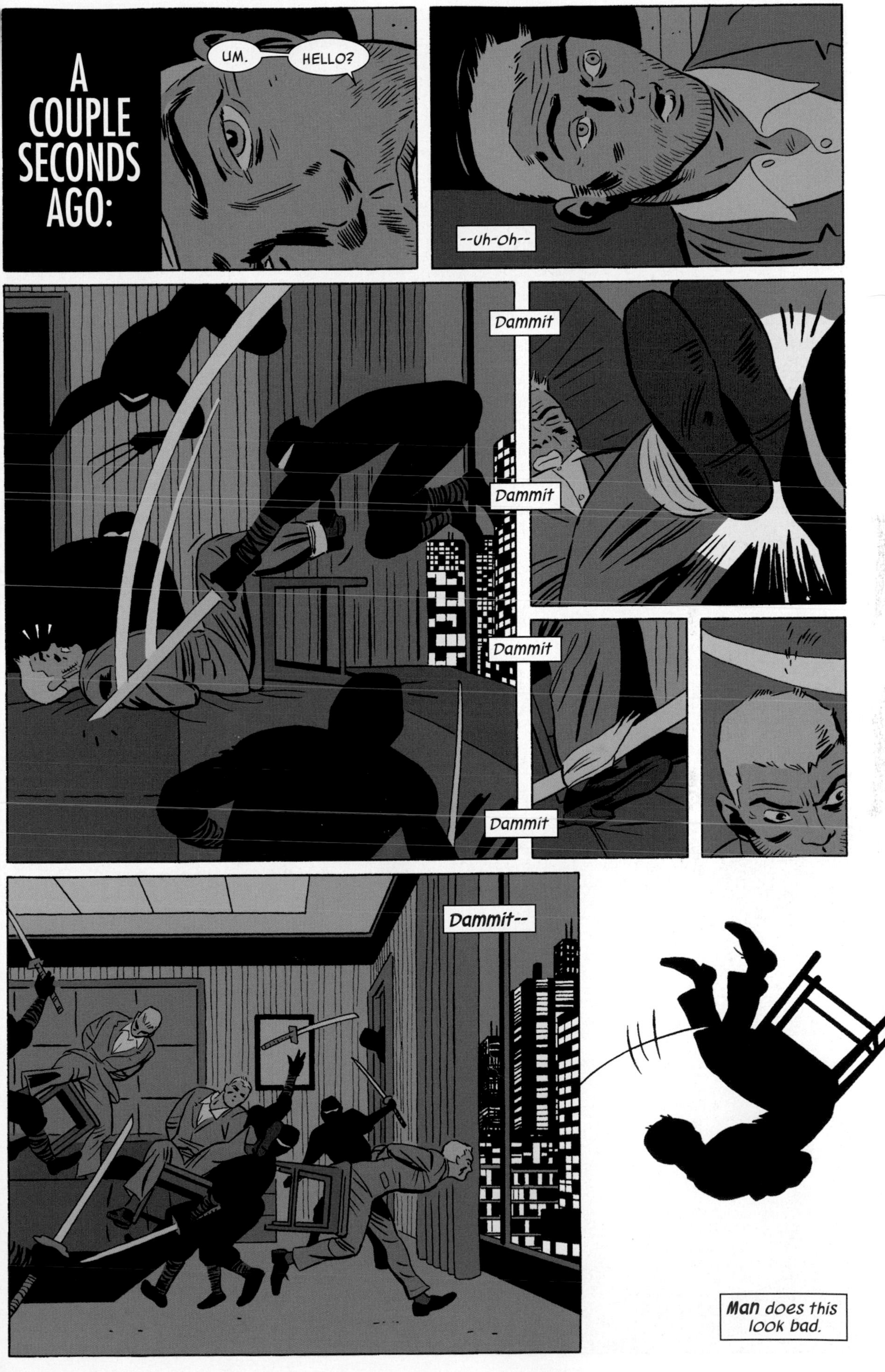
A COUPLE SECONDS AGO:
UM.
HELLO?
--Uh-Oh--
Dammit
Dammit
Dammit
Dammit
Dammit--
Man does this look bad.

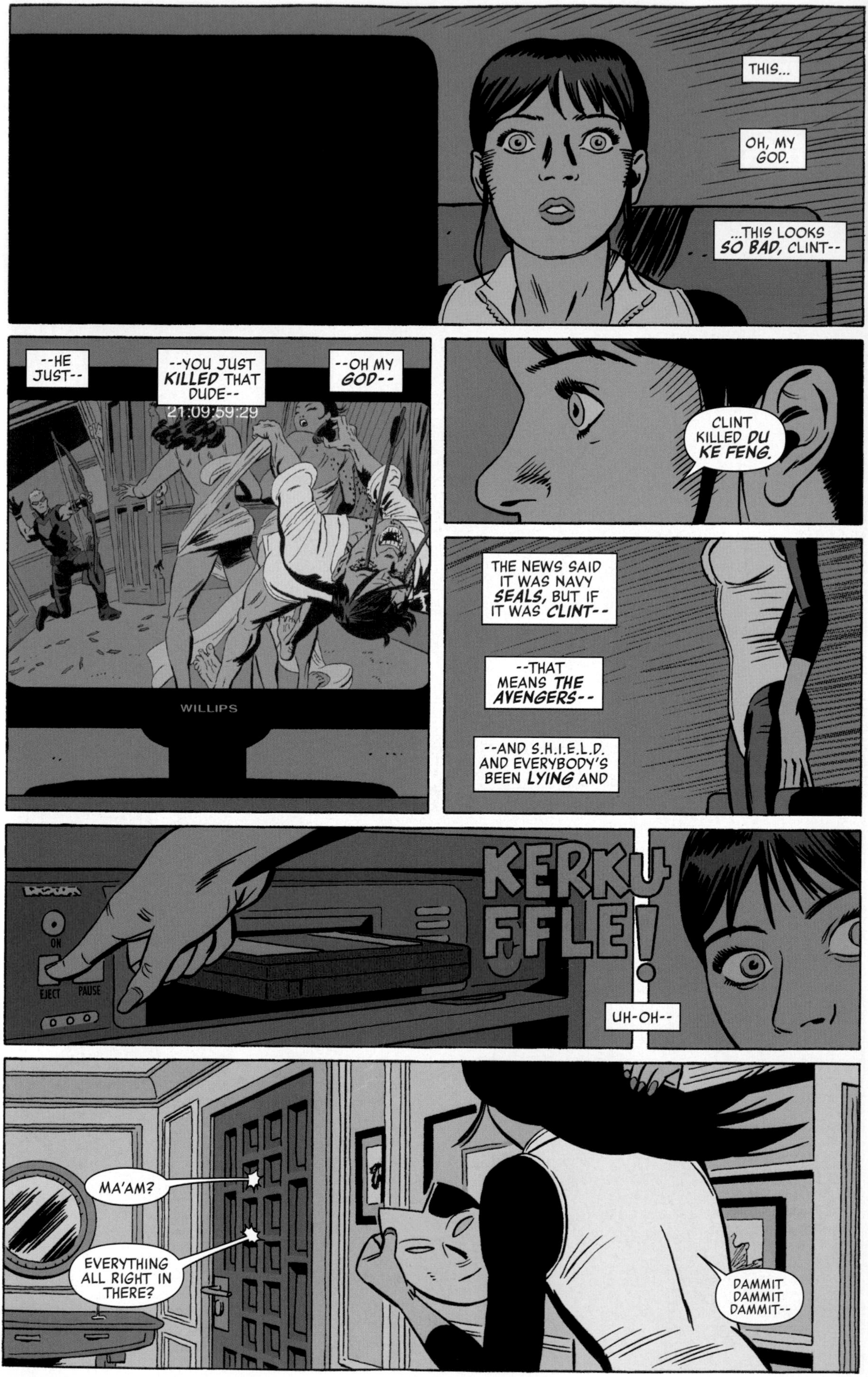
THIS...
OH, MY GOD.
...THIS LOOKS SO BAD, CLINT--
--HE JUST--
--YOU JUST KILLED THAT DUDE--
--OH MY GOD--
21:09:59:29
WILLIPS
CLINT KILLED DU KE FENG.
THE NEWS SAID IT WAS NAVY SEALS, BUT IF IT WAS CLINT--
--THAT MEANS THE AVENGERS--
--AND S.H.I.E.L.D. AND EVERYBODY'S BEEN LYING AND
KERKUFFLE!
ON
EJECT
PAUSE
UH-OH--
MA'AM?
EVERYTHING ALL RIGHT IN THERE?
DAMMIT DAMMIT DAMMIT--

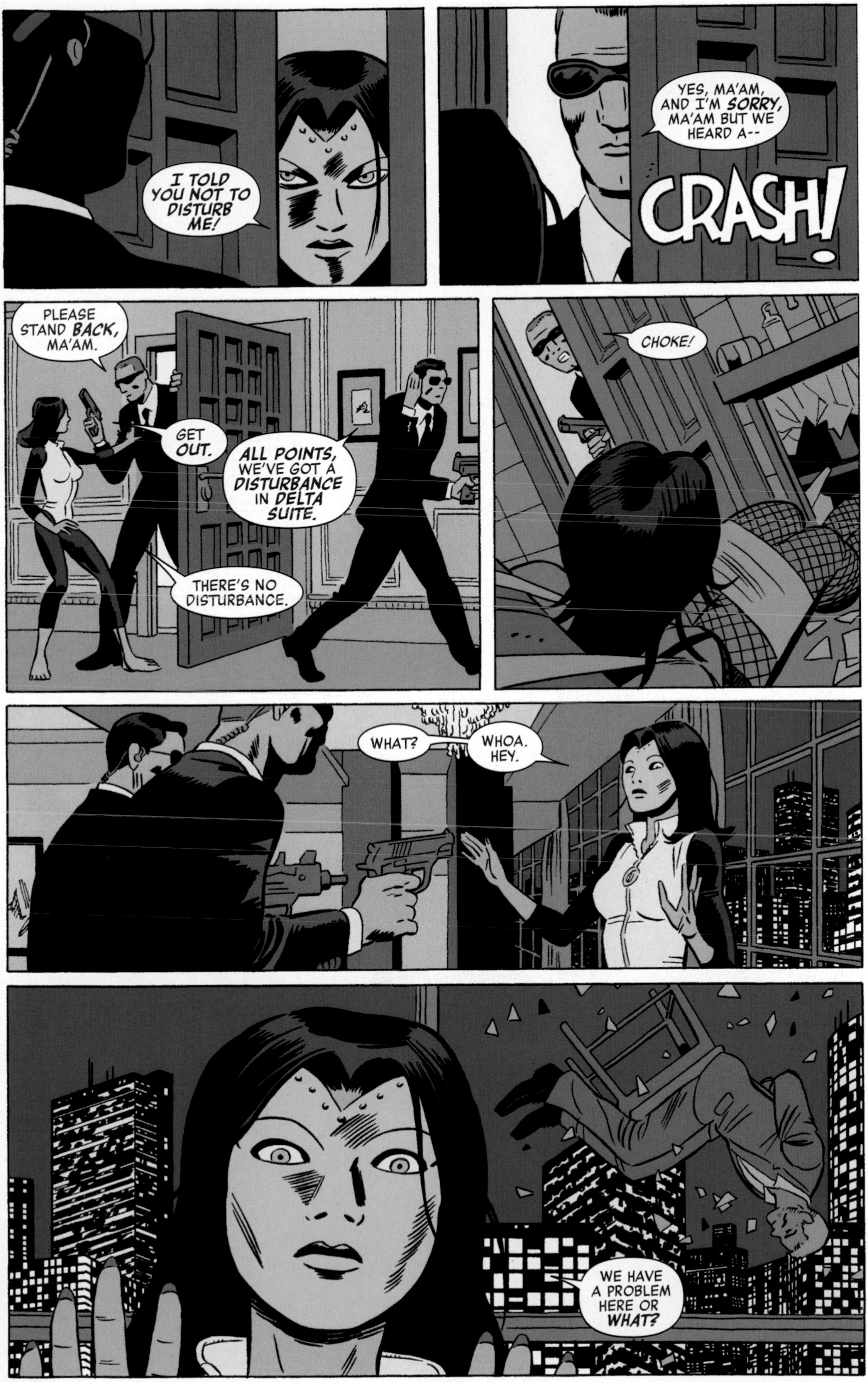
I TOLD YOU NOT TO DISTURB ME!
YES, MA'AM, AND I'M SORRY, MA'AM BUT WE HEARD A--
CRASH!
PLEASE STAND BACK, MA'AM.
GET OUT.
ALL POINTS, WE'VE GOT A DISTURBANCE IN DELTA SUITE.
THERE'S NO DISTURBANCE.
CHOKE!
WHAT?
WHOA. HEY.
WE HAVE A PROBLEM HERE OR WHAT?

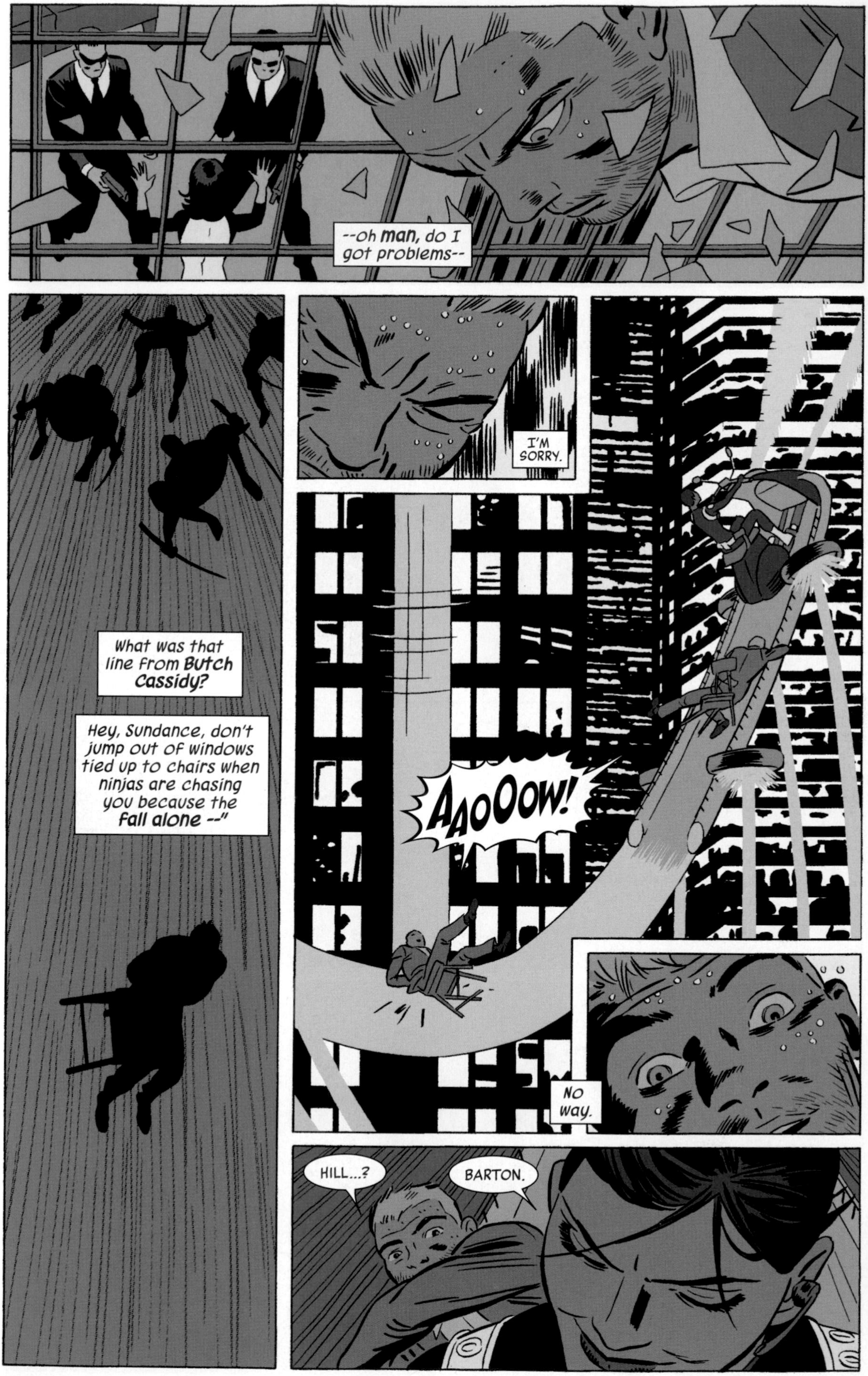

--oh man, do I got problems--
What was that line from Butch Cassidy?
Hey, Sundance, don't jump out of windows tied up to chairs when ninjas are chasing you because the fall alone --"
I'M SORRY.
AAOOOW!
No way.
HILL...?
BARTON.

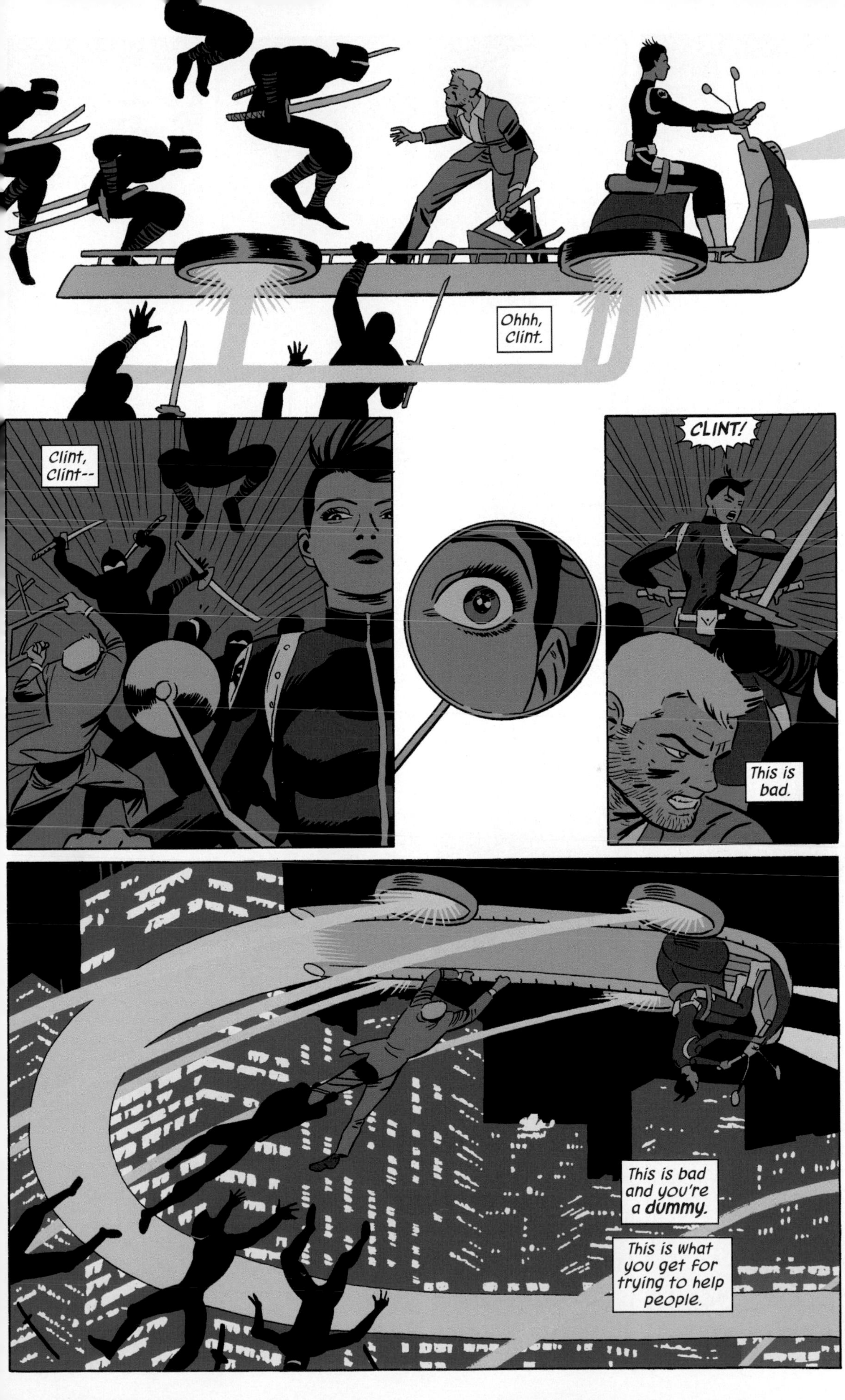
Ohhh, Clint.
Clint, Clint--
CLINT!
This is bad.
This is bad and you're a **dummy**.
This is what you get for trying to help people.

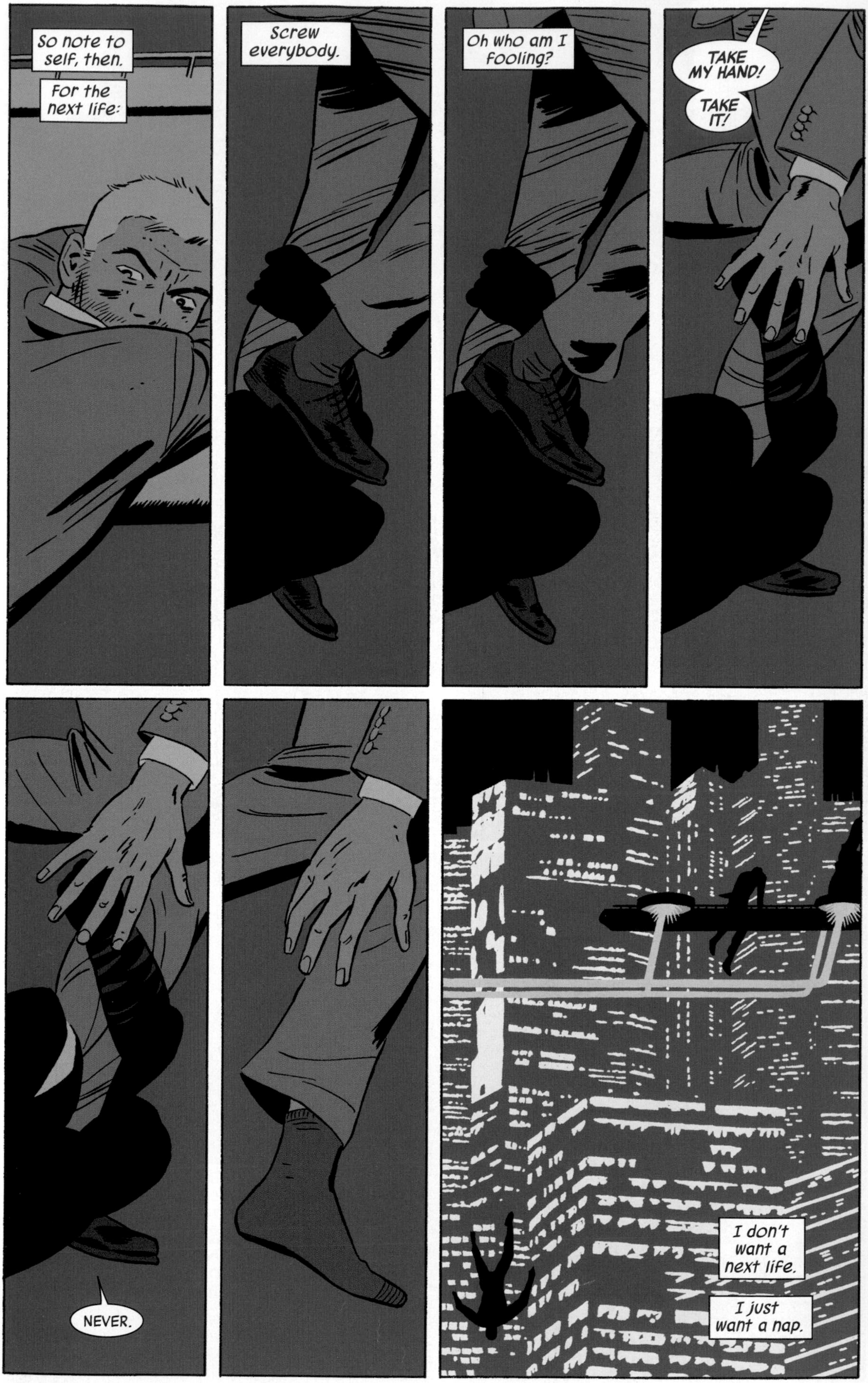
So note to self, then.
For the next life:
Screw everybody.
Oh who am I fooling?
TAKE MY HAND!
TAKE IT!
NEVER.
I don't want a next life.
I just want a nap.

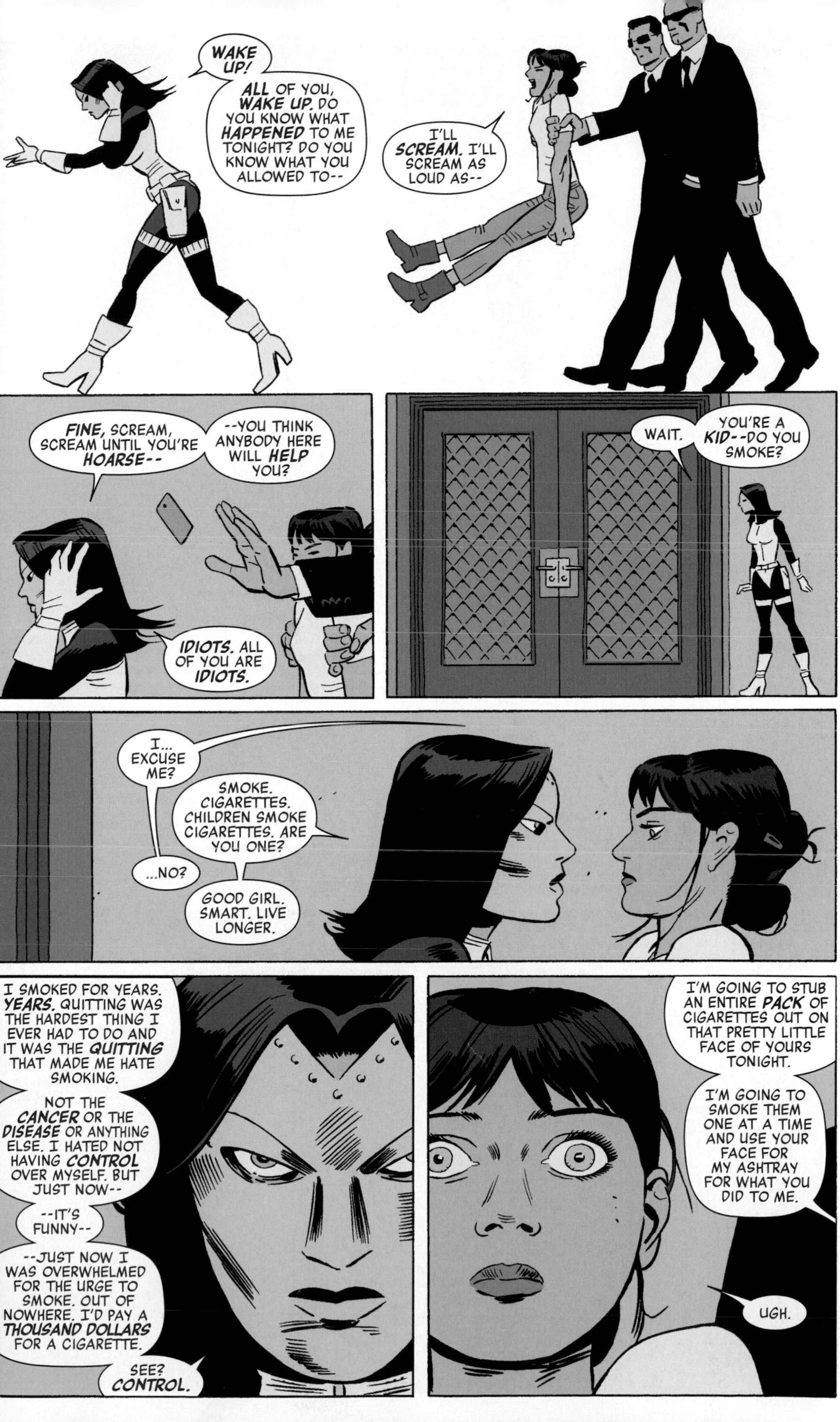
WAKE UP!
ALL OF YOU, WAKE UP. DO YOU KNOW WHAT HAPPENED TO ME TONIGHT? DO YOU KNOW WHAT YOU ALLOWED TO--
I'LL SCREAM. I'LL SCREAM AS LOUD AS--
FINE, SCREAM, SCREAM UNTIL YOU'RE HOARSE--
--YOU THINK ANYBODY HERE WILL HELP YOU?
IDIOTS. ALL OF YOU ARE IDIOTS.
WAIT.
YOU'RE A KID--DO YOU SMOKE?
I... EXCUSE ME?
SMOKE. CIGARETTES. CHILDREN SMOKE CIGARETTES. ARE YOU ONE?
...NO?
GOOD GIRL. SMART. LIVE LONGER.
I SMOKED FOR YEARS. YEARS. QUITTING WAS THE HARDEST THING I EVER HAD TO DO AND IT WAS THE QUITTING THAT MADE ME HATE SMOKING.
NOT THE CANCER OR THE DISEASE OR ANYTHING ELSE. I HATED NOT HAVING CONTROL OVER MYSELF. BUT JUST NOW--
--IT'S FUNNY--
--JUST NOW I WAS OVERWHELMED FOR THE URGE TO SMOKE. OUT OF NOWHERE. I'D PAY A THOUSAND DOLLARS FOR A CIGARETTE.
SEE? CONTROL.
I'M GOING TO STUB AN ENTIRE PACK OF CIGARETTES OUT ON THAT PRETTY LITTLE FACE OF YOURS TONIGHT.
I'M GOING TO SMOKE THEM ONE AT A TIME AND USE YOUR FACE FOR MY ASHTRAY FOR WHAT YOU DID TO ME.
UGH.

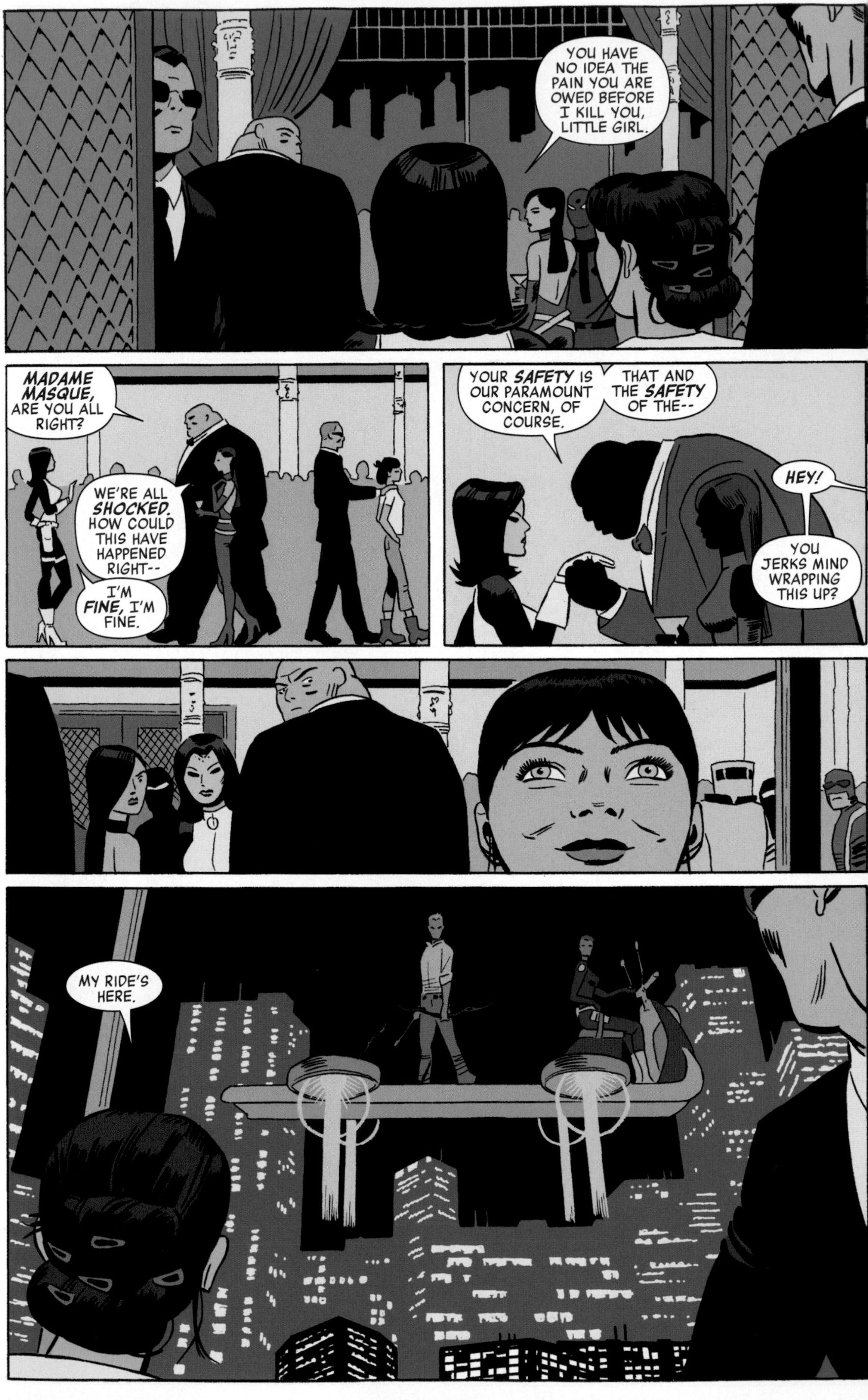
YOU HAVE NO IDEA THE PAIN YOU ARE OWED BEFORE I KILL YOU, LITTLE GIRL.
MADAME MASQUE, ARE YOU ALL RIGHT?
WE'RE ALL SHOCKED. HOW COULD THIS HAVE HAPPENED RIGHT--
I'M FINE, I'M FINE.
YOUR SAFETY IS OUR PARAMOUNT CONCERN, OF COURSE.
THAT AND THE SAFETY OF THE--
HEY!
YOU JERKS MIND WRAPPING THIS UP?
MY RIDE'S HERE.

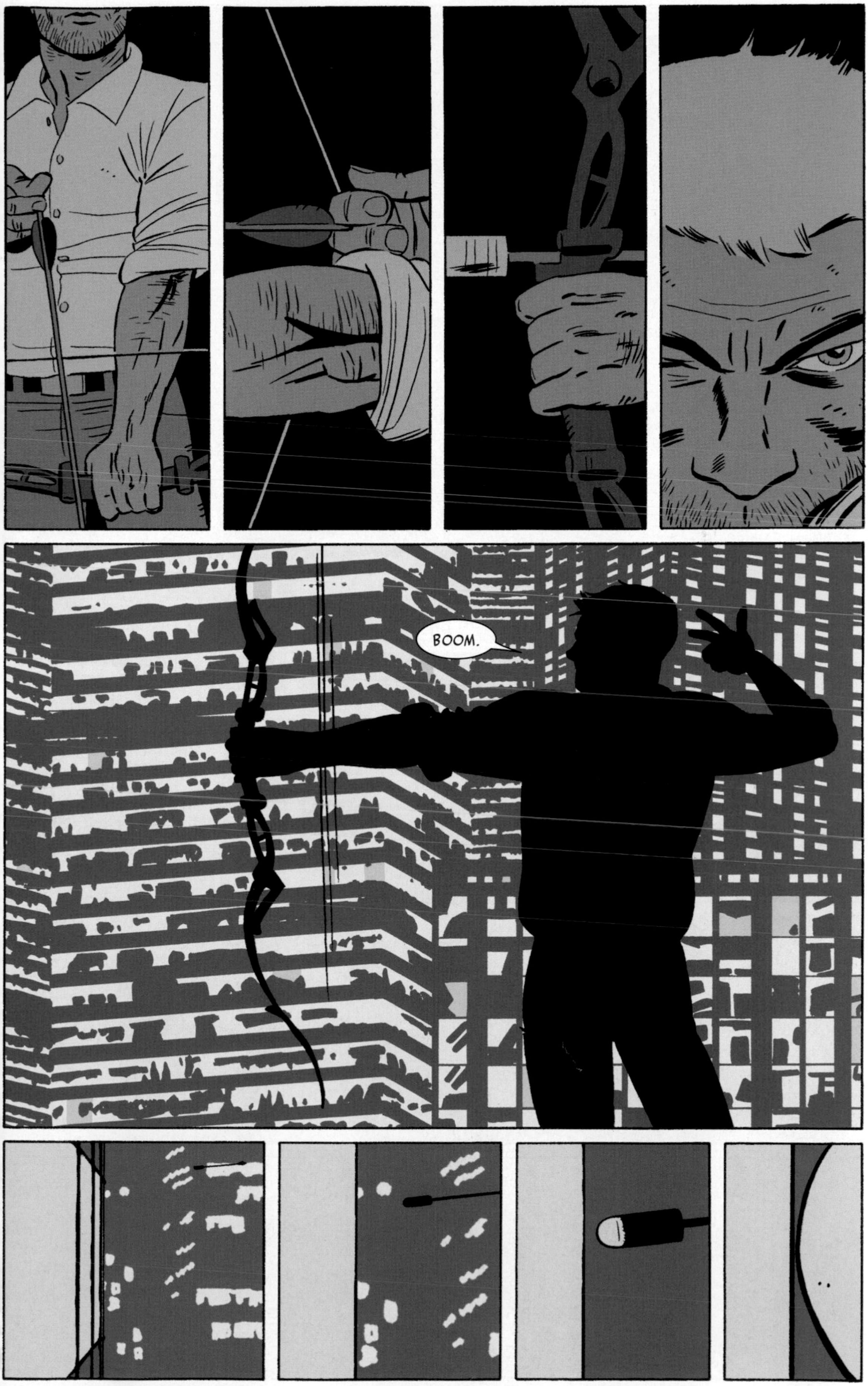
BOOM.

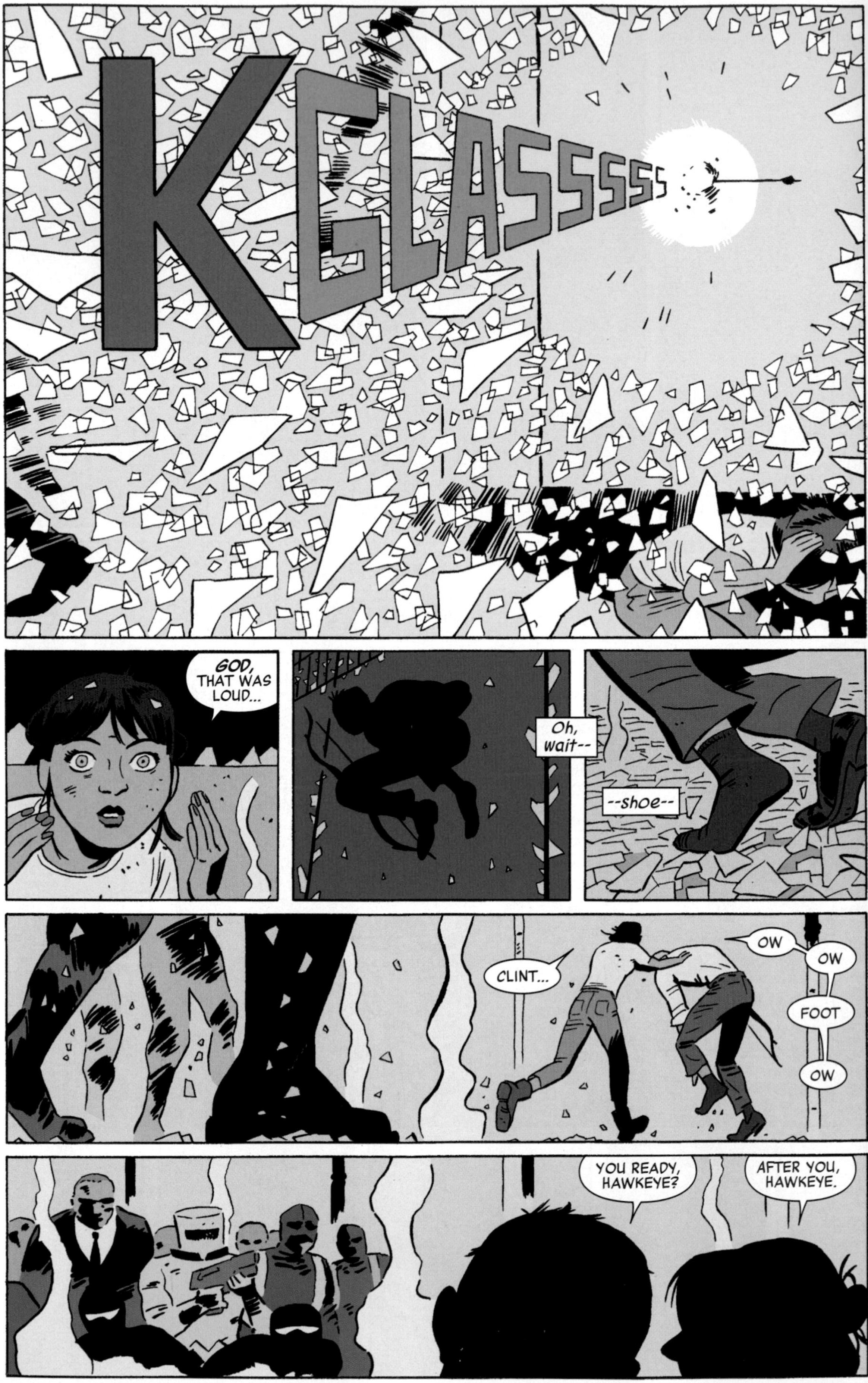
KGLASSSSS
GOD, THAT WAS LOUD...
Oh, wait--
--shoe--
CLINT...
OW
OW
FOOT
OW
YOU READY, HAWKEYE?
AFTER YOU, HAWKEYE.

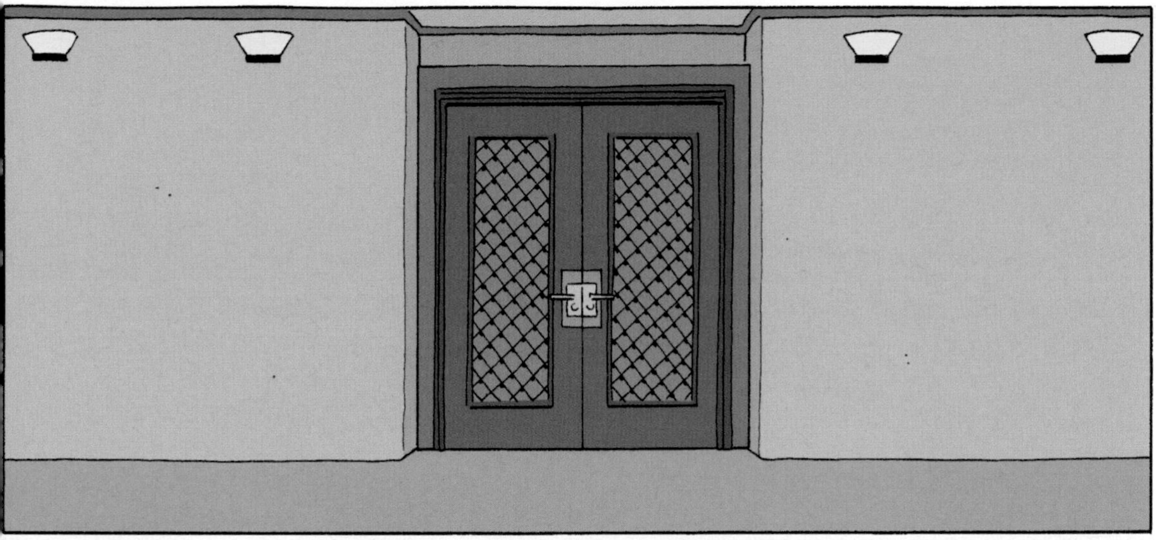

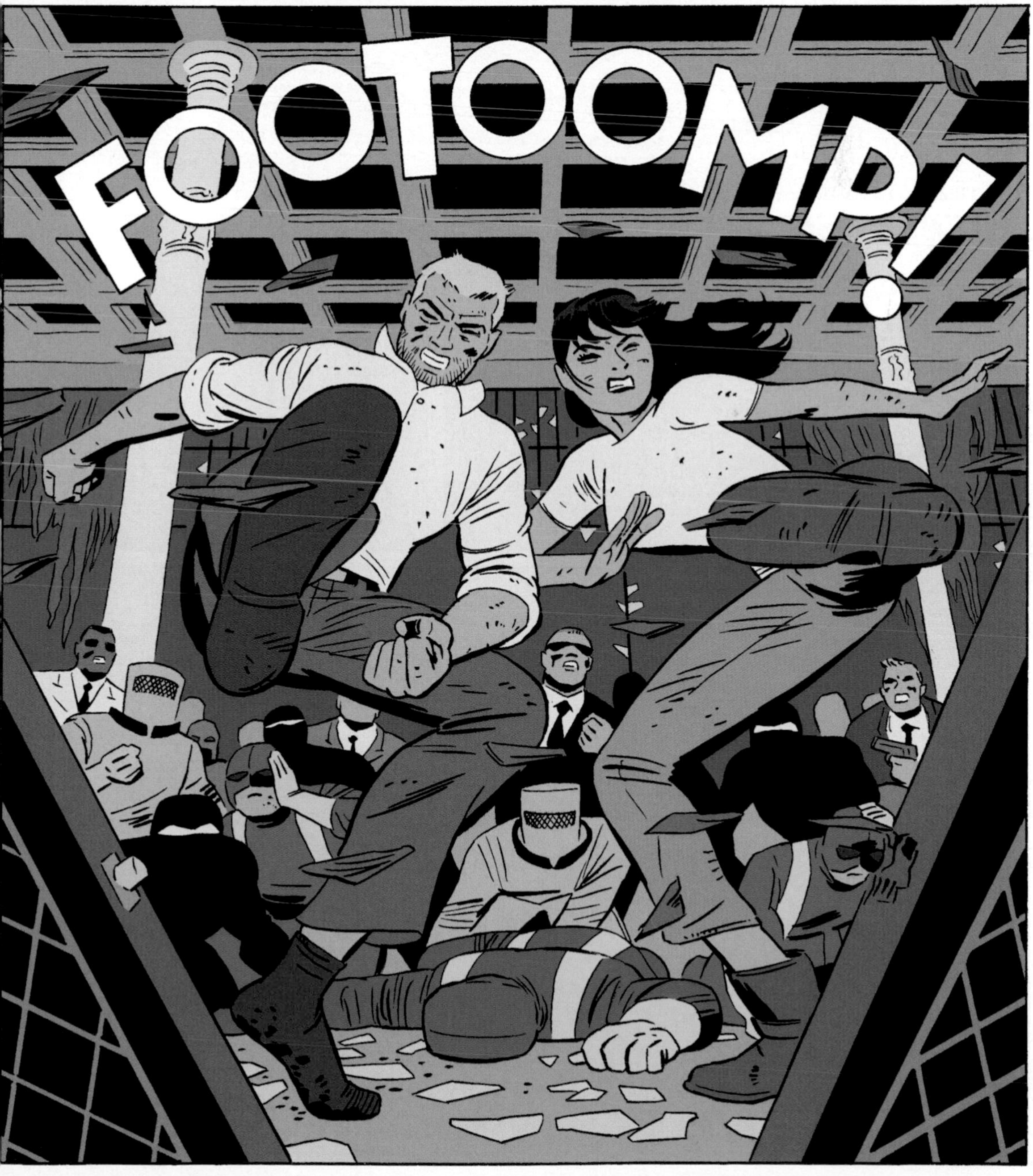
FOOTOOMP!

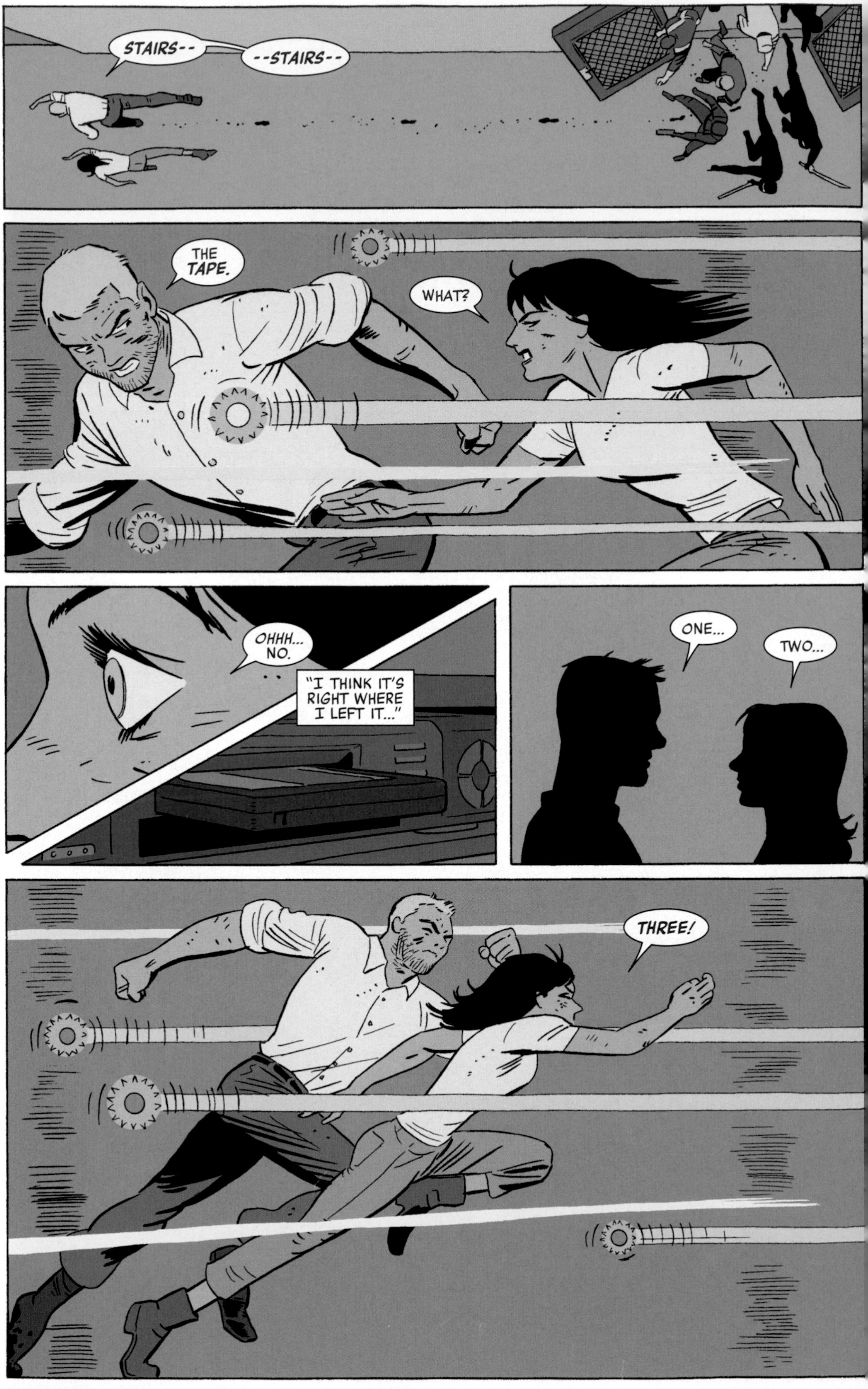
STAIRS--
--STAIRS--
THE TAPE.
WHAT?
OHHH... NO.
"I THINK IT'S RIGHT WHERE I LEFT IT..."
ONE...
TWO...
THREE!

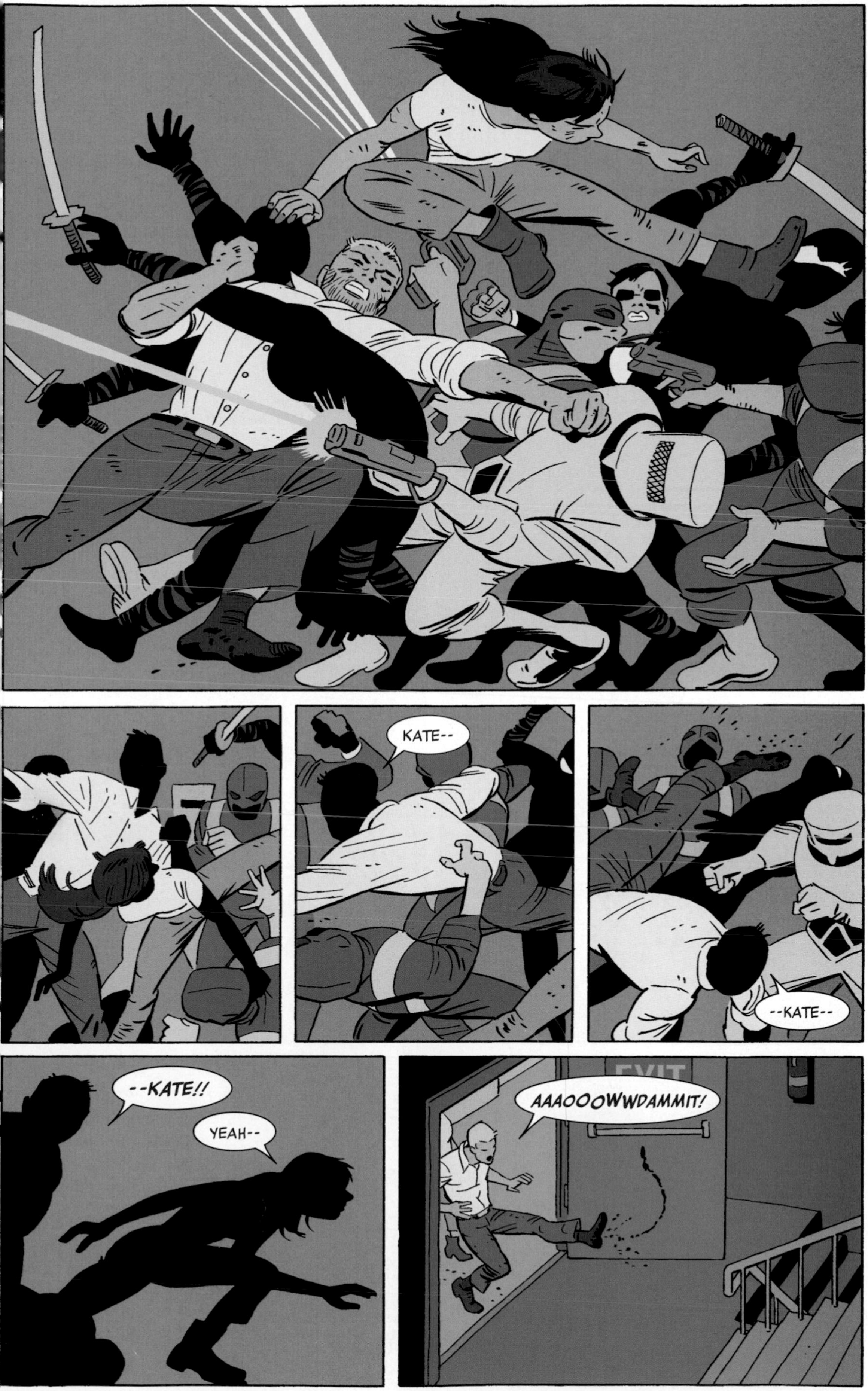
KATE--
--KATE--
--KATE!!
YEAH--
AAAOOOWWDAMMIT!

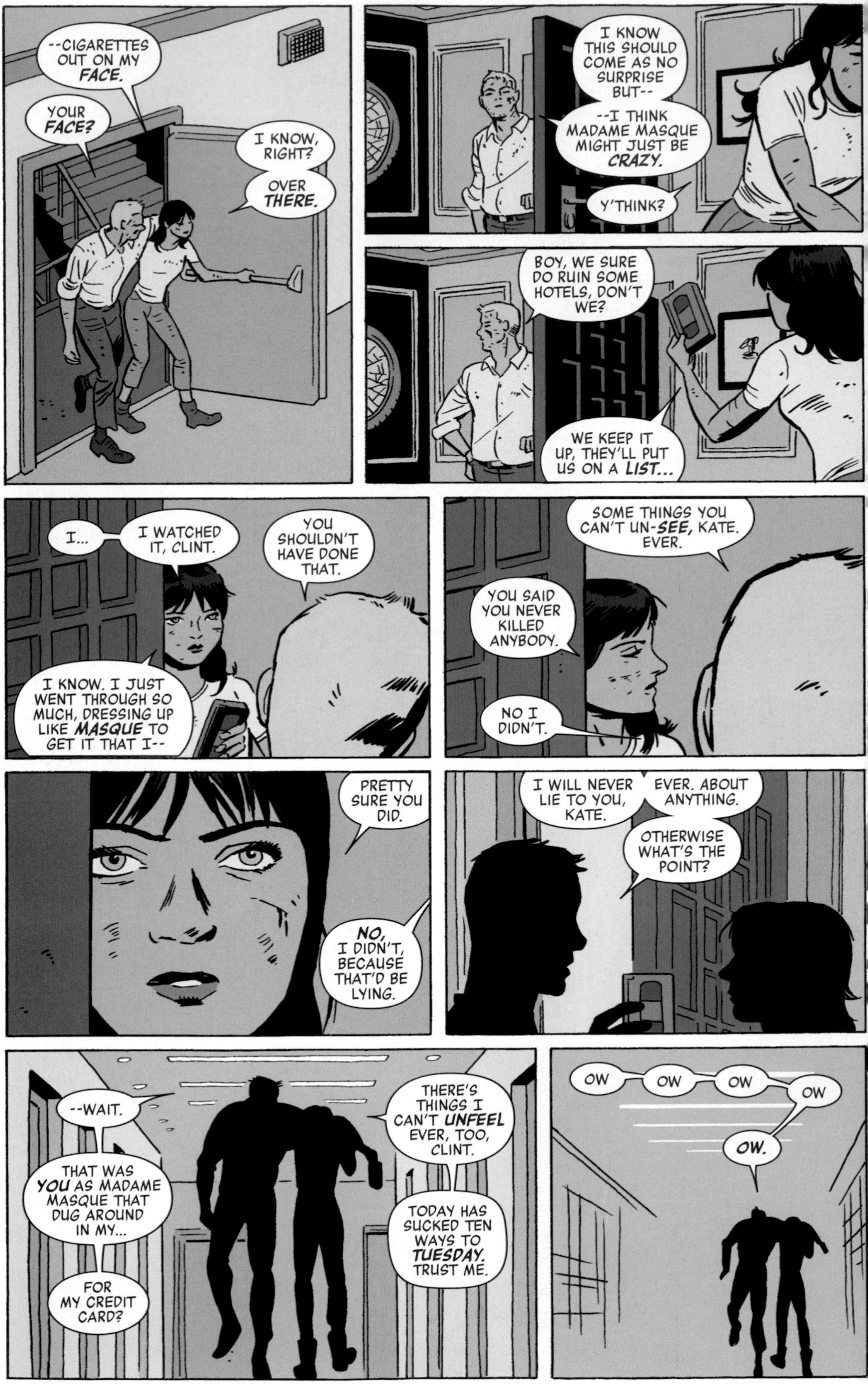
--CIGARETTES OUT ON MY FACE.
YOUR FACE?
I KNOW, RIGHT?
OVER THERE.
I KNOW THIS SHOULD COME AS NO SURPRISE BUT--
--I THINK MADAME MASQUE MIGHT JUST BE CRAZY.
Y'THINK?
BOY, WE SURE DO RUIN SOME HOTELS, DON'T WE?
WE KEEP IT UP, THEY'LL PUT US ON A LIST...
I...
I WATCHED IT, CLINT.
YOU SHOULDN'T HAVE DONE THAT.
I KNOW. I JUST WENT THROUGH SO MUCH, DRESSING UP LIKE MASQUE TO GET IT THAT I--
SOME THINGS YOU CAN'T UN-SEE, KATE. EVER.
YOU SAID YOU NEVER KILLED ANYBODY.
NO I DIDN'T.
PRETTY SURE YOU DID.
NO, I DIDN'T, BECAUSE THAT'D BE LYING.
I WILL NEVER LIE TO YOU, KATE.
EVER. ABOUT ANYTHING.
OTHERWISE WHAT'S THE POINT?
--WAIT.
THAT WAS YOU AS MADAME MASQUE THAT DUG AROUND IN MY...
FOR MY CREDIT CARD?
THERE'S THINGS I CAN'T UNFEEL EVER, TOO, CLINT.
TODAY HAS SUCKED TEN WAYS TO TUESDAY. TRUST ME.
OW
OW
OW
OW
OW.

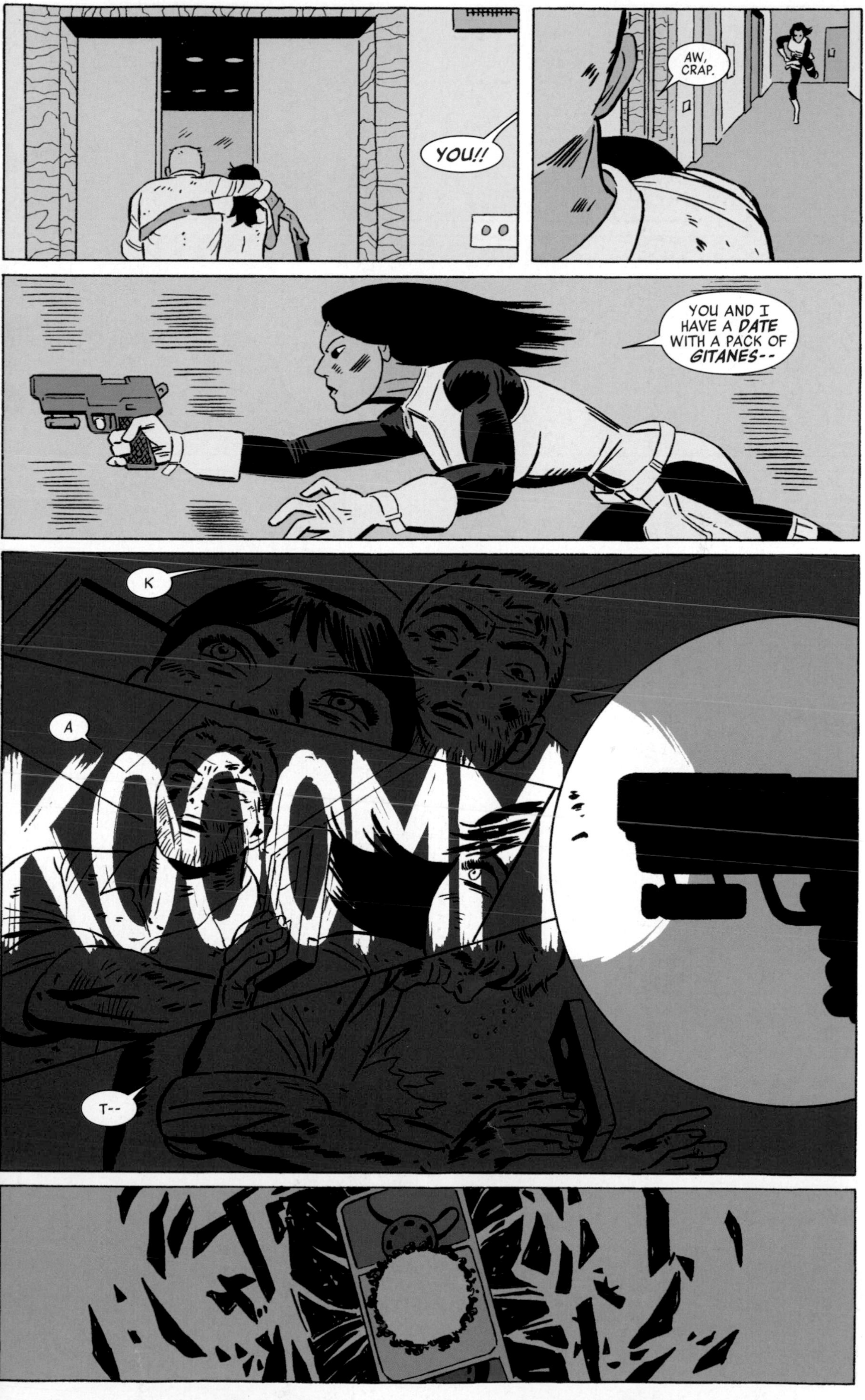
YOU!!
AW, CRAP.
YOU AND I HAVE A *DATE* WITH A PACK OF *GITANES*--
K
A
KOOOMM
T--

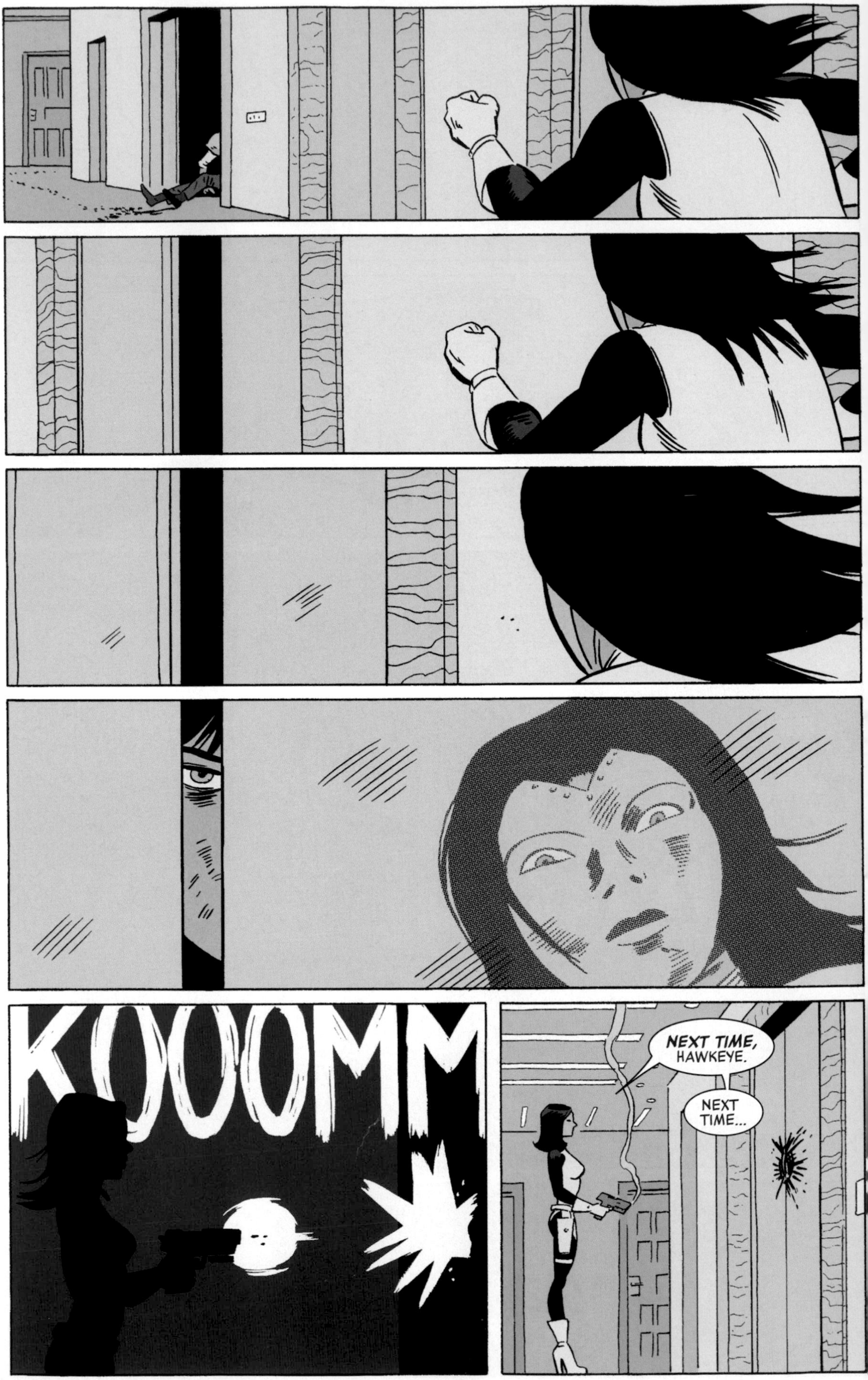
KOOOMM
NEXT TIME, HAWKEYE.
NEXT TIME...

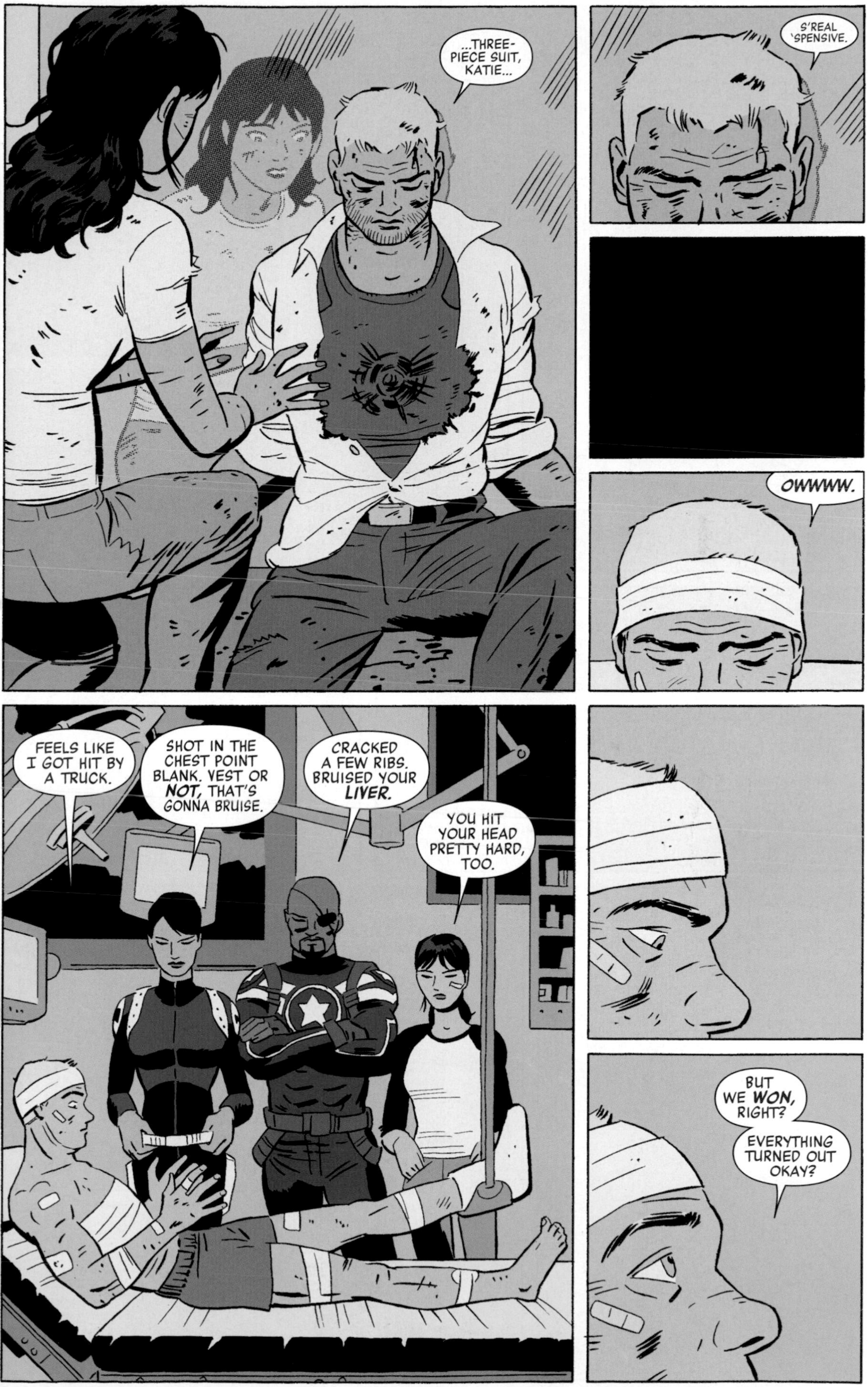
...THREE-PIECE SUIT, KATIE...
S'REAL 'SPENSIVE.
OWWWW.
FEELS LIKE I GOT HIT BY A TRUCK.
SHOT IN THE CHEST POINT BLANK. VEST OR NOT, THAT'S GONNA BRUISE.
CRACKED A FEW RIBS. BRUISED YOUR LIVER.
YOU HIT YOUR HEAD PRETTY HARD, TOO.
BUT WE WON, RIGHT?
EVERYTHING TURNED OUT OKAY?

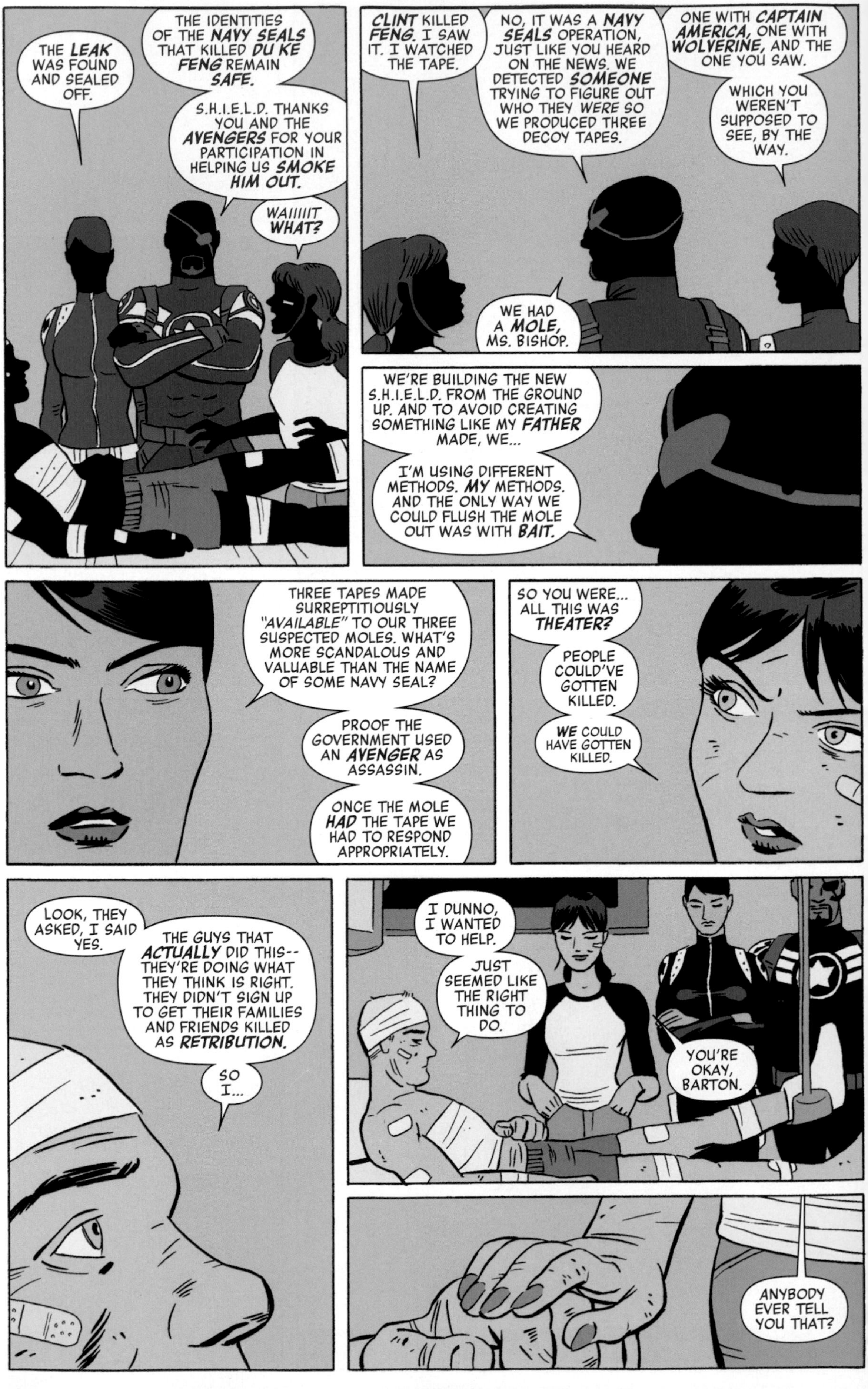
THE LEAK WAS FOUND AND SEALED OFF.
THE IDENTITIES OF THE NAVY SEALS THAT KILLED DU KE FENG REMAIN SAFE.
S.H.I.E.L.D. THANKS YOU AND THE AVENGERS FOR YOUR PARTICIPATION IN HELPING US SMOKE HIM OUT.
WAIIIIIT WHAT?
CLINT KILLED FENG. I SAW IT. I WATCHED THE TAPE.
NO, IT WAS A NAVY SEALS OPERATION, JUST LIKE YOU HEARD ON THE NEWS. WE DETECTED SOMEONE TRYING TO FIGURE OUT WHO THEY WERE SO WE PRODUCED THREE DECOY TAPES.
ONE WITH CAPTAIN AMERICA, ONE WITH WOLVERINE, AND THE ONE YOU SAW.
WHICH YOU WEREN'T SUPPOSED TO SEE, BY THE WAY.
WE HAD A MOLE, MS. BISHOP.
WE'RE BUILDING THE NEW S.H.I.E.L.D. FROM THE GROUND UP. AND TO AVOID CREATING SOMETHING LIKE MY FATHER MADE, WE...
I'M USING DIFFERENT METHODS. MY METHODS. AND THE ONLY WAY WE COULD FLUSH THE MOLE OUT WAS WITH BAIT.
THREE TAPES MADE SURREPTITIOUSLY "AVAILABLE" TO OUR THREE SUSPECTED MOLES. WHAT'S MORE SCANDALOUS AND VALUABLE THAN THE NAME OF SOME NAVY SEAL?
PROOF THE GOVERNMENT USED AN AVENGER AS ASSASSIN.
ONCE THE MOLE HAD THE TAPE WE HAD TO RESPOND APPROPRIATELY.
SO YOU WERE... ALL THIS WAS THEATER?
PEOPLE COULD'VE GOTTEN KILLED.
WE COULD HAVE GOTTEN KILLED.
LOOK, THEY ASKED, I SAID YES.
THE GUYS THAT ACTUALLY DID THIS-- THEY'RE DOING WHAT THEY THINK IS RIGHT. THEY DIDN'T SIGN UP TO GET THEIR FAMILIES AND FRIENDS KILLED AS RETRIBUTION.
SO I...
I DUNNO, I WANTED TO HELP.
JUST SEEMED LIKE THE RIGHT THING TO DO.
YOU'RE OKAY, BARTON.
ANYBODY EVER TELL YOU THAT?

"AS FAR AS PEOPLE GO, YOU'RE OKAY."

clint barton is

hawkeye

THE TAPE
2 OF 2

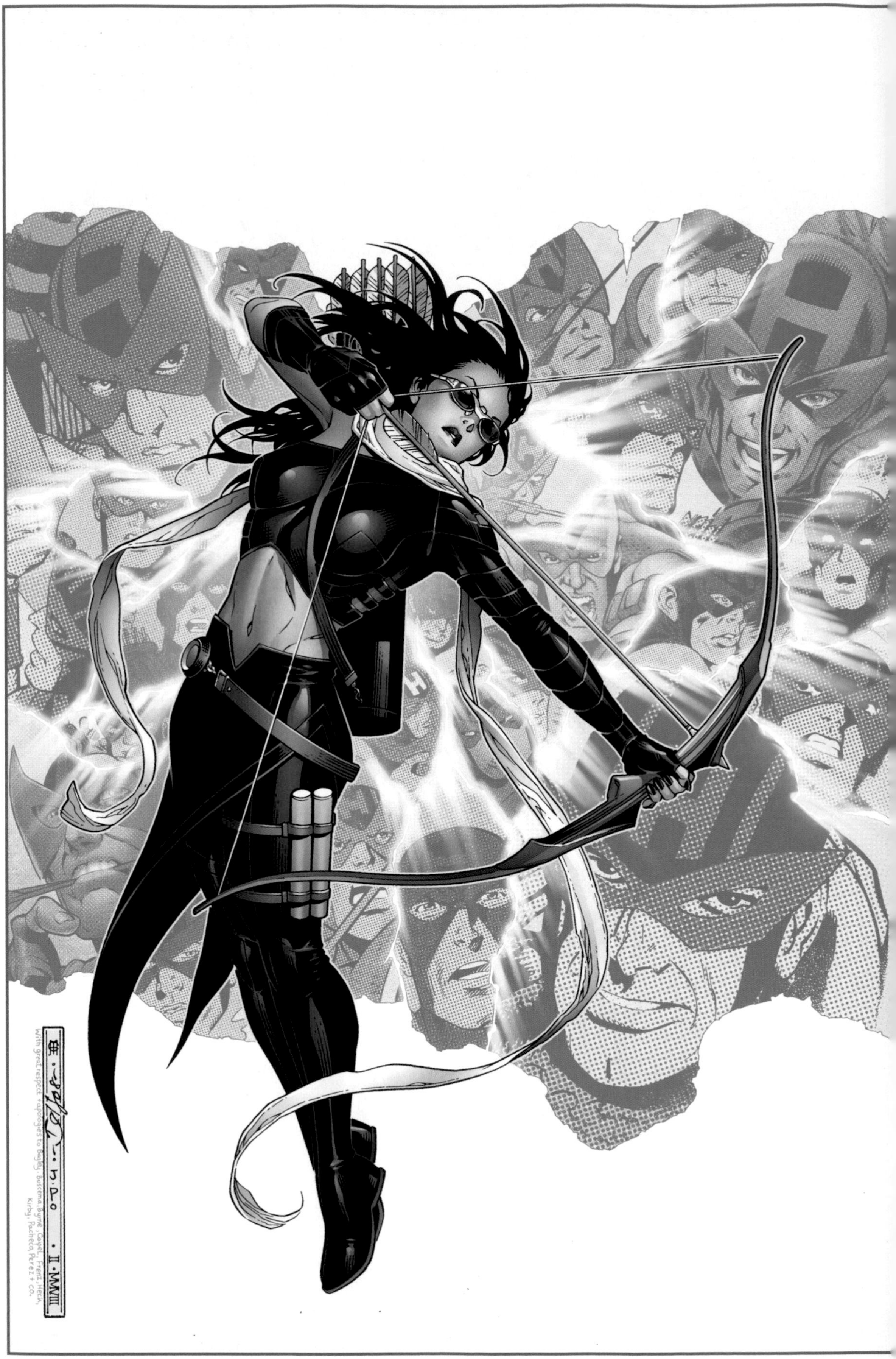
With great respect + apologies to Bagley, Buscema, Byrne, Coipel, Frenz, Heck, Kirby, Pacheco, Perez + co.
• II • MMVIII

YOUNG AVENGERS PRESENTS #6

United by friendship and bravery, Patriot, Hawkeye, Wiccan, Hulkling, Stature, Speed and the Vision are the Young Avengers, following in the footsteps of Earth's mightiest heroes! While superhuman registration temporarily caused the team to cease operations, they are ready to return to the streets to take on the threats no single super hero can withstand!

YOUNG AVENGERS
PRESENTS
HAWKEYE

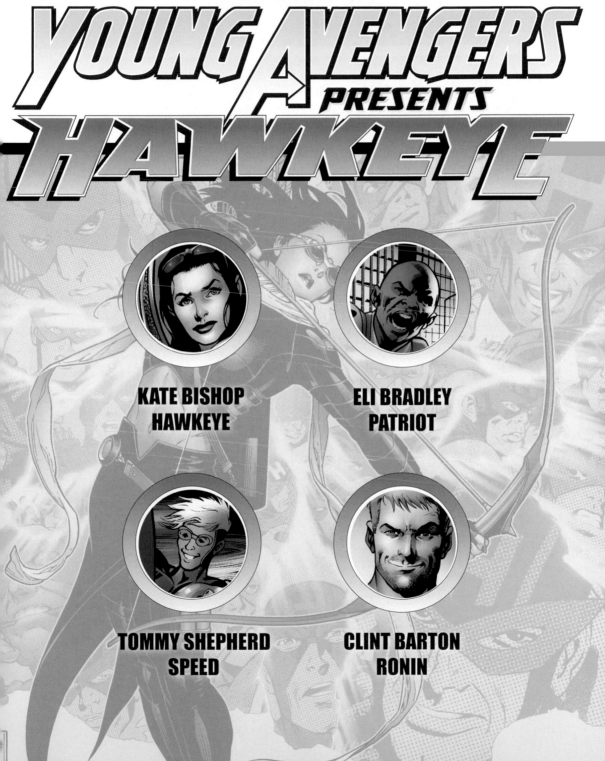

**KATE BISHOP
HAWKEYE**

**ELI BRADLEY
PATRIOT**

**TOMMY SHEPHERD
SPEED**

**CLINT BARTON
RONIN**

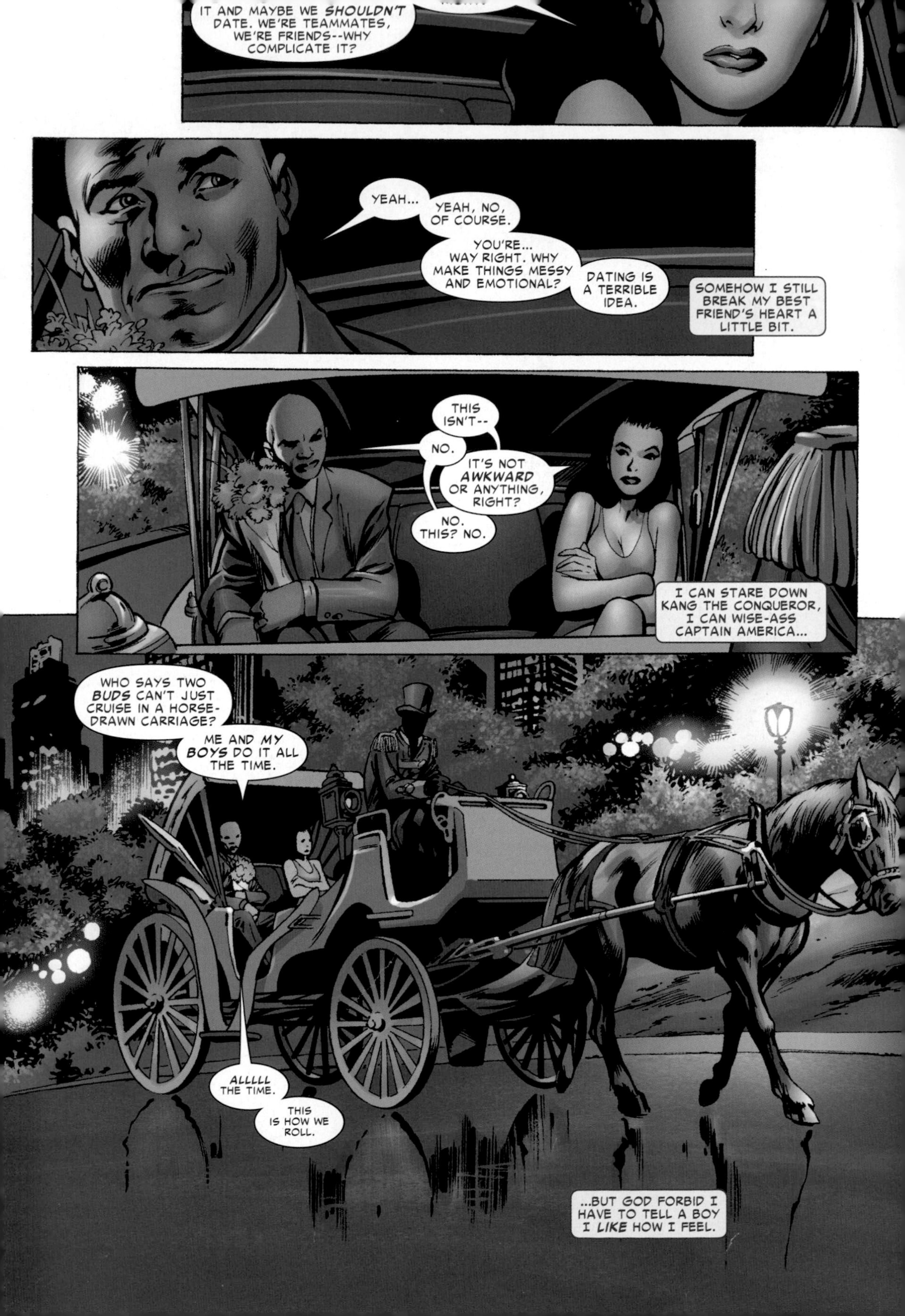
IT AND MAYBE WE SHOULDN'T DATE. WE'RE TEAMMATES, WE'RE FRIENDS--WHY COMPLICATE IT?
YEAH...
YEAH, NO, OF COURSE.
YOU'RE... WAY RIGHT. WHY MAKE THINGS MESSY AND EMOTIONAL?
DATING IS A TERRIBLE IDEA.
SOMEHOW I STILL BREAK MY BEST FRIEND'S HEART A LITTLE BIT.
THIS ISN'T--
NO.
IT'S NOT AWKWARD OR ANYTHING, RIGHT?
NO. THIS? NO.
I CAN STARE DOWN KANG THE CONQUEROR, I CAN WISE-ASS CAPTAIN AMERICA...
WHO SAYS TWO BUDS CAN'T JUST CRUISE IN A HORSE-DRAWN CARRIAGE?
ME AND MY BOYS DO IT ALL THE TIME.
ALLLLL THE TIME.
THIS IS HOW WE ROLL.
...BUT GOD FORBID I HAVE TO TELL A BOY I LIKE HOW I FEEL.

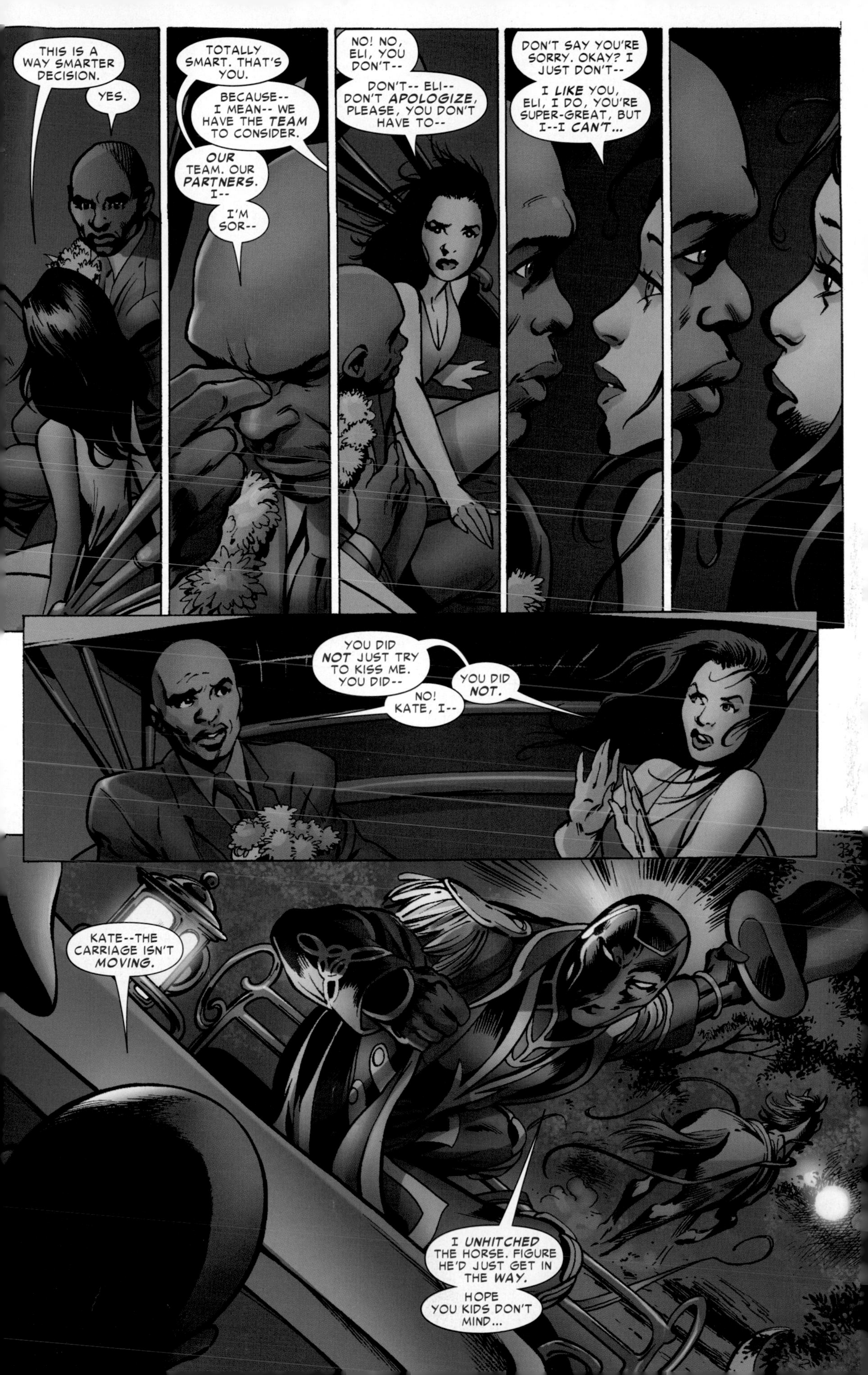
THIS IS A WAY SMARTER DECISION.
YES.
TOTALLY SMART. THAT'S YOU.
BECAUSE-- I MEAN-- WE HAVE THE *TEAM* TO CONSIDER.
OUR TEAM. OUR *PARTNERS*. I--
I'M SOR--
NO! NO, ELI, YOU DON'T--
DON'T-- ELI-- DON'T *APOLOGIZE*, PLEASE, YOU DON'T HAVE TO--
DON'T SAY YOU'RE SORRY. OKAY? I JUST DON'T--
I *LIKE* YOU, ELI, I DO, YOU'RE SUPER-GREAT, BUT I--I *CAN'T*...
YOU DID *NOT* JUST TRY TO KISS ME. YOU DID--
YOU DID *NOT*.
NO! KATE, I--
KATE--THE CARRIAGE ISN'T *MOVING*.
I *UNHITCHED* THE HORSE. FIGURE HE'D JUST GET IN THE *WAY*.
HOPE YOU KIDS DON'T MIND...

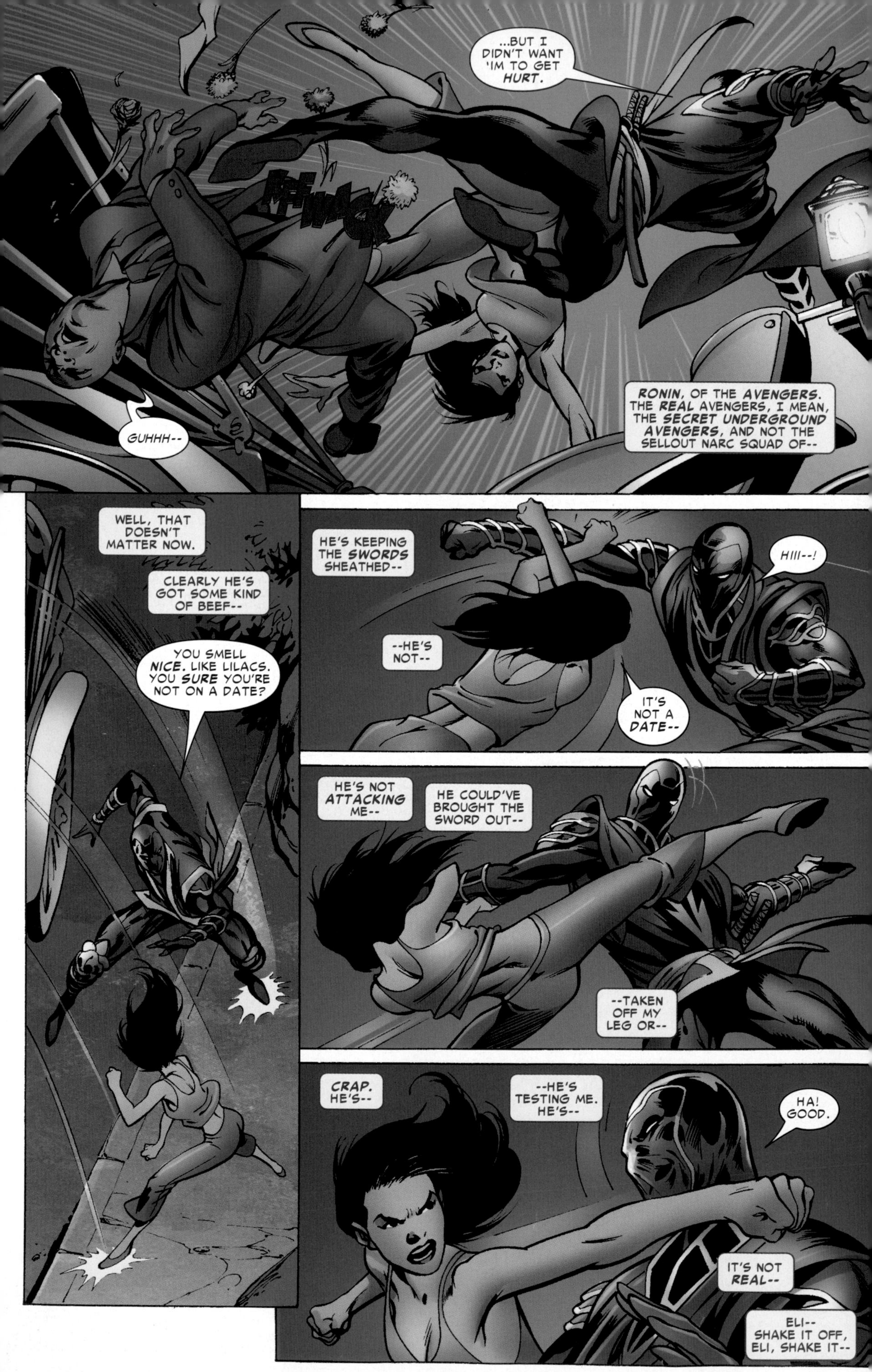
...BUT I DIDN'T WANT 'IM TO GET HURT.
FFFWACK
GUHHH--
RONIN, OF THE AVENGERS. THE REAL AVENGERS, I MEAN, THE SECRET UNDERGROUND AVENGERS, AND NOT THE SELLOUT NARC SQUAD OF--
WELL, THAT DOESN'T MATTER NOW.
CLEARLY HE'S GOT SOME KIND OF BEEF--
YOU SMELL NICE. LIKE LILACS. YOU SURE YOU'RE NOT ON A DATE?
HE'S KEEPING THE SWORDS SHEATHED--
HIII--!
--HE'S NOT--
IT'S NOT A DATE--
HE'S NOT ATTACKING ME--
HE COULD'VE BROUGHT THE SWORD OUT--
--TAKEN OFF MY LEG OR--
CRAP. HE'S--
--HE'S TESTING ME. HE'S--
HA! GOOD.
IT'S NOT REAL--
ELI-- SHAKE IT OFF, ELI, SHAKE IT--

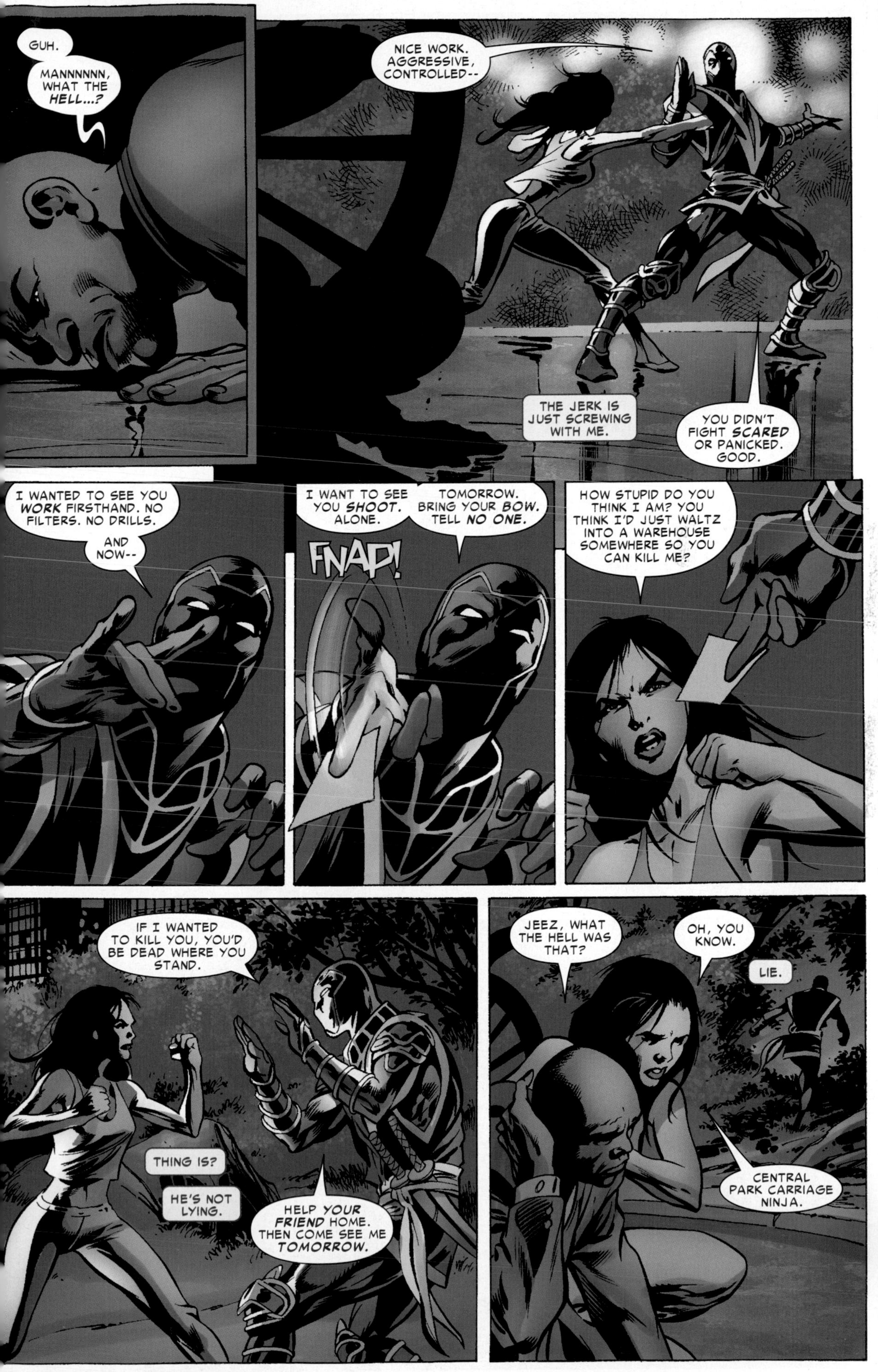
GUH.
MANNNNNN, WHAT THE HELL...?
NICE WORK. AGGRESSIVE, CONTROLLED--
THE JERK IS JUST SCREWING WITH ME.
YOU DIDN'T FIGHT SCARED OR PANICKED. GOOD.
I WANTED TO SEE YOU WORK FIRSTHAND. NO FILTERS. NO DRILLS.
AND NOW--
I WANT TO SEE YOU SHOOT. ALONE.
TOMORROW. BRING YOUR BOW. TELL NO ONE.
FNAP!
HOW STUPID DO YOU THINK I AM? YOU THINK I'D JUST WALTZ INTO A WAREHOUSE SOMEWHERE SO YOU CAN KILL ME?
IF I WANTED TO KILL YOU, YOU'D BE DEAD WHERE YOU STAND.
THING IS?
HE'S NOT LYING.
HELP YOUR FRIEND HOME. THEN COME SEE ME TOMORROW.
JEEZ, WHAT THE HELL WAS THAT?
OH, YOU KNOW.
LIE.
CENTRAL PARK CARRIAGE NINJA.

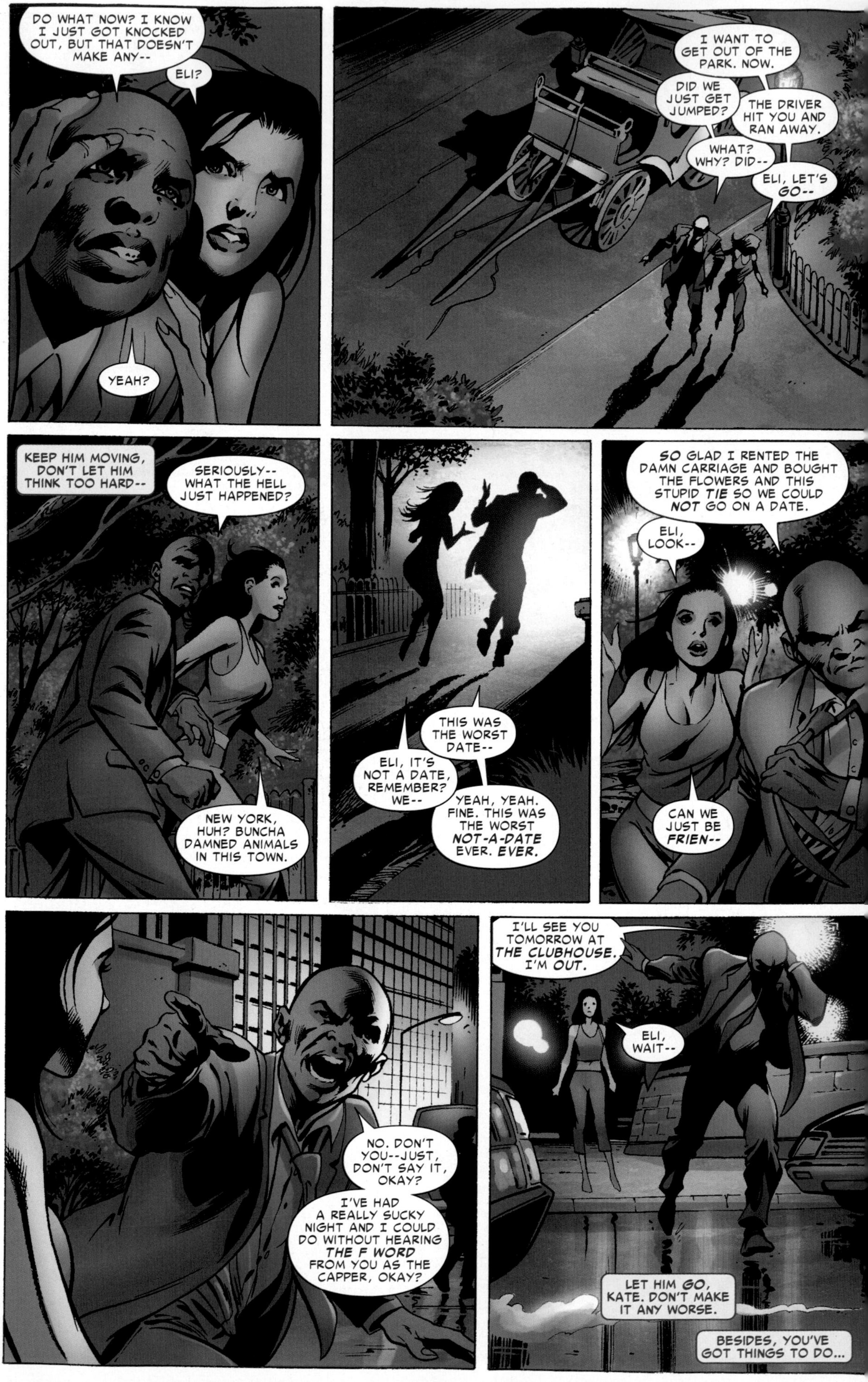
DO WHAT NOW? I KNOW I JUST GOT KNOCKED OUT, BUT THAT DOESN'T MAKE ANY--
ELI?
YEAH?
I WANT TO GET OUT OF THE PARK. NOW.
DID WE JUST GET JUMPED?
THE DRIVER HIT YOU AND RAN AWAY.
WHAT? WHY? DID--
ELI, LET'S GO--
KEEP HIM MOVING, DON'T LET HIM THINK TOO HARD--
SERIOUSLY-- WHAT THE HELL JUST HAPPENED?
NEW YORK, HUH? BUNCHA DAMNED ANIMALS IN THIS TOWN.
THIS WAS THE WORST DATE--
ELI, IT'S NOT A DATE, REMEMBER? WE--
YEAH, YEAH. FINE. THIS WAS THE WORST NOT-A-DATE EVER. EVER.
SO GLAD I RENTED THE DAMN CARRIAGE AND BOUGHT THE FLOWERS AND THIS STUPID TIE SO WE COULD NOT GO ON A DATE.
ELI, LOOK--
CAN WE JUST BE FRIEN--
NO. DON'T YOU--JUST, DON'T SAY IT, OKAY?
I'VE HAD A REALLY SUCKY NIGHT AND I COULD DO WITHOUT HEARING THE F WORD FROM YOU AS THE CAPPER, OKAY?
I'LL SEE YOU TOMORROW AT THE CLUBHOUSE. I'M OUT.
ELI, WAIT--
LET HIM GO, KATE. DON'T MAKE IT ANY WORSE.
BESIDES, YOU'VE GOT THINGS TO DO...

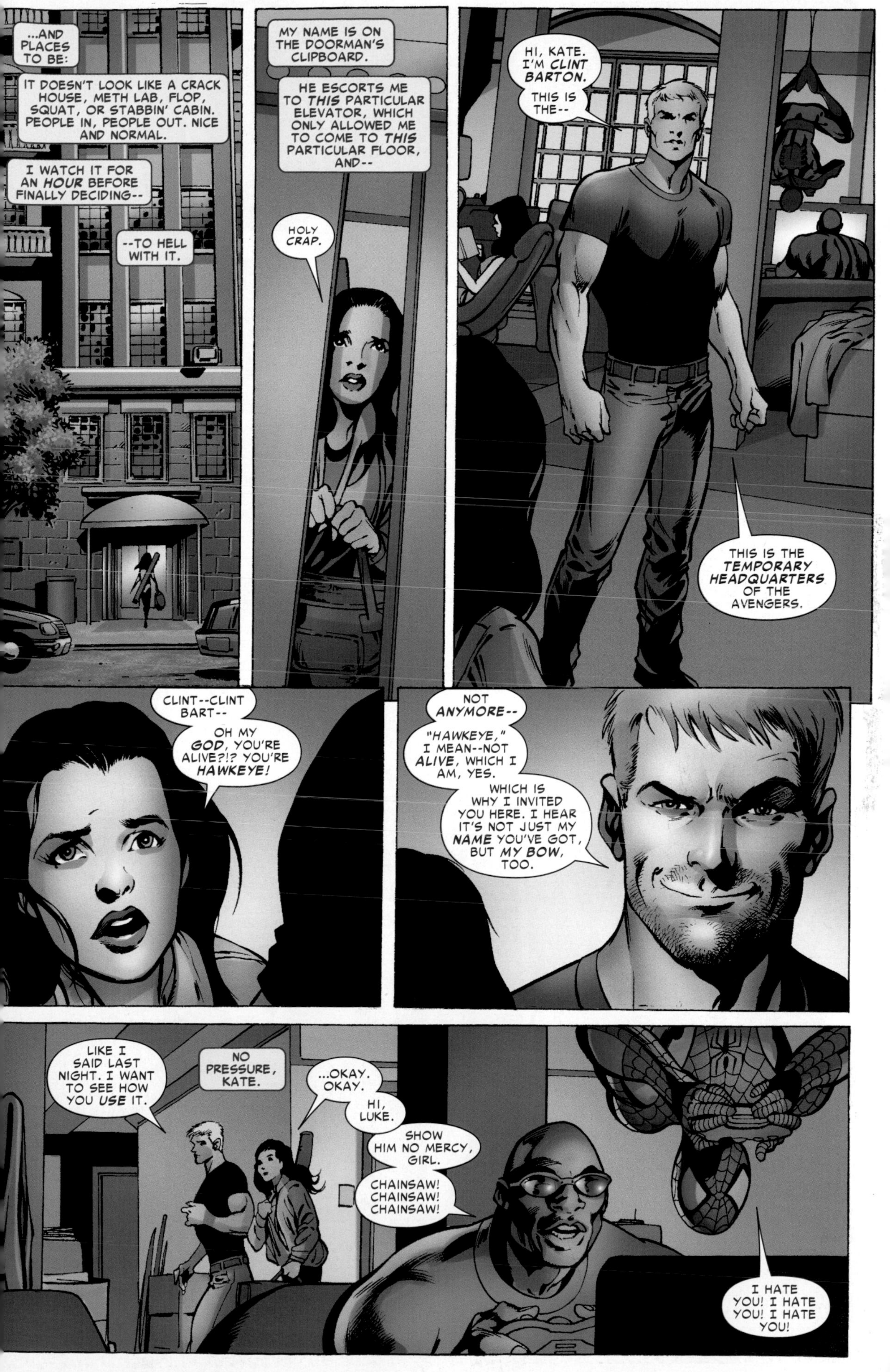
...AND PLACES TO BE:
IT DOESN'T LOOK LIKE A CRACK HOUSE, METH LAB, FLOP, SQUAT, OR STABBIN' CABIN. PEOPLE IN, PEOPLE OUT. NICE AND NORMAL.
I WATCH IT FOR AN HOUR BEFORE FINALLY DECIDING--
--TO HELL WITH IT.
MY NAME IS ON THE DOORMAN'S CLIPBOARD.
HE ESCORTS ME TO THIS PARTICULAR ELEVATOR, WHICH ONLY ALLOWED ME TO COME TO THIS PARTICULAR FLOOR, AND--
HOLY CRAP.
HI, KATE. I'M CLINT BARTON.
THIS IS THE--
THIS IS THE TEMPORARY HEADQUARTERS OF THE AVENGERS.
CLINT--CLINT BART--
OH MY GOD, YOU'RE ALIVE?!? YOU'RE HAWKEYE!
NOT ANYMORE--
"HAWKEYE," I MEAN--NOT ALIVE, WHICH I AM, YES.
WHICH IS WHY I INVITED YOU HERE. I HEAR IT'S NOT JUST MY NAME YOU'VE GOT, BUT MY BOW, TOO.
LIKE I SAID LAST NIGHT. I WANT TO SEE HOW YOU USE IT.
NO PRESSURE, KATE.
...OKAY. OKAY.
HI, LUKE.
SHOW HIM NO MERCY, GIRL.
CHAINSAW! CHAINSAW! CHAINSAW!
I HATE YOU! I HATE YOU! I HATE YOU!

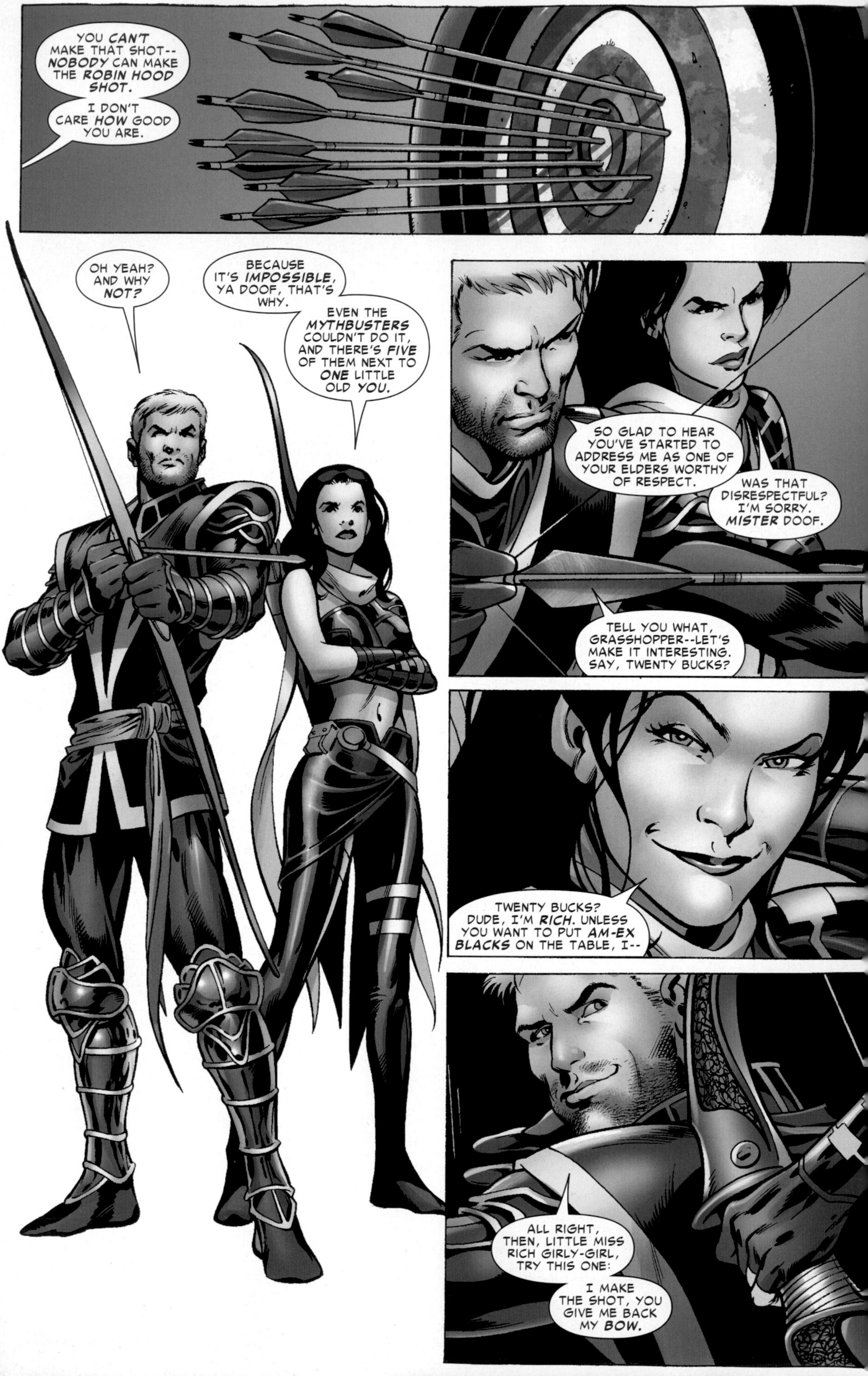
YOU CAN'T MAKE THAT SHOT-- NOBODY CAN MAKE THE ROBIN HOOD SHOT.
I DON'T CARE HOW GOOD YOU ARE.
OH YEAH? AND WHY NOT?
BECAUSE IT'S IMPOSSIBLE, YA DOOF, THAT'S WHY.
EVEN THE MYTHBUSTERS COULDN'T DO IT, AND THERE'S FIVE OF THEM NEXT TO ONE LITTLE OLD YOU.
SO GLAD TO HEAR YOU'VE STARTED TO ADDRESS ME AS ONE OF YOUR ELDERS WORTHY OF RESPECT.
WAS THAT DISRESPECTFUL? I'M SORRY. MISTER DOOF.
TELL YOU WHAT, GRASSHOPPER--LET'S MAKE IT INTERESTING. SAY, TWENTY BUCKS?
TWENTY BUCKS? DUDE, I'M RICH. UNLESS YOU WANT TO PUT AM-EX BLACKS ON THE TABLE, I--
ALL RIGHT, THEN, LITTLE MISS RICH GIRLY-GIRL, TRY THIS ONE:
I MAKE THE SHOT, YOU GIVE ME BACK MY BOW.

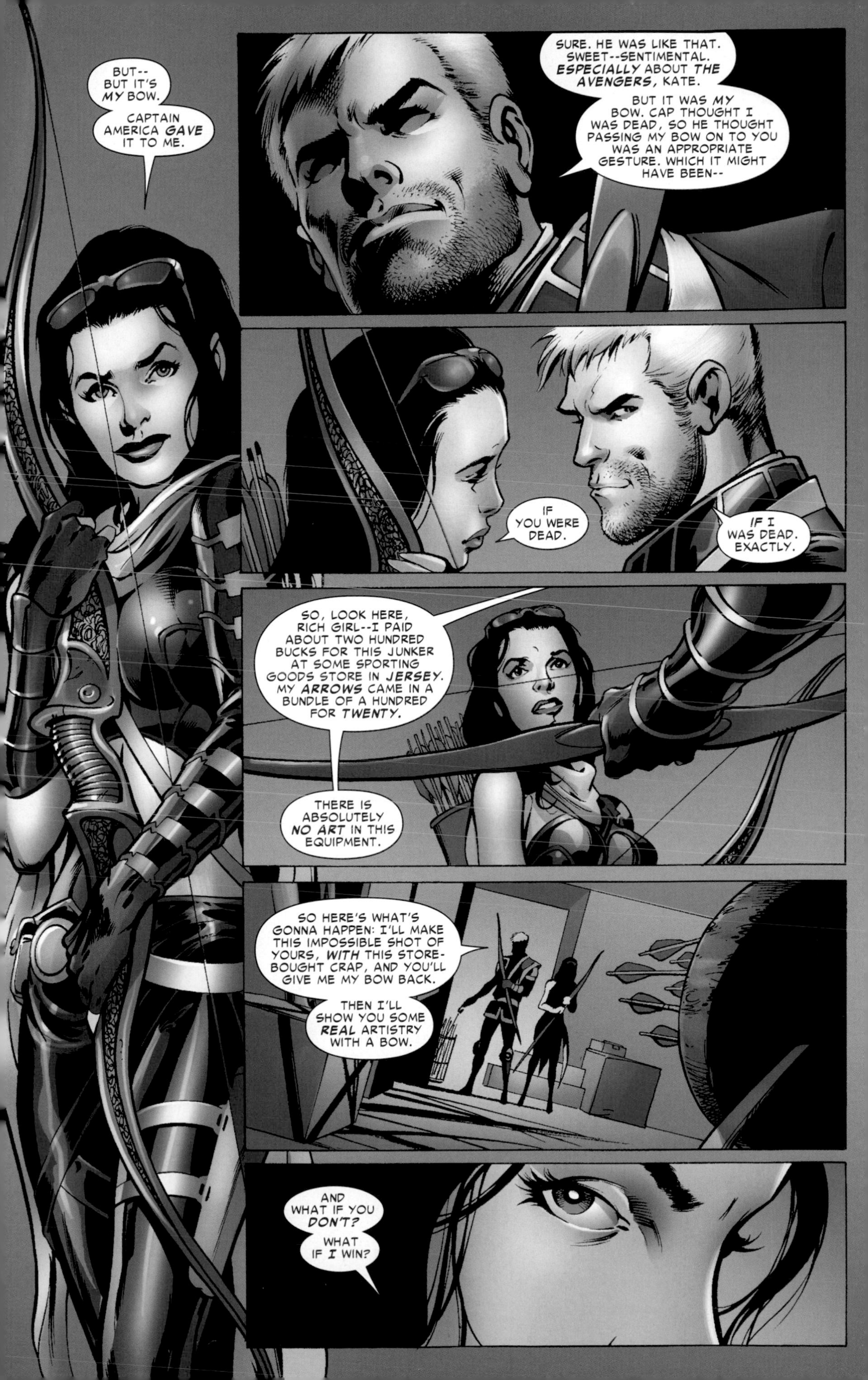
BUT-- BUT IT'S MY BOW.
CAPTAIN AMERICA GAVE IT TO ME.
SURE. HE WAS LIKE THAT. SWEET--SENTIMENTAL. ESPECIALLY ABOUT THE AVENGERS, KATE.
BUT IT WAS MY BOW. CAP THOUGHT I WAS DEAD, SO HE THOUGHT PASSING MY BOW ON TO YOU WAS AN APPROPRIATE GESTURE. WHICH IT MIGHT HAVE BEEN--
IF YOU WERE DEAD.
IF I WAS DEAD. EXACTLY.
SO, LOOK HERE, RICH GIRL--I PAID ABOUT TWO HUNDRED BUCKS FOR THIS JUNKER AT SOME SPORTING GOODS STORE IN JERSEY. MY ARROWS CAME IN A BUNDLE OF A HUNDRED FOR TWENTY.
THERE IS ABSOLUTELY NO ART IN THIS EQUIPMENT.
SO HERE'S WHAT'S GONNA HAPPEN: I'LL MAKE THIS IMPOSSIBLE SHOT OF YOURS, WITH THIS STORE-BOUGHT CRAP, AND YOU'LL GIVE ME MY BOW BACK.
THEN I'LL SHOW YOU SOME REAL ARTISTRY WITH A BOW.
AND WHAT IF YOU DON'T?
WHAT IF I WIN?

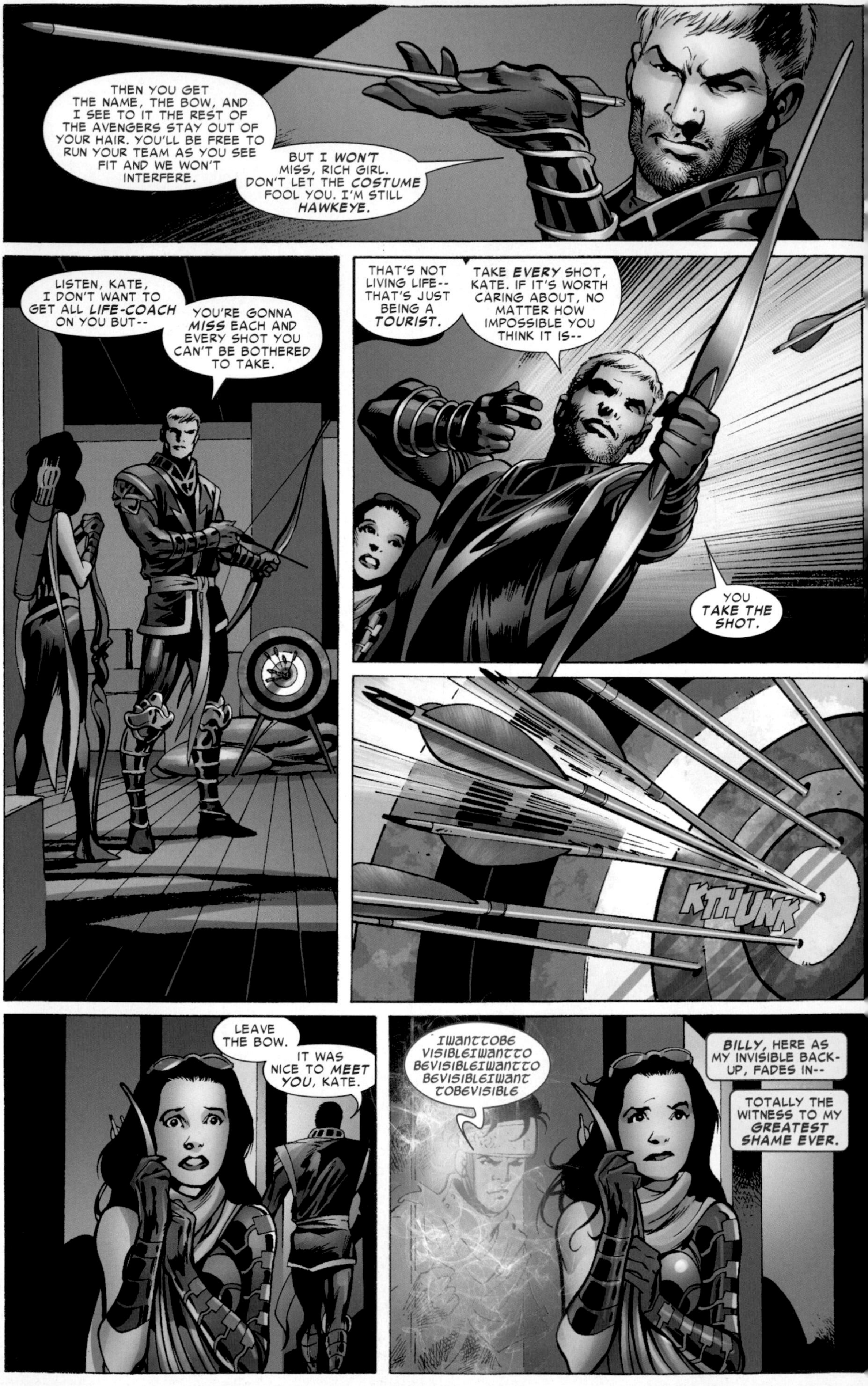

THEN YOU GET THE NAME, THE BOW, AND I SEE TO IT THE REST OF THE AVENGERS STAY OUT OF YOUR HAIR. YOU'LL BE FREE TO RUN YOUR TEAM AS YOU SEE FIT AND WE WON'T INTERFERE.
BUT I WON'T MISS, RICH GIRL. DON'T LET THE COSTUME FOOL YOU. I'M STILL HAWKEYE.
LISTEN, KATE, I DON'T WANT TO GET ALL LIFE-COACH ON YOU BUT--
YOU'RE GONNA MISS EACH AND EVERY SHOT YOU CAN'T BE BOTHERED TO TAKE.
THAT'S NOT LIVING LIFE-- THAT'S JUST BEING A TOURIST.
TAKE EVERY SHOT, KATE. IF IT'S WORTH CARING ABOUT, NO MATTER HOW IMPOSSIBLE YOU THINK IT IS--
YOU TAKE THE SHOT.
KTHUNK
LEAVE THE BOW.
IT WAS NICE TO MEET YOU, KATE.
IWANTTOBE VISIBLEIWANTTO BEVISIBLEIWANTTO BEVISIBLEIWANT TOBEVISIBLE
BILLY, HERE AS MY INVISIBLE BACK-UP, FADES IN--
TOTALLY THE WITNESS TO MY GREATEST SHAME EVER.

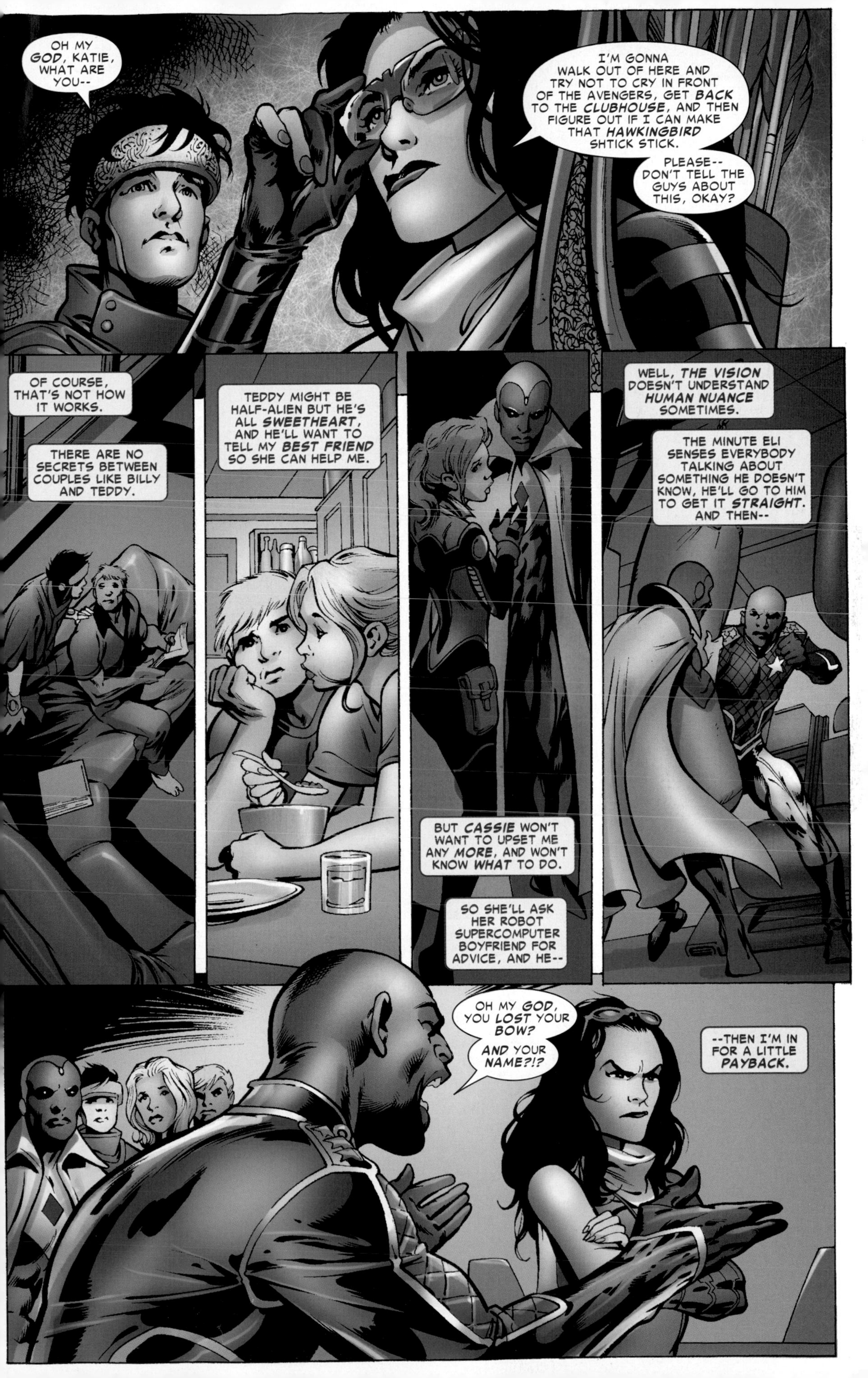

OH MY GOD, KATIE, WHAT ARE YOU--
I'M GONNA WALK OUT OF HERE AND TRY NOT TO CRY IN FRONT OF THE AVENGERS, GET BACK TO THE CLUBHOUSE, AND THEN FIGURE OUT IF I CAN MAKE THAT HAWKINGBIRD SHTICK STICK.
PLEASE-- DON'T TELL THE GUYS ABOUT THIS, OKAY?
OF COURSE, THAT'S NOT HOW IT WORKS.
THERE ARE NO SECRETS BETWEEN COUPLES LIKE BILLY AND TEDDY.
TEDDY MIGHT BE HALF-ALIEN BUT HE'S ALL SWEETHEART, AND HE'LL WANT TO TELL MY BEST FRIEND SO SHE CAN HELP ME.
BUT CASSIE WON'T WANT TO UPSET ME ANY MORE, AND WON'T KNOW WHAT TO DO.
SO SHE'LL ASK HER ROBOT SUPERCOMPUTER BOYFRIEND FOR ADVICE, AND HE--
WELL, THE VISION DOESN'T UNDERSTAND HUMAN NUANCE SOMETIMES.
THE MINUTE ELI SENSES EVERYBODY TALKING ABOUT SOMETHING HE DOESN'T KNOW, HE'LL GO TO HIM TO GET IT STRAIGHT. AND THEN--
OH MY GOD, YOU LOST YOUR BOW?
AND YOUR NAME?!?
--THEN I'M IN FOR A LITTLE PAYBACK.

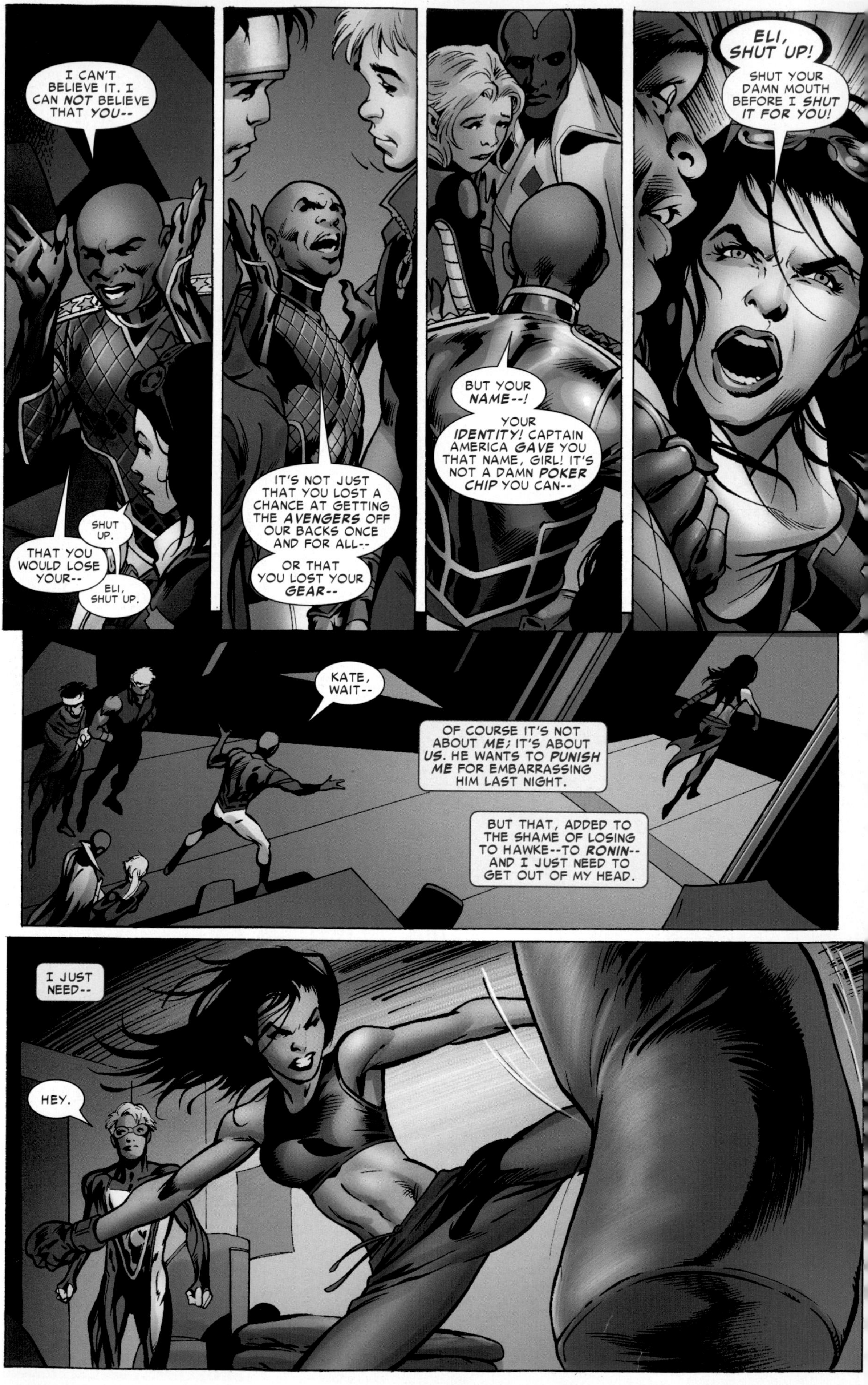
I CAN'T BELIEVE IT. I CAN NOT BELIEVE THAT YOU--
THAT YOU WOULD LOSE YOUR--
SHUT UP.
ELI, SHUT UP.
IT'S NOT JUST THAT YOU LOST A CHANCE AT GETTING THE AVENGERS OFF OUR BACKS ONCE AND FOR ALL--
OR THAT YOU LOST YOUR GEAR--
BUT YOUR NAME--!
YOUR IDENTITY! CAPTAIN AMERICA GAVE YOU THAT NAME, GIRL! IT'S NOT A DAMN POKER CHIP YOU CAN--
ELI, SHUT UP!
SHUT YOUR DAMN MOUTH BEFORE I SHUT IT FOR YOU!
KATE, WAIT--
OF COURSE IT'S NOT ABOUT ME; IT'S ABOUT US. HE WANTS TO PUNISH ME FOR EMBARRASSING HIM LAST NIGHT.
BUT THAT, ADDED TO THE SHAME OF LOSING TO HAWKE--TO RONIN--AND I JUST NEED TO GET OUT OF MY HEAD.
I JUST NEED--
HEY.

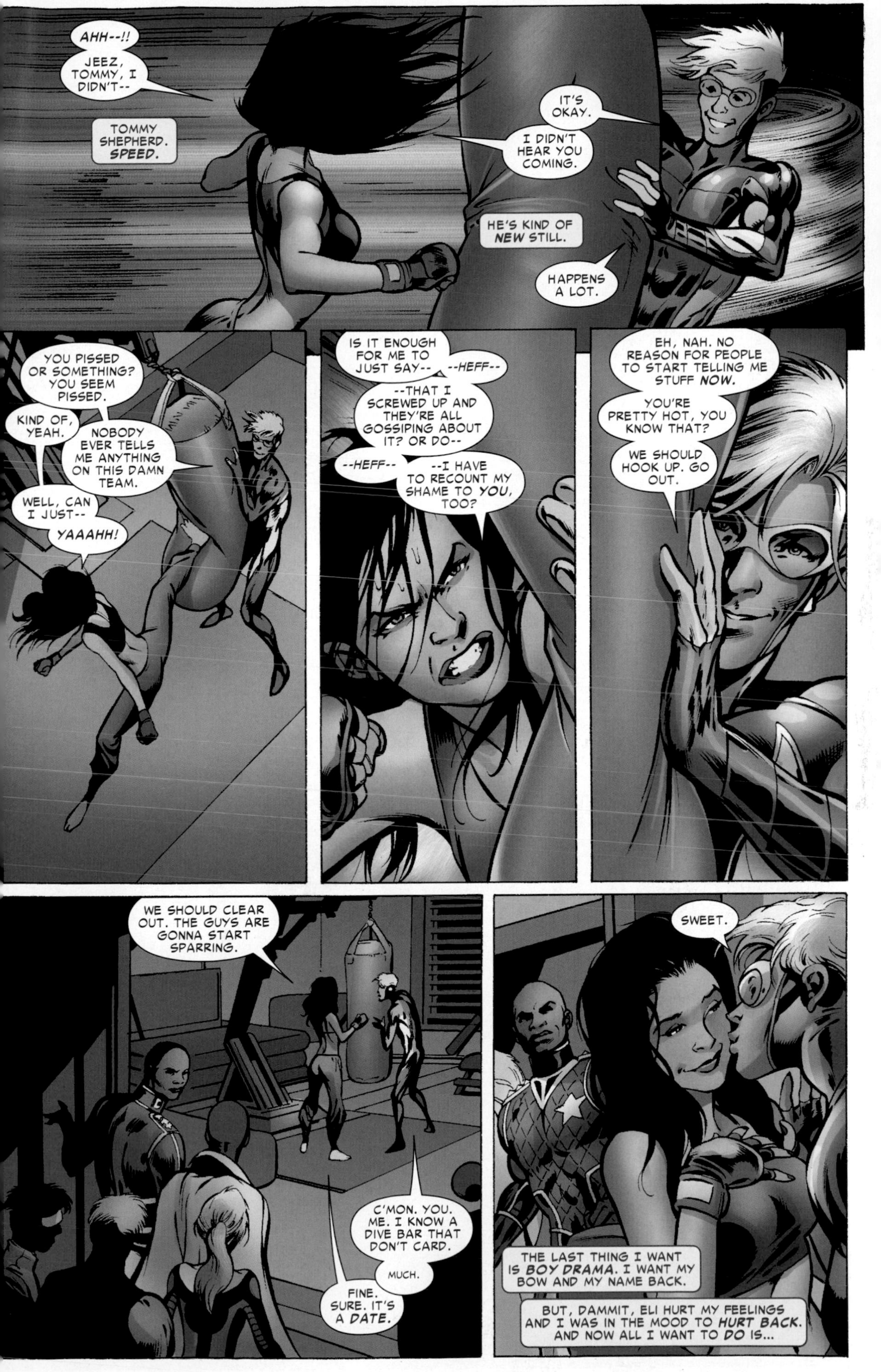

AHH--!!
JEEZ, TOMMY, I DIDN'T--
TOMMY SHEPHERD. SPEED.
IT'S OKAY.
I DIDN'T HEAR YOU COMING.
HE'S KIND OF NEW STILL.
HAPPENS A LOT.
YOU PISSED OR SOMETHING? YOU SEEM PISSED.
KIND OF, YEAH.
NOBODY EVER TELLS ME ANYTHING ON THIS DAMN TEAM.
WELL, CAN I JUST--
YAAAHH!
IS IT ENOUGH FOR ME TO JUST SAY--
--HEFF--
--THAT I SCREWED UP AND THEY'RE ALL GOSSIPING ABOUT IT? OR DO--
--HEFF--
--I HAVE TO RECOUNT MY SHAME TO YOU, TOO?
EH, NAH. NO REASON FOR PEOPLE TO START TELLING ME STUFF NOW.
YOU'RE PRETTY HOT, YOU KNOW THAT?
WE SHOULD HOOK UP. GO OUT.
WE SHOULD CLEAR OUT. THE GUYS ARE GONNA START SPARRING.
C'MON. YOU. ME. I KNOW A DIVE BAR THAT DON'T CARD.
MUCH.
FINE. SURE. IT'S A DATE.
SWEET.
THE LAST THING I WANT IS BOY DRAMA. I WANT MY BOW AND MY NAME BACK.
BUT, DAMMIT, ELI HURT MY FEELINGS AND I WAS IN THE MOOD TO HURT BACK. AND NOW ALL I WANT TO DO IS...

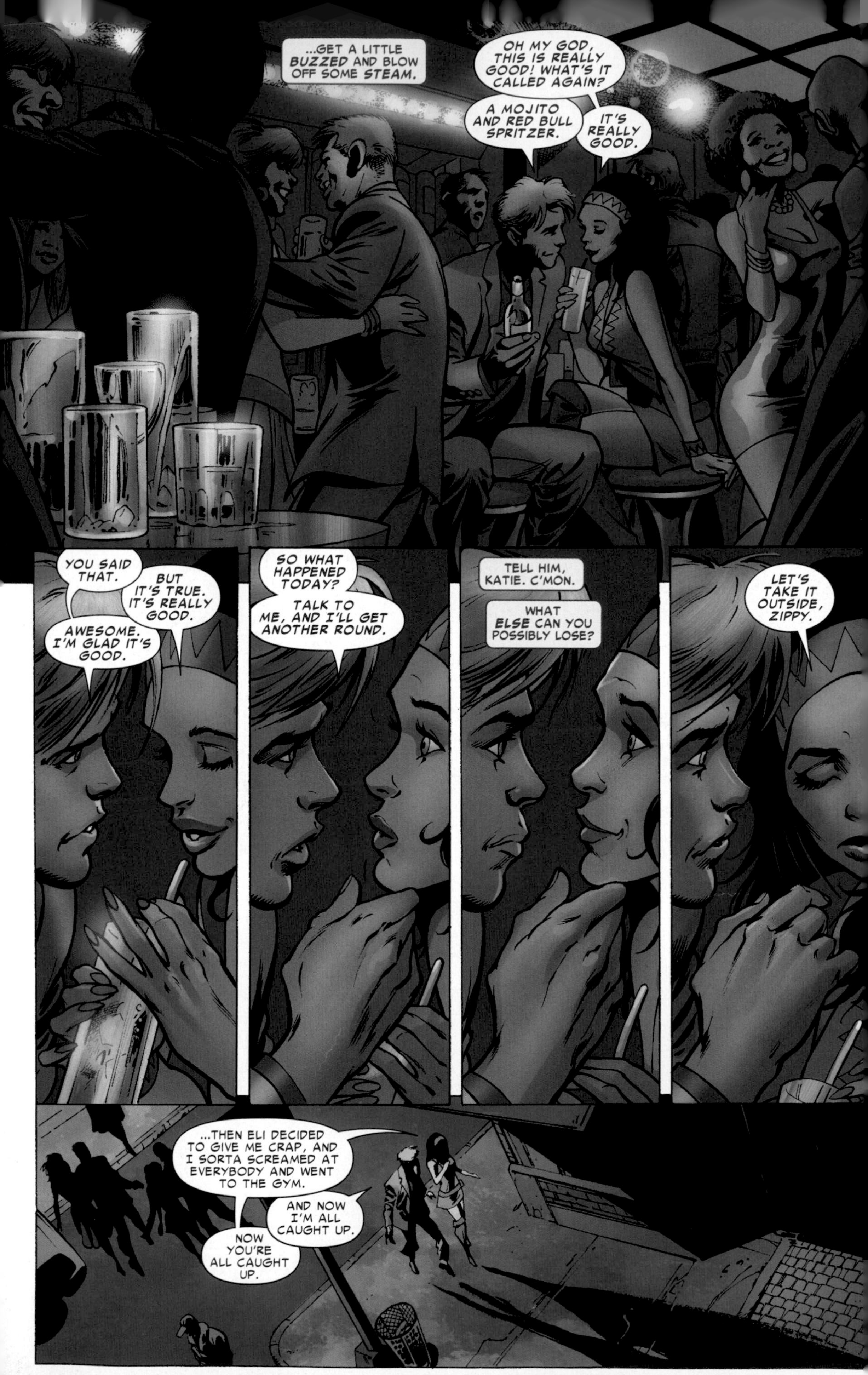
...GET A LITTLE BUZZED AND BLOW OFF SOME STEAM.
OH MY GOD, THIS IS REALLY GOOD! WHAT'S IT CALLED AGAIN?
A MOJITO AND RED BULL SPRITZER.
IT'S REALLY GOOD.
YOU SAID THAT.
BUT IT'S TRUE. IT'S REALLY GOOD.
AWESOME. I'M GLAD IT'S GOOD.
SO WHAT HAPPENED TODAY?
TALK TO ME, AND I'LL GET ANOTHER ROUND.
TELL HIM, KATIE. C'MON.
WHAT ELSE CAN YOU POSSIBLY LOSE?
LET'S TAKE IT OUTSIDE, ZIPPY.
...THEN ELI DECIDED TO GIVE ME CRAP, AND I SORTA SCREAMED AT EVERYBODY AND WENT TO THE GYM.
AND NOW I'M ALL CAUGHT UP.
NOW YOU'RE ALL CAUGHT UP.

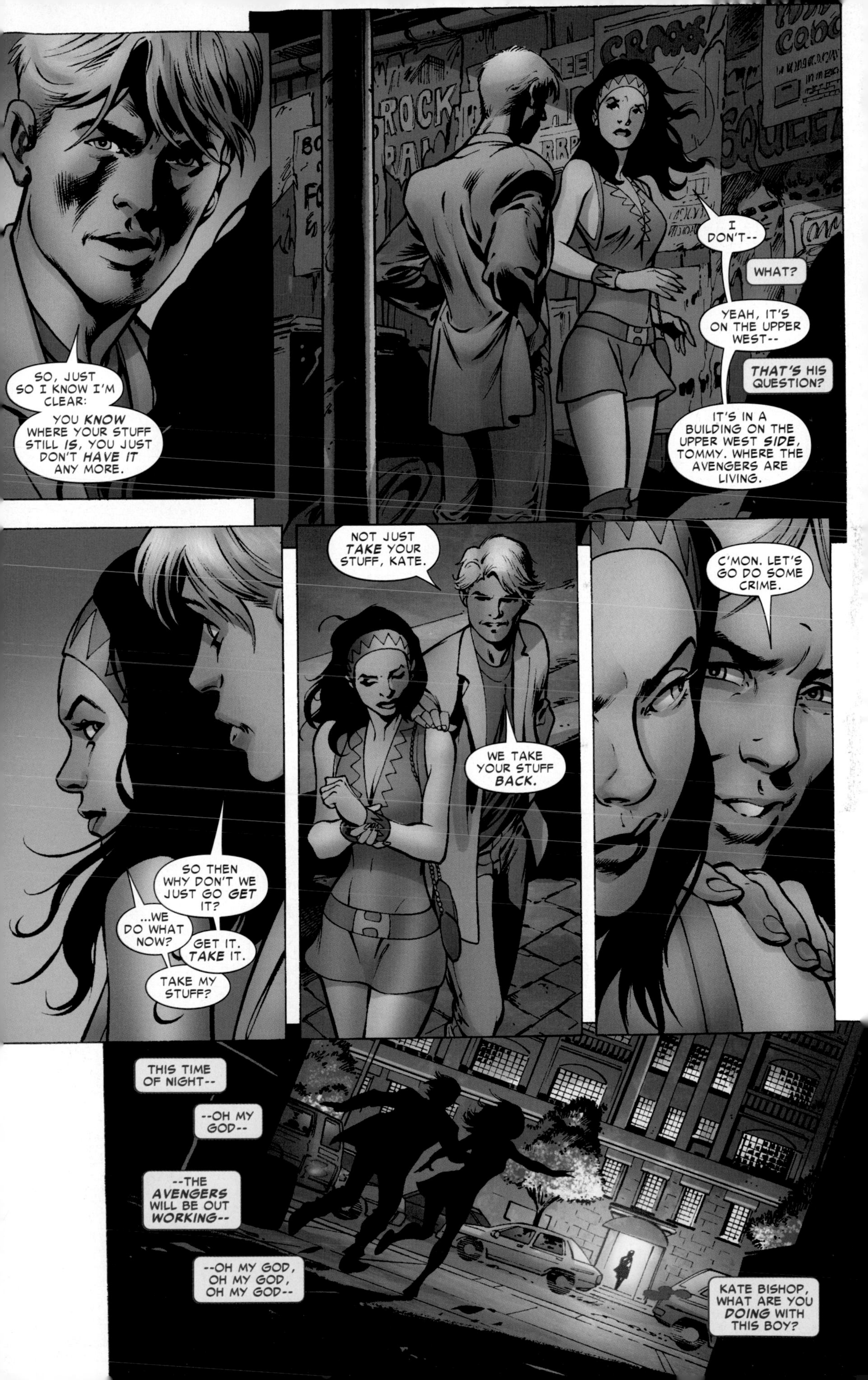

SO, JUST SO I KNOW I'M CLEAR:
YOU KNOW WHERE YOUR STUFF STILL IS, YOU JUST DON'T HAVE IT ANY MORE.
I DON'T--
WHAT?
YEAH, IT'S ON THE UPPER WEST--
THAT'S HIS QUESTION?
IT'S IN A BUILDING ON THE UPPER WEST SIDE, TOMMY. WHERE THE AVENGERS ARE LIVING.
SO THEN WHY DON'T WE JUST GO GET IT?
...WE DO WHAT NOW?
GET IT. TAKE IT.
TAKE MY STUFF?
NOT JUST TAKE YOUR STUFF, KATE.
WE TAKE YOUR STUFF BACK.
C'MON. LET'S GO DO SOME CRIME.
THIS TIME OF NIGHT--
--OH MY GOD--
--THE AVENGERS WILL BE OUT WORKING--
--OH MY GOD, OH MY GOD, OH MY GOD--
KATE BISHOP, WHAT ARE YOU DOING WITH THIS BOY?

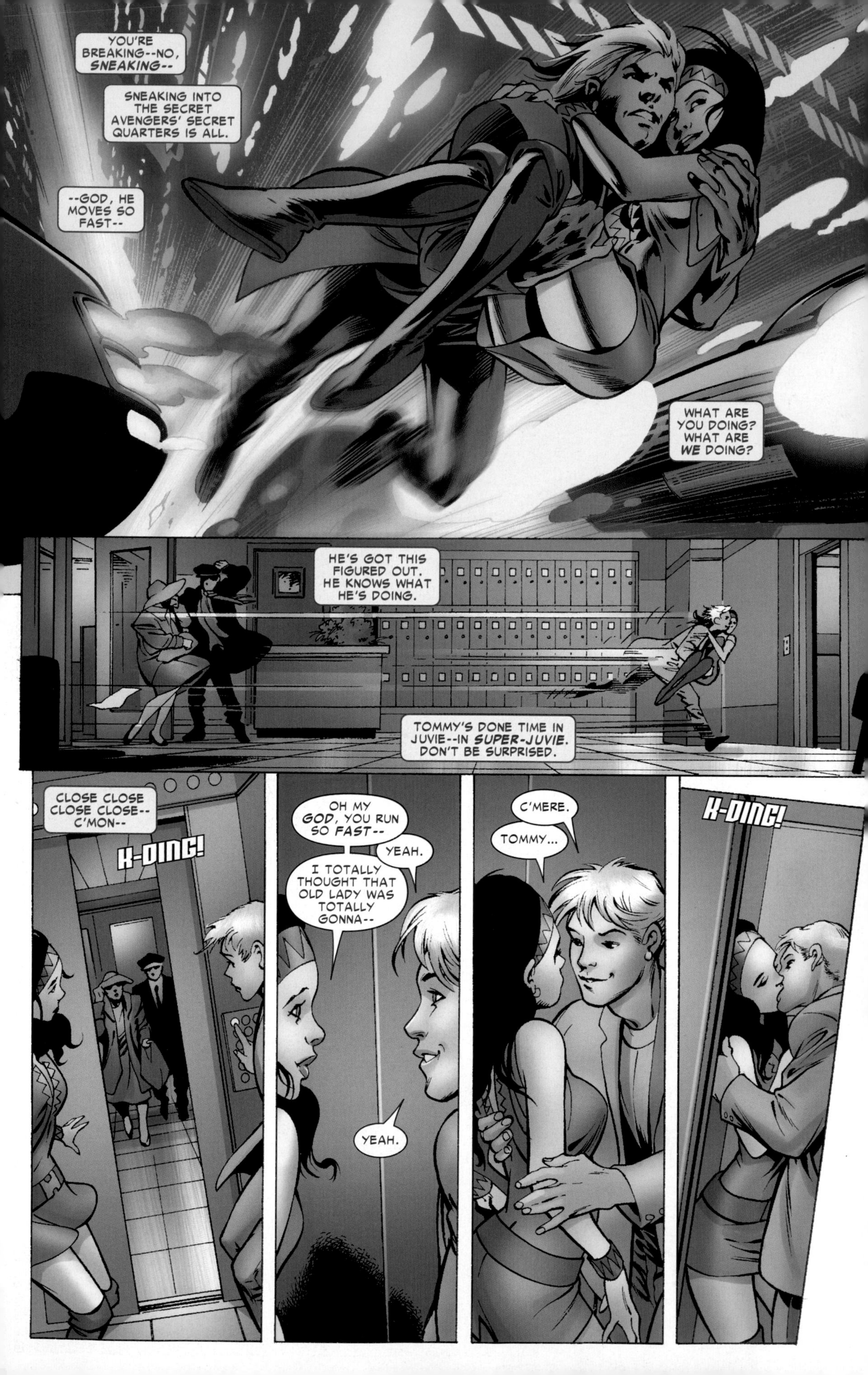
YOU'RE BREAKING--NO, SNEAKING--
SNEAKING INTO THE SECRET AVENGERS' SECRET QUARTERS IS ALL.
--GOD, HE MOVES SO FAST--
WHAT ARE YOU DOING? WHAT ARE WE DOING?
HE'S GOT THIS FIGURED OUT. HE KNOWS WHAT HE'S DOING.
TOMMY'S DONE TIME IN JUVIE--IN SUPER-JUVIE. DON'T BE SURPRISED.
CLOSE CLOSE CLOSE CLOSE-- C'MON--
K-DING!
OH MY GOD, YOU RUN SO FAST--
YEAH.
I TOTALLY THOUGHT THAT OLD LADY WAS TOTALLY GONNA--
YEAH.
C'MERE.
TOMMY...
K-DING!

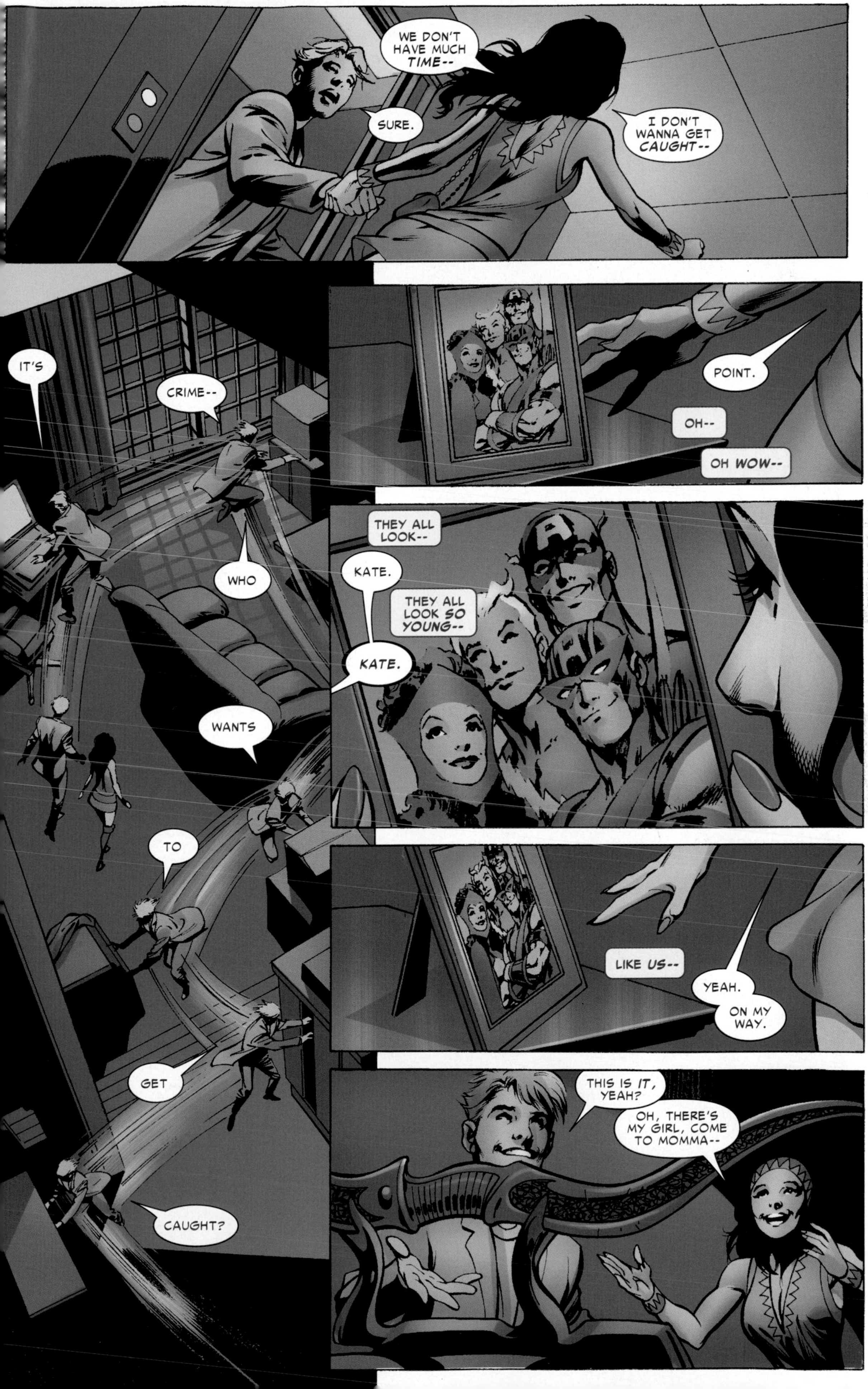
WE DON'T HAVE MUCH TIME--
SURE.
I DON'T WANNA GET CAUGHT--
IT'S
CRIME--
WHO
WANTS
TO
GET
CAUGHT?
POINT.
OH--
OH WOW--
THEY ALL LOOK--
KATE.
THEY ALL LOOK SO YOUNG--
KATE.
LIKE US--
YEAH.
ON MY WAY.
THIS IS IT, YEAH?
OH, THERE'S MY GIRL, COME TO MOMMA--

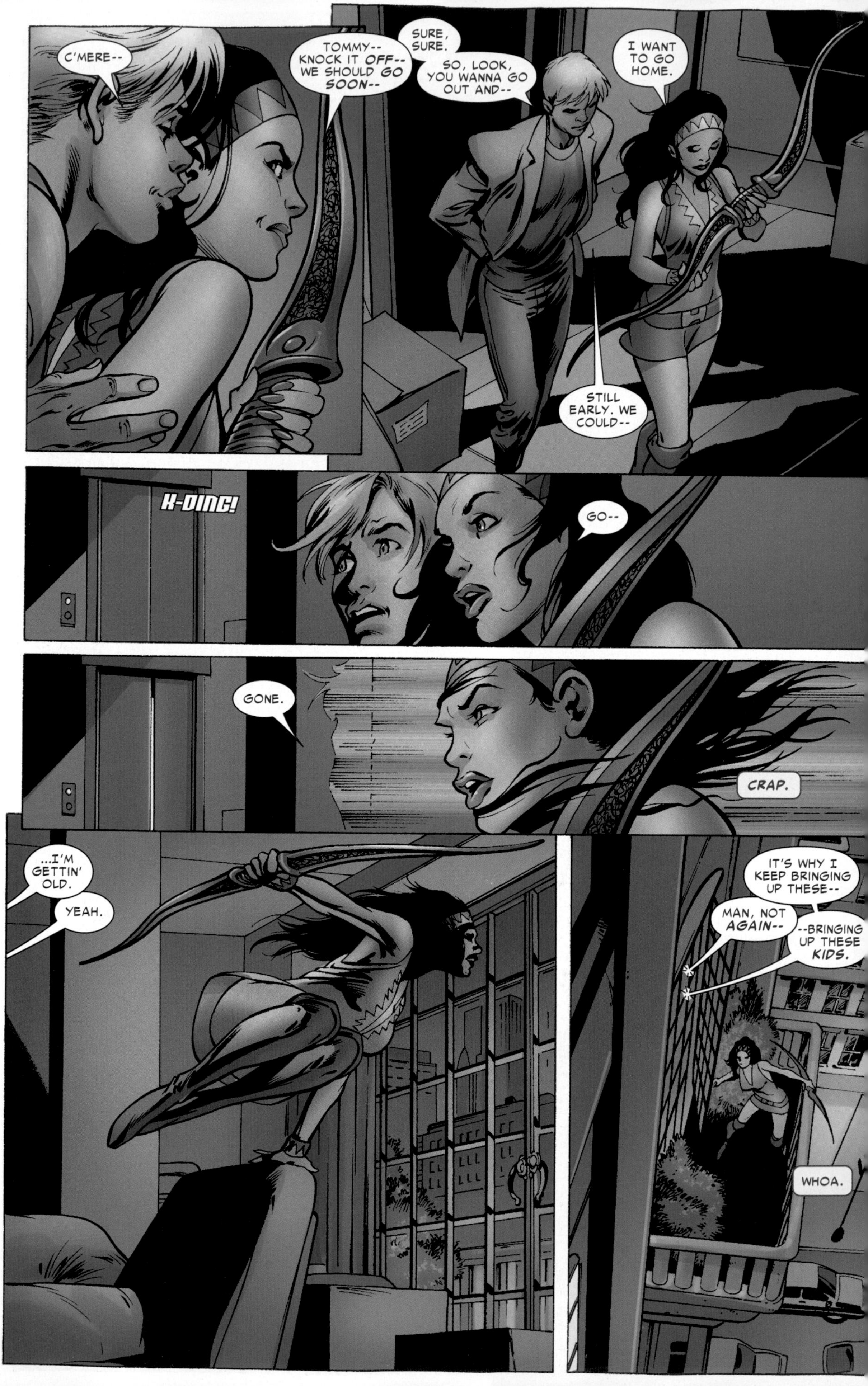
C'MERE--
TOMMY-- KNOCK IT OFF-- WE SHOULD GO SOON--
SURE, SURE.
SO, LOOK, YOU WANNA GO OUT AND--
I WANT TO GO HOME.
STILL EARLY. WE COULD--
K-DING!
GO--
GONE.
CRAP.
...I'M GETTIN' OLD.
YEAH.
IT'S WHY I KEEP BRINGING UP THESE--
MAN, NOT AGAIN--
--BRINGING UP THESE KIDS.
WHOA.

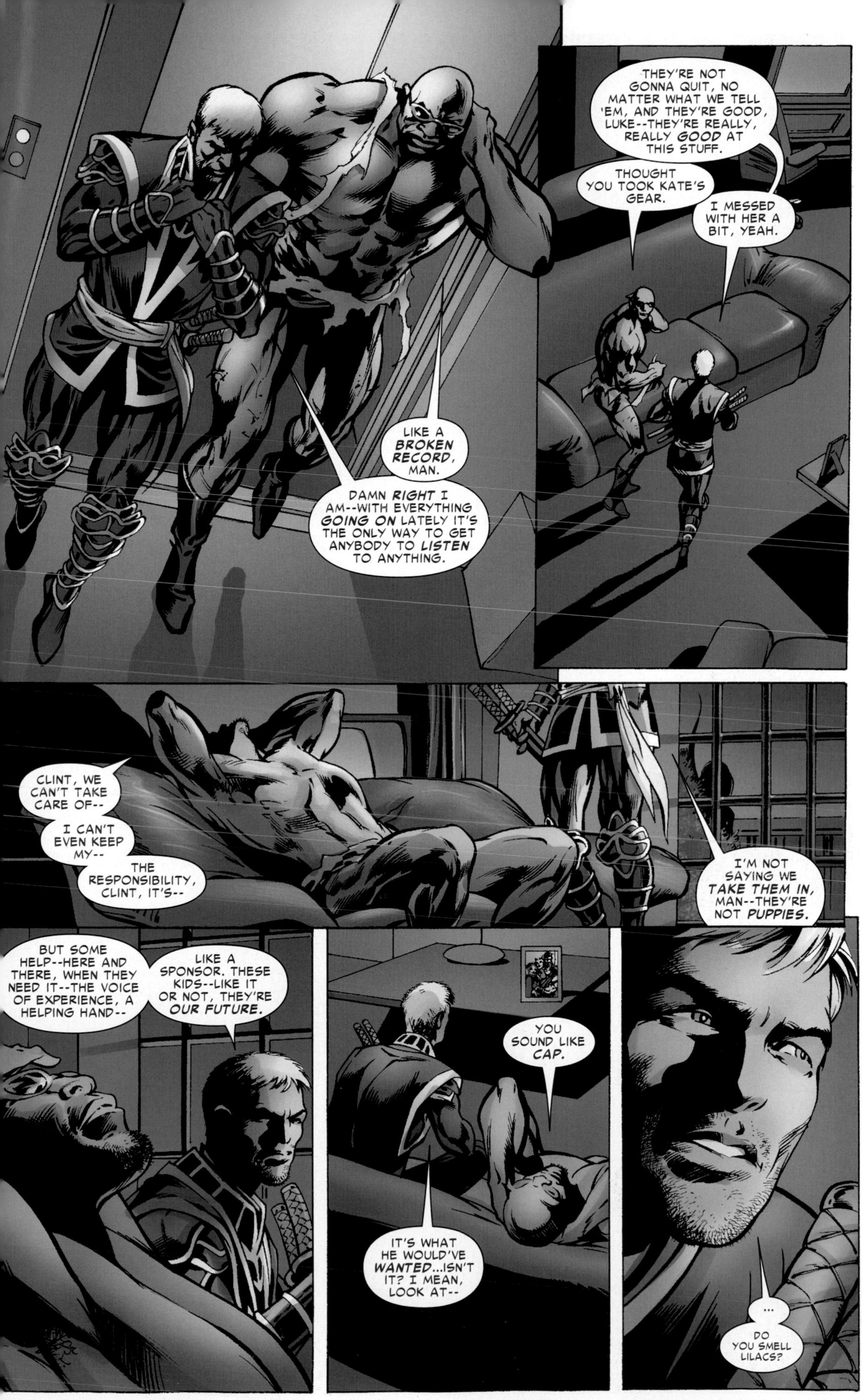
THEY'RE NOT GONNA QUIT, NO MATTER WHAT WE TELL 'EM, AND THEY'RE GOOD, LUKE--THEY'RE REALLY, REALLY GOOD AT THIS STUFF.
THOUGHT YOU TOOK KATE'S GEAR.
I MESSED WITH HER A BIT, YEAH.
LIKE A BROKEN RECORD, MAN.
DAMN RIGHT I AM--WITH EVERYTHING GOING ON LATELY IT'S THE ONLY WAY TO GET ANYBODY TO LISTEN TO ANYTHING.
CLINT, WE CAN'T TAKE CARE OF--
I CAN'T EVEN KEEP MY--
THE RESPONSIBILITY, CLINT, IT'S--
I'M NOT SAYING WE TAKE THEM IN, MAN--THEY'RE NOT PUPPIES.
BUT SOME HELP--HERE AND THERE, WHEN THEY NEED IT--THE VOICE OF EXPERIENCE, A HELPING HAND--
LIKE A SPONSOR. THESE KIDS--LIKE IT OR NOT, THEY'RE OUR FUTURE.
YOU SOUND LIKE CAP.
IT'S WHAT HE WOULD'VE WANTED...ISN'T IT? I MEAN, LOOK AT--
...
DO YOU SMELL LILACS?

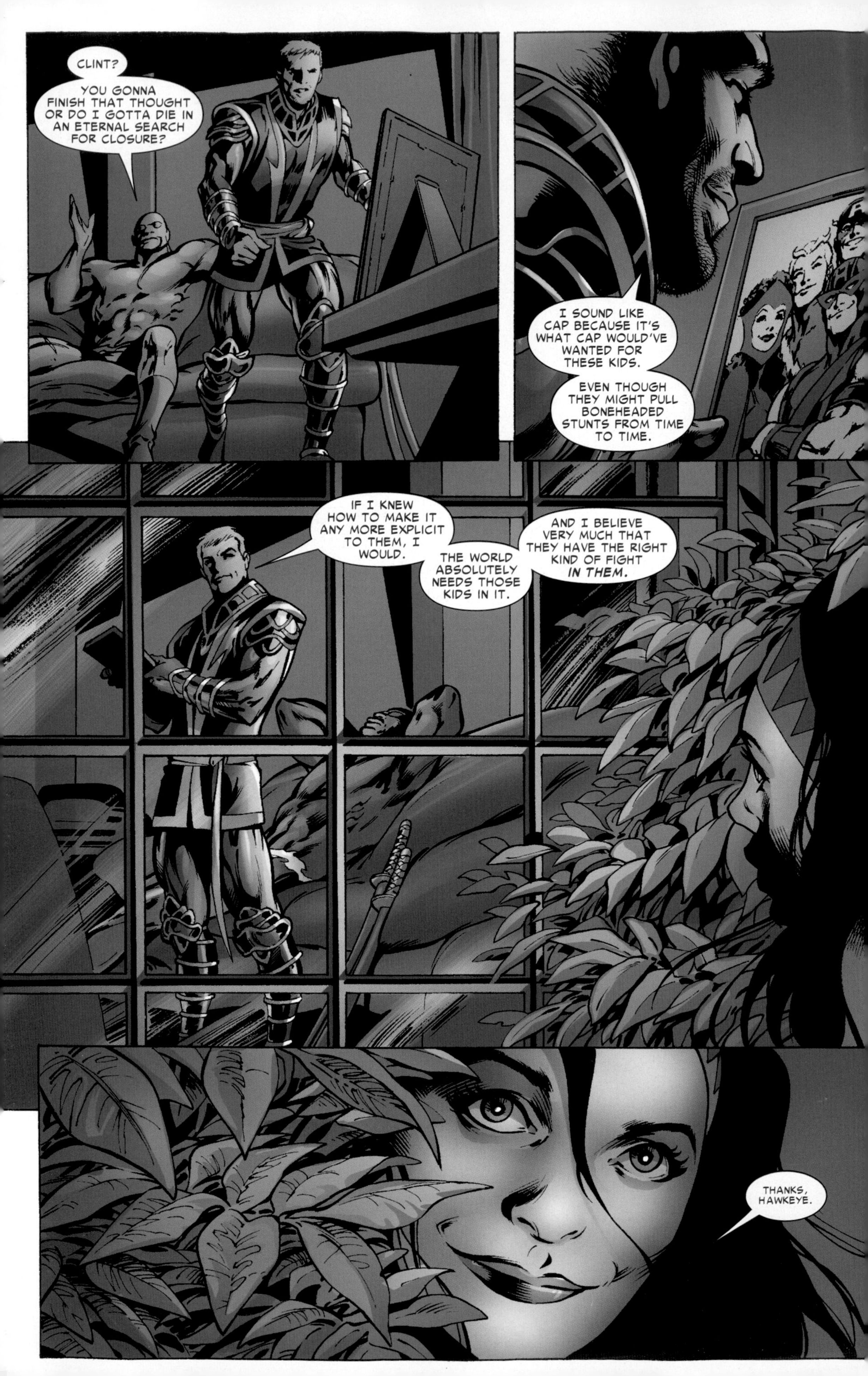
CLINT?
YOU GONNA FINISH THAT THOUGHT OR DO I GOTTA DIE IN AN ETERNAL SEARCH FOR CLOSURE?
I SOUND LIKE CAP BECAUSE IT'S WHAT CAP WOULD'VE WANTED FOR THESE KIDS.
EVEN THOUGH THEY MIGHT PULL BONEHEADED STUNTS FROM TIME TO TIME.
IF I KNEW HOW TO MAKE IT ANY MORE EXPLICIT TO THEM, I WOULD.
THE WORLD ABSOLUTELY NEEDS THOSE KIDS IN IT.
AND I BELIEVE VERY MUCH THAT THEY HAVE THE RIGHT KIND OF FIGHT *IN THEM.*
THANKS, HAWKEYE.

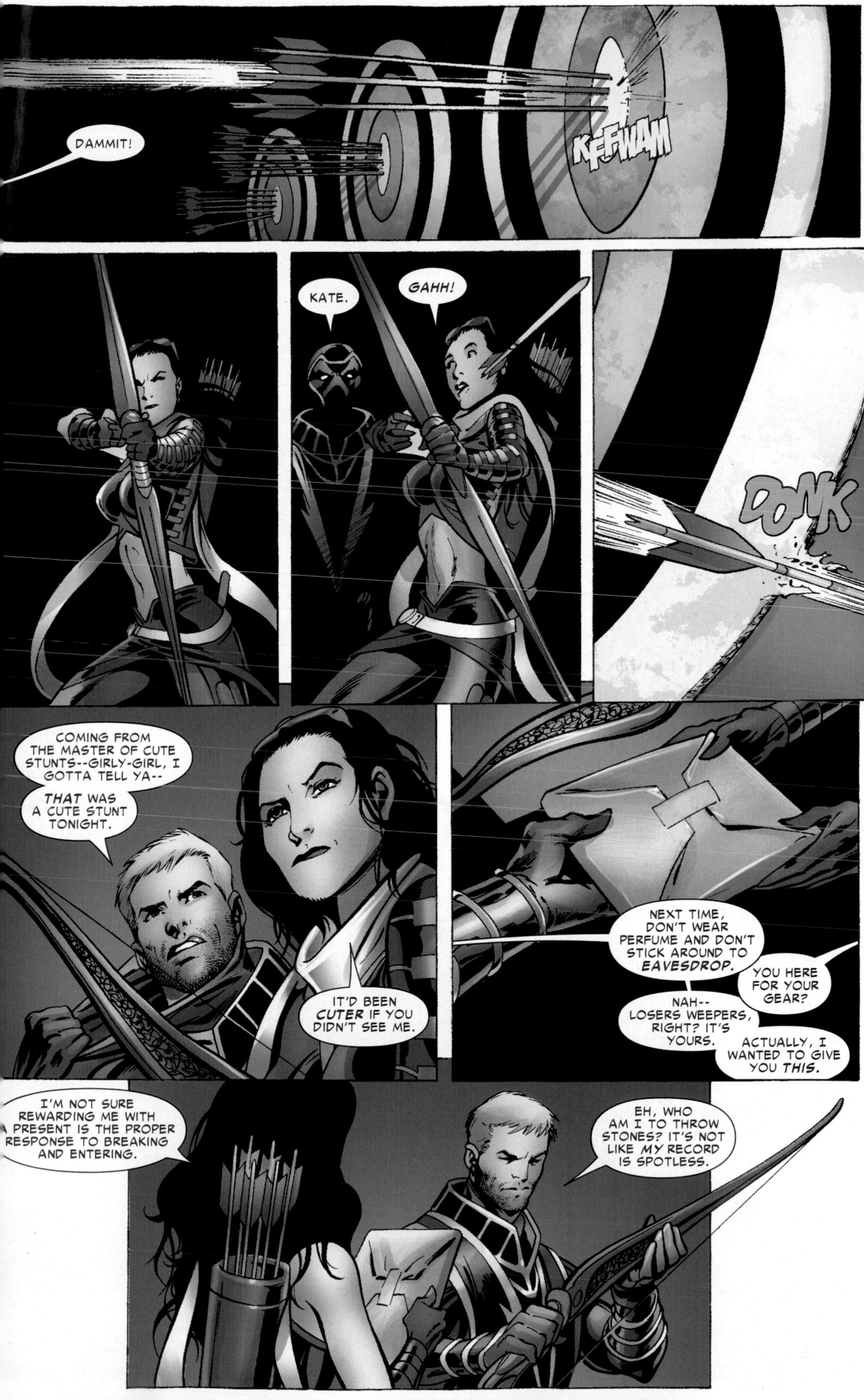
DAMMIT!
KFFWAM
KATE.
GAHH!
DONK
COMING FROM THE MASTER OF CUTE STUNTS--GIRLY-GIRL, I GOTTA TELL YA--
THAT WAS A CUTE STUNT TONIGHT.
IT'D BEEN CUTER IF YOU DIDN'T SEE ME.
NEXT TIME, DON'T WEAR PERFUME AND DON'T STICK AROUND TO EAVESDROP.
YOU HERE FOR YOUR GEAR?
NAH-- LOSERS WEEPERS, RIGHT? IT'S YOURS.
ACTUALLY, I WANTED TO GIVE YOU THIS.
I'M NOT SURE REWARDING ME WITH A PRESENT IS THE PROPER RESPONSE TO BREAKING AND ENTERING.
EH, WHO AM I TO THROW STONES? IT'S NOT LIKE MY RECORD IS SPOTLESS.

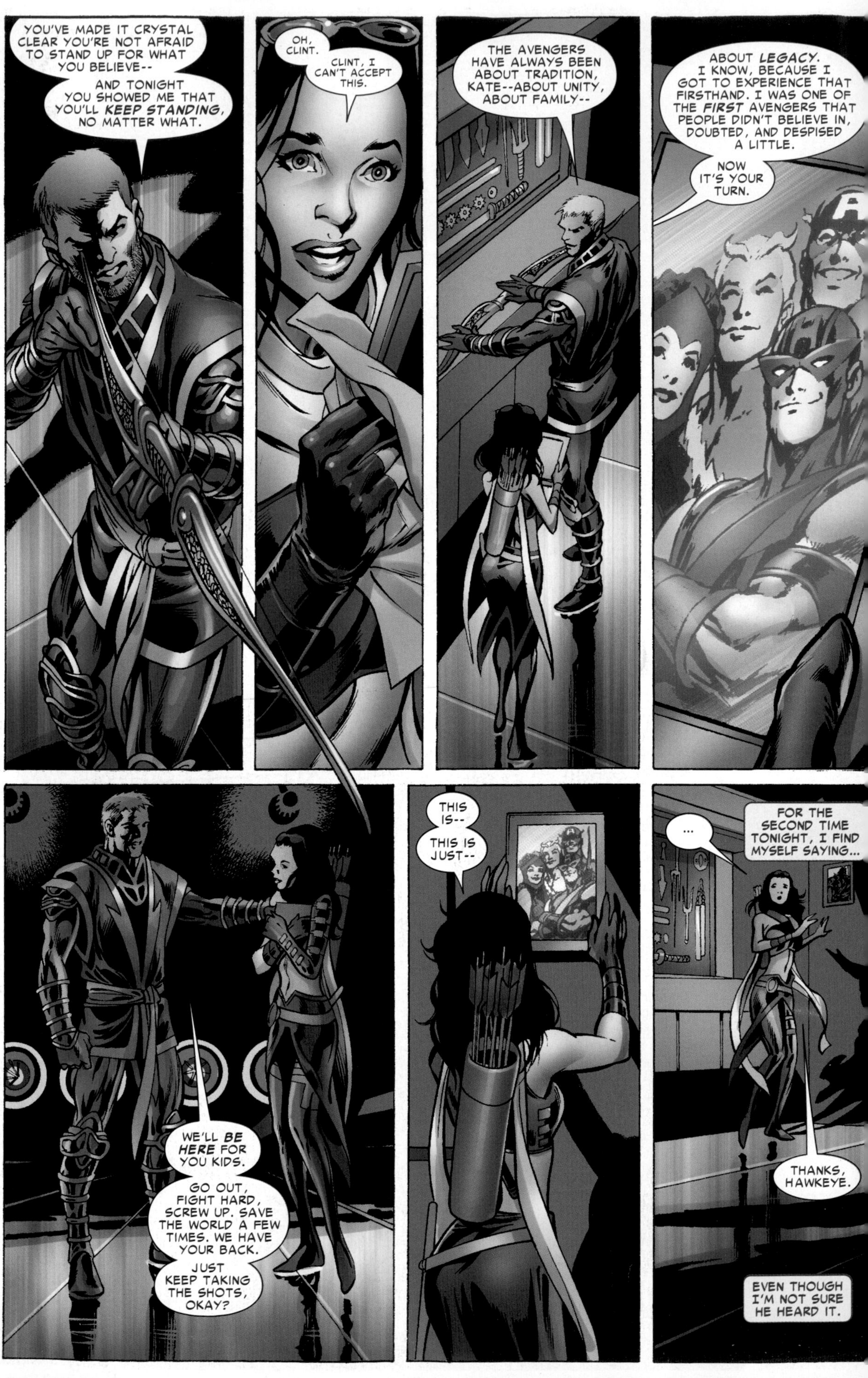

YOU'VE MADE IT CRYSTAL CLEAR YOU'RE NOT AFRAID TO STAND UP FOR WHAT YOU BELIEVE--
AND TONIGHT YOU SHOWED ME THAT YOU'LL KEEP STANDING, NO MATTER WHAT.
OH, CLINT.
CLINT, I CAN'T ACCEPT THIS.
THE AVENGERS HAVE ALWAYS BEEN ABOUT TRADITION, KATE--ABOUT UNITY, ABOUT FAMILY--
ABOUT LEGACY. I KNOW, BECAUSE I GOT TO EXPERIENCE THAT FIRSTHAND. I WAS ONE OF THE FIRST AVENGERS THAT PEOPLE DIDN'T BELIEVE IN, DOUBTED, AND DESPISED A LITTLE.
NOW IT'S YOUR TURN.
WE'LL BE HERE FOR YOU KIDS.
GO OUT, FIGHT HARD, SCREW UP. SAVE THE WORLD A FEW TIMES. WE HAVE YOUR BACK.
JUST KEEP TAKING THE SHOTS, OKAY?
THIS IS--
THIS IS JUST--
...
FOR THE SECOND TIME TONIGHT, I FIND MYSELF SAYING...
THANKS, HAWKEYE.
EVEN THOUGH I'M NOT SURE HE HEARD IT.

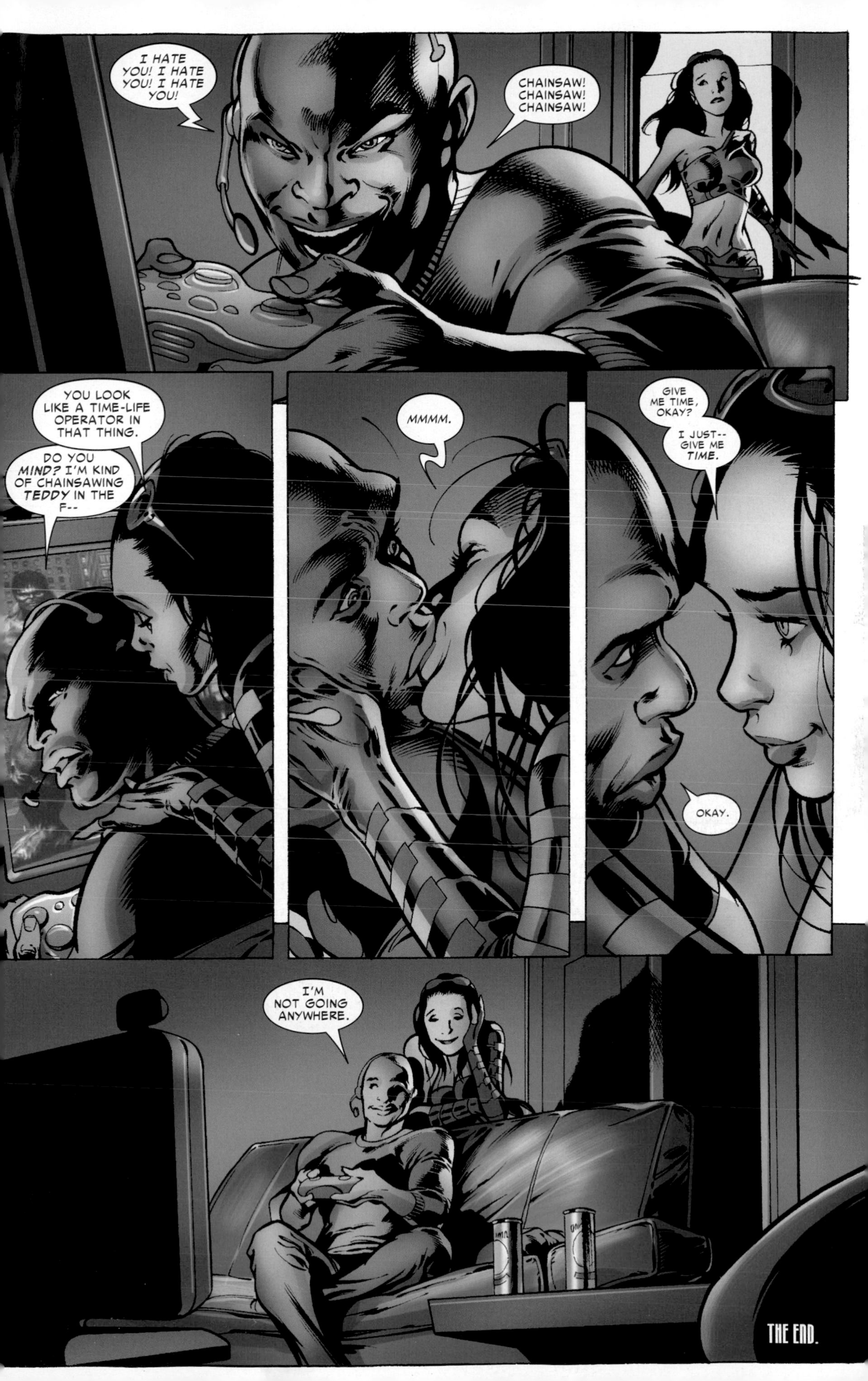
I HATE YOU! I HATE YOU! I HATE YOU!
CHAINSAW! CHAINSAW! CHAINSAW!
YOU LOOK LIKE A TIME-LIFE OPERATOR IN THAT THING.
DO YOU *MIND?* I'M KIND OF CHAINSAWING *TEDDY* IN THE F--
MMMM.
GIVE ME TIME, OKAY?
I JUST-- GIVE ME *TIME.*
OKAY.
I'M NOT GOING ANYWHERE.
THE END.

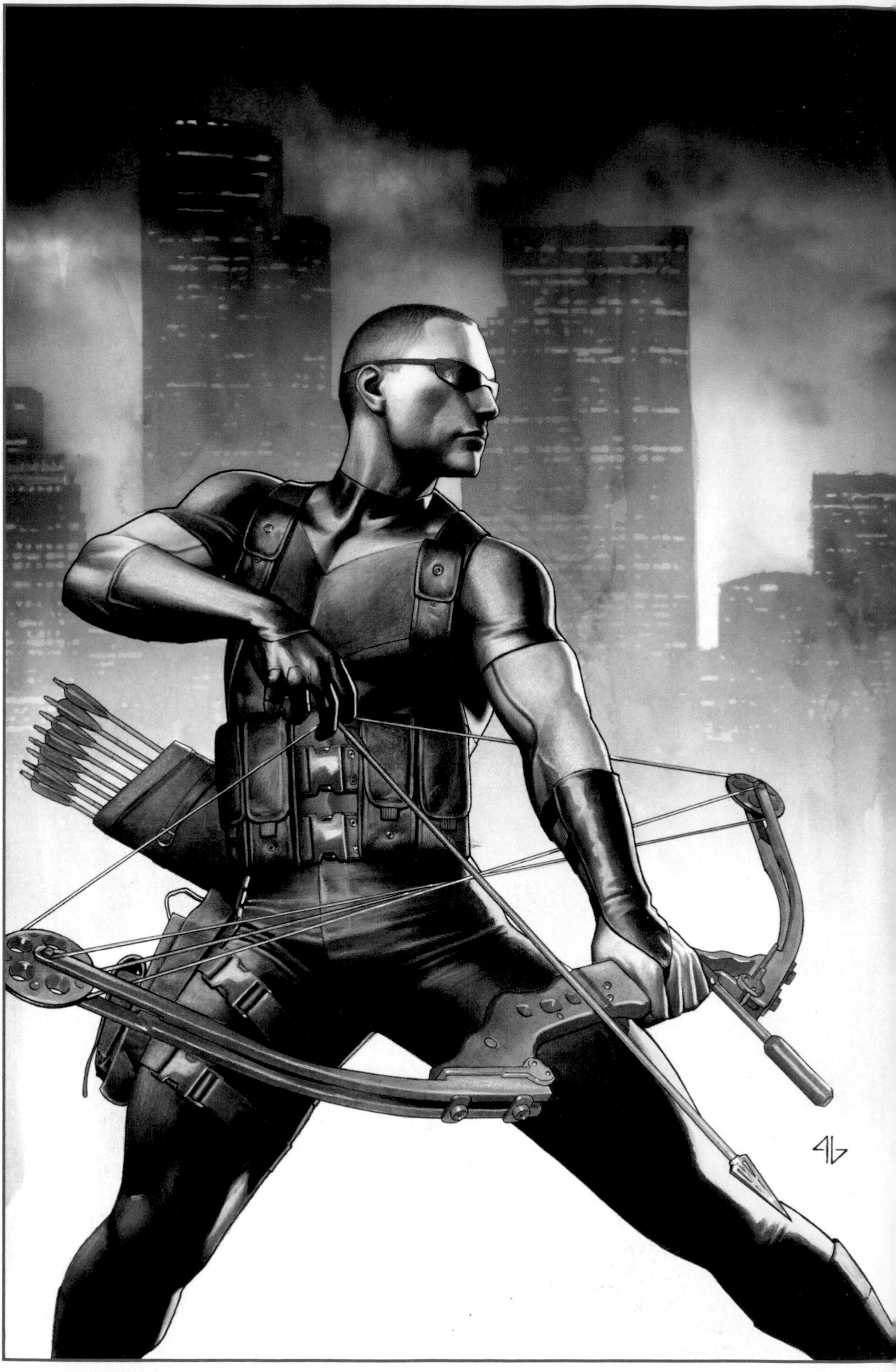

HAWKEYE #1 VARIANT
BY ADI GRANOV

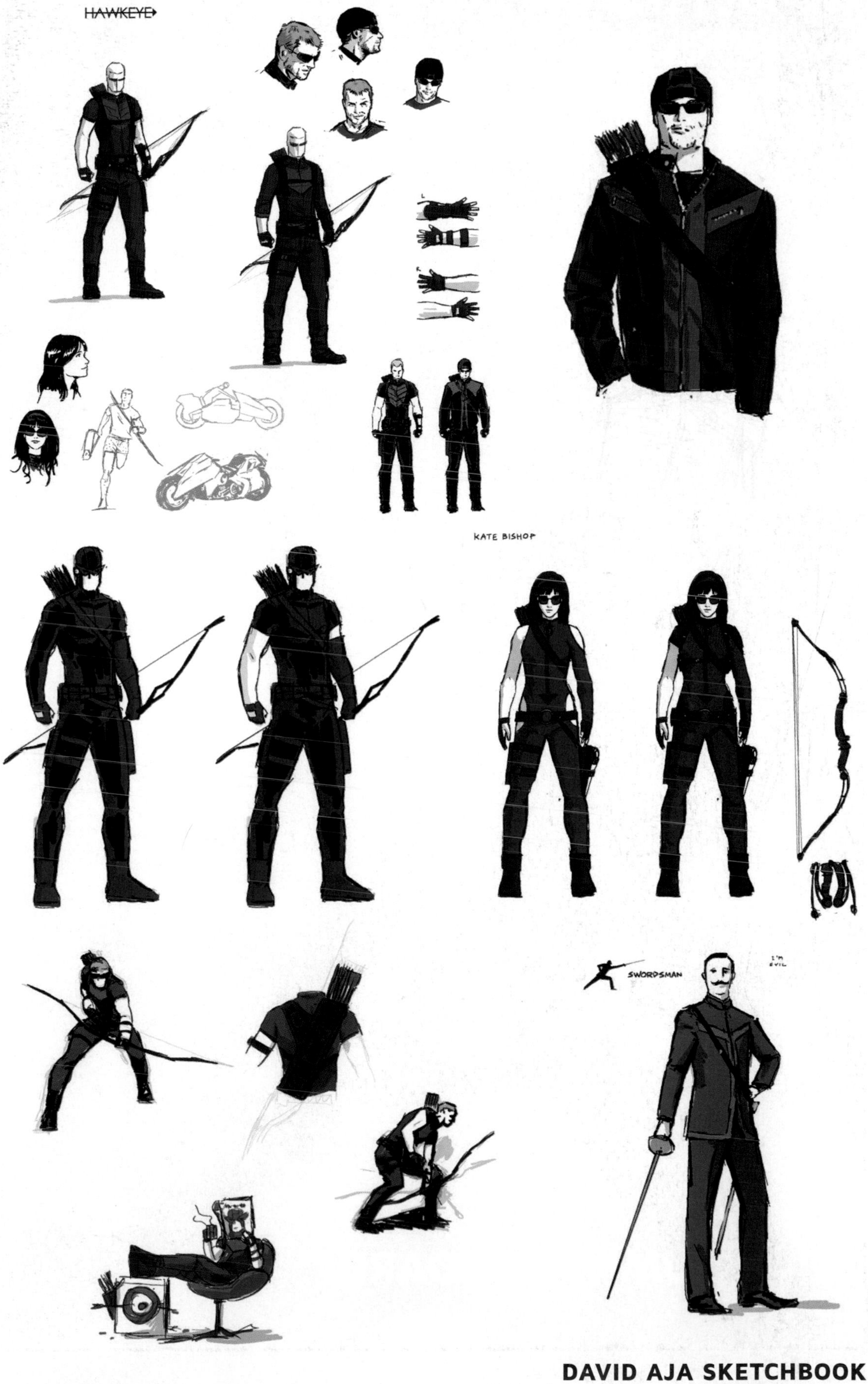
HAWKEYE
KATE BISHOP
SWORDSMAN
I'M EVIL

DAVID AJA SKETCHBOOK